Children Like Us

A Métis Woman's Memoir of Family, Identity and Walking Herself Home

Brittany Penner

A REGALO PRESS BOOK
ISBN: 979-8-89565-497-2
ISBN (eBook): 979-8-89565-498-9

Children Like Us:
A Métis Woman's Memoir of Family, Identity and Walking Herself Home

Cover and text design by Talia Abramson
Typesetting by Daniella Zanchetta
Cover images: (trees) Dian / Adobe Stock; (grass) johnpluto, (fireflies) An Chubenko / Shutterstock

Publishing Team:
Founder and Publisher – Gretchen Young
Managing Editor – Caitlin Burdette
Production Manager – Kate Harris
Production Editor – Rachel Paul

Certain names and identifying details have been changed to protect individuals' privacy.

Content warning: This memoir contains mentions of or allusions to child abuse, child sexual abuse, death, eating disorders, hate speech, miscarriage, misogyny, murder, racism, rape, self-harm, suicide and violence against animals.

The photographs on the part openers (of the author with Grandma, page 7; with Baba, page 107; and with her biological grandmother, page 201) are from the author's personal collection.

This book, as well as any other Regalo Press publications, may be purchased in bulk quantities at a special discounted rate. Contact orders@regalopress.com for more information.

As part of the mission of Regalo Press, a donation is being made to the American Indian College Fund, as chosen by the author. Find out more about this organization at https://collegefund.org.

Regalo Press
New York • Nashville
regalopress.com

Published in the United States of America
1 2 3 4 5 6 7 8 9 10

Everything I put forth into the world is done in honour of every Indigenous child, every Indigenous family, whose stories have remained largely unseen and unheard.

This book is for my brothers and my sisters and my cousins. Especially George.

And for every Indigenous child currently in the foster care system.

A WORD ON LANGUAGE

For generations, the Canadian government referred to Métis Peoples as "half-breeds." "Indian" is another weaponized term that was enshrined in laws created to subjugate Indigenous Peoples and used by settlers for centuries. In the 1990s and 2000s, I grew up with the labels "Native" and "Aboriginal." These terms are now largely considered to be outdated. Today, "Indigenous" is generally the preferred umbrella term that includes all First Nations, Métis Peoples and Inuit—but ideally, one would refer to Indigenous nations and communities by their specific chosen names. I, for instance, am a member of the Red River Métis of Manitoba, and am of Métis, Anishinaabe, Cree and European descent.

Although I can't say it ever felt empowering when people called me or my family members "Natives," it was familiar. I tried to honour that experience throughout this book, which is why I use "Native" and "Aboriginal" in the sections that describe my childhood, adolescence and young adulthood. Throughout this book, I try to authentically replicate the ways in which terminology has changed throughout my life.

A WORD ON HOPE

This is not a memoir seeking to highlight the importance of kinship or the beauty of adoption—although I hope you'll find strands of both these perspectives woven throughout the coming pages.

It is not a memoir wherein I ask you to choose a side in the age-old question of nurture versus nature. My life and my story, like those of so many fostered and adopted individuals, cannot possibly be confined to such neat corridors.

I'll admit, this is a memoir that carries the weight of some difficult truths and painful realities. But it's also a memoir that holds so much love for all those who have loved me or tried to love me.

I recognize it's bold to ask anything of you as a reader, but if you would grant me one request (and let's be honest—you're already here with me, aren't you?): With each flip of the page, will you remain open? Open to hope. And if not quite open to it, perhaps open to the possibility of it. Hope for us all to hold the capacity for difficult stories, our own and others'. For complicated relationships, joys and pains and fears and tiny triumphs to weave themselves in beautiful nuance.

CHILDREN LIKE US

Prologue

The car door closing sends echoes through the trees. It's the middle of the afternoon on a November prairie day, and no one is around. The sun is shining so brightly my eyes begin to sting. The air has grown cool in the last few weeks, the kind that crawls under your skin and needles itself into your bones. Manitoba weather is like this. The sun has a tendency to lure you outdoors, only for your body to realize within seconds that it was all a ruse. Of course, this is no trick at all on the part of the land. This is just how life is here. Full of contradictions.

With winters so cold we have to leave our vehicles running for twenty minutes before we can climb inside them, and with snow piled so high in our yards we can't see out our front windows, there is no shortage of reasons to leave this place. Yet, somehow, there has always been, there will always be, reason enough to stay.

My eyes focus on a weathered path between tall pine trees, and I can feel my feet carrying me toward it. I have just come from my grandmother's funeral. A grandmother I never really knew.

A grandmother who, for most of my life, I never had the chance to know. Her name and identity, much like my own, were taken from me shortly after I was born.

The leaves crackle beneath my feet. It's as though a curtain is pulled in around me, dimming the light. I have been here before, in this wild bush that sits midway between the hometown in which I was raised and the hometown in which I could have been raised.

My grandmother died almost two weeks ago. I wish my husband could be here with me, but it is—we are—over. Our life together, over a decade, suddenly finished—and now my grandmother is gone too. In these woods, I am surrounded by so much. I'm held by the trees and the bush, growing barer by the day—by the hardened earth beneath my feet. By the straggling geese overhead, the last to migrate. I am trying, struggling, to understand how to hold any of it.

Some days, like today, I don't set out to come to this place. I settle into my car, a list of errands in hand, and, instead, I find myself here again. I feel alone here. In some ways, I feel abandoned here. This feels fitting, somehow, and, in recognizing the truth in that, I find that I can breathe easier here.

I inhale, closing my eyes, and I am five years old. Suddenly, I am five and I am eleven and I am thirteen and I am eighteen and I am twenty-five and I am thirty-three. I am all of these versions of myself. Somehow, I am all of these versions of myself in this moment.

I am walking on the land that some of my people have lived on for generations. My ancestors. My grandmothers who have given birth on this land, who have birthed this land, for thousands of years. My grandfathers who have hunted on these lands, who have given back to these lands, who have travelled these lands, kept warm by bison hides, their stomachs filled with bannock and deer and lard and berries.

This is also the land upon which my people, my *other* people, settled. Where they cut down trees and built homesteads and raised animals and farmed and prayed, ruling their houses with a firm fist and an even firmer belief of what is right and what is wrong in the eyes of the Lord. A land to which they fled, away from the violence of their own homeland—perhaps unaware, or perhaps not much bothered, by the violence that afforded them opportunities here. But can I call these people my people? This is a question with which I've wrestled my entire life.

I inhale the scent of wet bark and it reaches deep into my lungs. Are these bushes that surround me like the ones my great-grandmother hid inside with her newborn daughter, my grandmother, while the government agents raided their home? They were in search of an Indian baby born to an Indian mother, a sin for which there was legislated punishment at the time. I picture my great-grandmother holding her child tight against her chest as she crouched low. A woman with thick, dark hair like my own and eyes I wish I could have had the chance to stare into at least once. Do these trees resemble the ones that shielded the two of them that day? Does this earth still hold the memory of that moment? Does it still hold the memory of her? Does my body, in some way I have yet to figure out, carry within it the possibility for me to remember a great-grandmother I have never known?

I can't see through the thicket of birch trees raising their arms tall into the sky, but splinters from the tangerine sun poke through as if waving to me.

I see you, they beckon.

I cannot even see myself, I reply.

I'm searching for home. I walk and I seek but I cannot see past the trees that surround me. I look to the skies above, like I did whenever I prayed as a child. Everyone else—my father, my grandfather, my mother, my grandmother—always bowed their heads instead. As Mennonites, there is no greater show of respect than a bowed head, an averted gaze. Solemnity. Reverence. As early as I could formulate questions, I wondered—at first aloud, and then silently, as I grew to learn that questions were inappropriate—*Why must I hide my face? What a funny thing,* I thought, *that I must look away from God.*

My head upturned, I see nothing but the copper sun in the cotton-candy-blue sky. I am searching for home but I cannot find it. *Perhaps it would be helpful,* I think, *if I knew what home looked like.*

I keep walking.

PART ONE

Chapter One

It begins with a child. Or, perhaps, it begins with the pregnancy of a teenage girl. Or with a couple deemed medically infertile, waiting year after year after year for that coveted call from Child and Family Services. Or, maybe, it all begins long before any of that. This story, like so many others, reaches back to a time when European settlers colonized this land and deemed its people, my people, savages. A problem. An "Indian problem."

Regardless, now there is a child over whom guardianship must be determined. And *to whom* this child should belong is a very real question.

My entrance into this world is a quiet farewell song whispered into hospital corridors. No relatives flock to my mother's side, anxiously awaiting their turn to hold me, welcoming me into the family. My birth is one of closed doors and shuttered windows.

The two of us leave the hospital, my mother and I, through different doors, into different worlds. She steps out, no longer calling herself a mother. I am carried out in the arms of a social worker. A ward of the province; a daughter of the government. A child yet to be gifted a name that will stay.

I have yet to be offered to a mother and a father who might call me their own or a variation of that. I am a child without a culture, a history, a family. All of these, the government says, can simply be written anew.

The day the couple receives the call from Child and Family Services does not begin spectacularly, by any means. The woman's mother hasn't spoken of having peculiar dreams in the days preceding it, premonitions—as she's been known to have—hinting that something life-changing was soon to come. Or if she has felt something, she's mentioned it to no one, and it does not become a part of this story.

The week has been ordinary: the woman attending her shifts at Stylerite, the department store in town; the man working at the local building centre. And then, of course, the call changes everything.

A social worker is on the other end when the woman picks up her cordless telephone. She hurriedly scribbles down the little information the agent provides before running the fifty yards to reach her husband outside by the woodstove.

"A baby!" she cries.

"A baby?" he asks.

"A baby, a baby," she says. "We have a baby!"

The child they prayed for, pleaded with God for in the dark of the night, has come. Finally born. Officially surrendered.

The couple, my soon-to-be parents, have been driving for forty minutes now. My new mother—can she call herself a mother already? she wonders. It's only been two days since they learned of my existence and she hasn't yet met me—but they *are* on their way to pick me up, so, yes, she decides, she can call herself a mother. This mother can barely contain her excitement.

Sure, she would have loved to have a biological child of her own. But she'd always known *this* was a possibility. Her mother-in-law had even warned her before she got married. "You know, my sons can't have children." My mother had assumed as much—four of her husband's five living biological brothers had adopted children. Her doctor had been curious about the wider family history of infertility and offered to test the whole family, but her husband firmly said no. It was much too invasive a request, in his mind. It was not the Mennonite way.

What will her mother say when she sees the baby? And her father? "Just don't bring home an Indian baby," he'd said when she first told him that she and her husband were applying to adopt. He knew, as she did all too well, that the system was filled with Native kids. But it has been so many years and she has waited so long for this day, they have all waited so long for this day, so who really cares at this point? Plus, the baby, her new daughter, is only part-Native.

She shrugs her shoulders at all these thoughts. Nothing can bring her down today. Finally, she has a baby. Finally, she is a mother. She may not have felt like the prettiest girl growing up. Or the smartest. She never much cared about being the smartest, anyway. God and her mother know she has never been the skinniest. But now she is a mother and no one can take that away from her.

What a stupid thing to say, my new father thinks to himself, one hand tightly gripping the bottom of the steering wheel and the other holding ten o'clock. He holds this position whenever he is concentrating on the road. *What a stupid thing to say,* he thinks again, shaking his head. *Give the child back—who does that?*

"We'll give you some time to see if the child fits into your home," the social worker had told him and his wife on the phone.

"Well, what are we gonna do?" he spat out. "Give the baby back?"

"Sometimes things don't work out. We want to give you time to adjust to being a new family."

"Naw." The word sprang from his mouth. A mix between his native Low German "nay" and "no." He will forever be mixing the two languages. "That's not right."

He shakes his head again at the memory. Family doesn't do that. He'd thought it then and he thinks it today as he drives to meet his child. Family doesn't give family back. It doesn't matter if the baby has a crooked toe or, well, whatever issues the baby might have. Crooked toe or not, family is family. Whether you're related by blood or not. He nods decisively at the thought as the car whizzes by bright canola fields glistening in the sun. There's right and there's wrong. Family is family, and of all the right and wrong things in this world, that's probably the rightest thing he can think of.

My mother reminds herself to breathe, the excitement palpitating in her chest, her heart skipping entire beats, jolting along with the rhythm of the old highway cracked from the heat of the Manitoba sun.

She feels like she is in the opening scene of a movie. The main character, a middle-aged woman (twenty-nine is middle-aged, isn't it?), an air of elegance surrounding her even in moments of stress like this, is driving with her sweet husband to pick up her very own child. She is driving off into the sunset to meet her baby.

Yes, this is the opening scene of her life. But there is one question nagging her. It has gnawed at her mind since the day they applied to adopt so many years ago. Will the child still love her, even when she learns that she is not her "real" mother? Will the child still love her, even then?

Chapter Two

The woodpecker is jackhammering away at a tree outside her bedroom window, but she doesn't hear it. She's particularly talented at ignoring any sound she doesn't want to hear, like the chime of the grandfather clock her husband built, which rings throughout the house every fifteen minutes—at pretending something doesn't exist simply by telling herself it is so.

It's a humid midsummer morning. The heat curls Mom's bangs and the tiny hairs at the nape of her neck. The rest of her ash-blonde hair is pulled tight to the back of her head, smoothed with a comb and gelled twice over. She's sitting on her bed. Her shoulders are hunched over as she holds a small compact mirror a foot from her face. The rays from the egg-yolk sun dance against the blue wallpaper strewn with white wildflowers. This farmhouse five miles south of town may not have cost much when my parents bought it eight years ago, but they will be making payments on it for the rest of their lives, remortgaging it as money gets tighter and tighter, painting its walls whenever the mood strikes my mother. "I can't afford to move," she will say, "so, I change what it looks like just a little." No one can say she hasn't made this house a home. Now, the coos of a fussing baby girl travel from the small room just down the hall. If someone would have told her a month ago this is how her life would look, Mom wouldn't have believed them.

She reaches into her black makeup bag and pulls out a cross-stitch needle. She repositions herself on the bed so she can steady her elbow against her knee, and brings the mirror in closer so it's just inches from her face. She holds the needle so its tip floats just below her lash line. I will scold her for this for years, starting when I'm six years old. "You're gonna poke your eye out!" I will say, mindful not to startle her and cause her to do just as I fear. "Oh, Brit," she'll always reply with a sigh, while running the needle through the clumps in her mascara, separating lash from lash. It's a practice she's perfected with the precision of a surgeon separating fascia from tissue—a ritual with which she begins each day.

It's the morning of her baby shower, a day for which she has waited nearly a decade. She doesn't care that her daughter is not "her own," because, really, by now, she's spent more time with me than my birth mother ever did, and isn't that what makes a mother? Someone who rocks her baby to sleep, who's awoken by her child's cries, someone who's present to—well, admittedly, she hasn't *exactly* changed a diaper yet. The smell and texture are too much for her to bear. She did try once when I'd been home just over a week. My father was out by the barn when he heard her screaming from the house. He ran as hard as his asthma allowed, his breath clogged with that wheezy cough. He was certain something tragic had happened—the baby not even home a week!—so he was surprised when he reached the door to find his wife wearing a kitchen towel tied around her lower face.

"What happened?" he shouted. "Where's the baby?"

My mother could not form the words. Each time she tried, she felt certain she would vomit, acid rising from her stomach. She shook her head and waved him inside the house with her hand. "Just go," she managed, before her stomach began heimliching itself again.

Dad walked into the house to find me lying on the nursery floor upstairs unbothered, dirty diaper half undone. "It wasn't even a big poop," he will say for years to come.

"What was I supposed to do?" she will reply, giggling, palms upturned to the ceiling.

Since that day, my father has changed every diaper—except when he's been away from home. In those cases, Mom calls in the neighbour across the road. But so what? That doesn't make her any less of a mother—or her daughter any less her own. She tries not to concern herself with my life before. My biological family merely gave me my gene pool. Anything more than that will come from her and her husband, she's decided. How could it not? And my father agrees, holding firm to the belief that a child's life is shaped primarily by the people who raise her. His world has always consisted of what he can see and touch around him. That is where God is to be found. In the food on the table, in the snow you clear from a neighbour's driveway, in bills that are paid. Anything beyond that merely complicates life.

My mother returns the needle to her makeup bag. She refocuses her pupils, the irises green like ripe avocado, and begins to line her lids with a thick brown pencil. Next, her lips, with a deep shade of burgundy. Her signature for years to come. Despite having converted to her husband's Mennonite faith, she has relinquished neither her makeup nor her gold jewellery.

Once her makeup is just right, her lips as evenly marked as they can be, she wanders to the baby's room next door. She's owned a crib for years, but until recently it was filled only with a stuffed bear to look back at her. Now, she stands over the crib, watching me, and smiles. She doesn't think she's ever felt this happy before. Her father, her mother, her grandparents who were so present in her own upbringing—they are all so happy. Everyone is happy for her and my father. *I did that.* The thought is perhaps what makes her smile the most. *I've made them this happy.* This is all she has ever wanted since she was a young child playing dress-up with her doll.

She wonders what I will look like as I grow older. She was given a brief description of my birth mother that first day they received the call from the social worker: *dark hair, dark eyes, part-Native.* But how Native will I look? Not that it matters, of course. *Still, it would be nice—for Brittany,* she thinks, *convenient, even, if she doesn't look too Native.* She doesn't want people to assume bad things about me.

Although her father had urged her not to bring home an Indian baby, upon meeting me he'd cried and laughed in a way she'd never seen before. The fact that I was Native, or part-Native, was never mentioned, and she was grateful.

Before they leave, she'll dress me in a white onesie, a pink bow on my head, and she and Dad will drive to her parents' house in town, where the shower is to be held. Today is just one of many days worthy of celebration lately.

JULY 30, 1989
PHOTOGRAPH

I'm four weeks old, swaddled in a pink receiving blanket in Mom's arms. She plays the part well—a relaxed ease to her shoulders. And she's nothing if not photogenic. She smiles brightly like she always will for photos, her teeth showing, her cheeks plump and flushed.

I will call the tiny woman with freshly coloured deep-brown hair to Mom's right "Baba," the Ukrainian word for grandmother. Mauve nail polish and gold rings adorn her fingers. What she lacks in stature, she well makes up for in spirit. Mom has always known she inherited more from her father's side than her mother's, in more ways than one. A stranger would not make them out to be mother and daughter. Mom has hips and a bust Baba will be forever criticizing. And Mom's retorts to Baba's barbs will always go unexpressed. Such is the nature of their relationship.

Grandma, Dad's mother, stands to Mom's left. She is sixteen years older than Baba, although the generational gap between the two women is overshadowed by the cultural one. Grandma's grey hair is covered with first a hairnet and then a black head scarf. She is hidden beneath a shapeless white dress she has sewn for herself. She smiles modestly, baring no teeth. She rarely, if ever, betrays her emotions. Her features are soft, her demeanour gentle.

I will spend moments of my childhood to come looking at my mother and then my father, observing the obvious differences between their two worlds. I will wonder what force it was exactly that drew them together. How did my conservative Mennonite father come to marry my quippy Ukrainian-Catholic mother? Mom was raised in a tight-knit, polka-dancing, fiddle-playing, vodka-drinking family in a one-road southern Manitoban town settled by Ukrainian and Polish immigrants. Dad was raised on a one-room homestead on a small plot of land bordered tightly by well-kept crops in an area settled decades earlier by Old Colony Mennonites. My father's ancestors were among the first Mennonites to settle this stolen Anishinaabe and Métis land, their influence reverberating through time.

There is nothing like new life to align two seemingly disjointed worlds, if only for a moment. It is the day of my baby shower and all three women are proud, though they wear it differently.

AUGUST 6, 1989
PHOTOGRAPH

Someone has placed me on an aged brown-and-beige loveseat between two of my male cousins, the adopted sons of two of Dad's brothers. I am clearly struggling to hold up my head. George, ten months older than I am, is on my left; he has pudgy cheeks and round teddy bear eyes that will forever betray his attempts at Mennonite stoicism.

Wyatt, born almost three months before me, sits to my right; he has a head of thick black hair that would be the envy of all my uncles, most of whom began balding in their twenties, if Mennonites allowed themselves to feel such an emotion.

The resemblance we three share is far greater than that which we share with our parents. We will grow up side by side, spending the next several years chasing each other through the wet grass on our grandparents' farm and sledding down big snow hills Dad will pile high with his tractor at the end of our driveway.

I imagine that three mothers stand behind the camera, just outside the frame. Three fathers sit at the kitchen table, sipping instant coffee and eating schnetke *in familiar silence. Hope is what has brought us all together.*

Chapter Three

James and Marion join our family shortly after my second birthday. Even though I was the first, I'm the youngest—my brother two years and my sister thirteen months older—and I fall in love with them almost as soon as we become family. Everyone falls in love with them, even my father. Mom finally has the three children—two girls and a boy—she's always wanted, and it's clear that Dad enjoys raising a larger family too. He is especially fond of James, whose smile has the power to soften even his temper. With his light-brown hair, olive skin, and eyes a swirl of caramel and brown, James certainly looks like my brother, and he takes his role seriously. He is strong and well-behaved, and always a good example for his younger sisters.

It's a Saturday afternoon in late summer, and while the mosquitoes and the horseflies fall into a slumber and the cows graze in the fenced pasture a few feet from us, Marion and I play in the sandbox in our backyard. Dad built this sandbox a few weeks ago, with four tall pillars and a roof to shade us from the sun. The farm cats have quickly claimed it as a glorified litterbox, but we love it just the same. Whenever we spot a piece of poop in the sand, we simply flick it out of the box with one of our toy shovels and continue playing. We're building a strip of houses when, suddenly, I hear James cry out. I look up to see him across the yard in Dad's scrap pile of plywood and metal, clutching his leg below the knee and crouching low to the ground.

Dad, hammering at something a few feet away in his dark denim coveralls and weathered baseball cap, drops his tool and runs over to my brother. He calmly scoops James up into his arms and walks assuredly, though unhurriedly, into the house. Marion and I toss our shovels aside, jump up and run as fast as our legs allow.

In the kitchen, we find James sitting on the counter, his right foot hanging over the sink, his rubber boots on the floor. There's a trail of mud across the linoleum that leads to Dad, beside the sink. Mom is in the hallway covering her mouth with her hands, the way she does when she watches something frightening on TV. She's the first to admit she can't cope with any sort of pain, whether it's her own or another person's. My father, meanwhile, is calm and methodical as he readies the hydrogen peroxide. It's the ultimate healing tonic in our family, like holy water or a sacred tincture passed down through the generations.

"What happened?" I ask, standing on tiptoe to better see what Dad is doing.

"Never mind what happened," he says.

"I stepped on a nail," James replies. My eyes widen and I peer over at James's boots on the floor, wondering if there's a hole in one of the heels.

James winces but there are no tears running down his face. Now is not the time for tears. It is never the time for tears—an unspoken rule my siblings and I have learned to obey. A rule that Mom has never quite been able to follow. In my teenage years and beyond, I will wonder how my parents make it work, with such fundamental differences in the way they see and interact with the world. Sometimes, I will wonder whether each acts to balance out the other. For every word my father does not speak, my mother shares a lusciously woven tale. For every hysterical reaction Mom has to a simple sliver, Dad washes a deep wound, douses it with peroxide, and bandages it up without complaint.

My skin tingles as I watch Dad pour the peroxide over my brother's heel, which begins to bubble. James lets out a little whimper and his face scrunches. He lets an aberrant teardrop escape, but Dad doesn't seem to notice. I lean in a bit closer.

"Brit," Dad barks. "Back!"

My body reflexively jolts backward. I'm disappointed I can no longer see what's happening. I wish I had a magnifying glass. I've watched James and our cousin George hold theirs under the sun, directing rays onto ants on the driveway (we then eat them like they're chicken-flavoured poppy seeds).

"There. Stay off it and it'll be like new again soon." He helps James onto his feet before walking out the door and back to the barn.

"How about some iced tea?" Mom asks, finally entering the room.

We're all so thirsty and the three of us scurry to the table—James a little slowly—and wait for our mother to fill our cups.

AUGUST 27, 1991
HOME VIDEO

The video camera is shaky, as it always will be when she films. Baba's essential hand tremor began in her early fifties, and it will only get worse as she ages. The camcorder whips through the kitchen and homes in on the dining table, where Dad is sitting close to Marion. His arms are crossed and his expression solemn. My sister has never been a "good" eater, and there is nothing more sinful or perplexing to my father than the sight of food left on a plate. Dad refuses to allow Marion to leave the table until she's finished everything.

James and I are playing in the living room. Gida is smoking, reclining into a corner of the couch, and Mom is on the loveseat cross-stitching. "There's James and Brittany doing a puzzle," Baba says from behind the camcorder. "Wave to the camera."

She walks over to the kitchen and zooms in on Marion's face. My sister's cheeks are full of mashed potatoes and she looks like she's in the thick of a marathon she does not believe she can win. A more encouraging father might cheer his daughter on with "dig deep!" or "this is what we trained for!" Actually, I'm not sure what a more encouraging father might say. Dad sits there silently, his arms still crossed, now extending his look of displeasure to Baba and her camcorder.

"Ah, try smiling," she says, huffing, as she spins around and walks back to the living room.

An hour later, Dad and Marion have finally stepped away from the table, my sister's plate washed and put away. She and I are both sitting on a swivel armchair and squealing as our father tickles us. He is rarely this playful and I will struggle to remember him being this playful with us again. But today we are here, and Baba is recording, and our father is laughing right along with us.

We are a family of five and we fit together as we should. Me and my brother and my sister. Mom with the three children she's always wanted, playing in the background as she tells her parents a story. One hand on her chest to steady herself and the other stretched out wide, she regales them with the details of how James nearly escaped death this past week. "The sink—oh my God, the sink!"—she winces—"you should have seen the blood! His foot"—she shivers—"I couldn't even look!"

My Gida smiles, inhaling on his cigarette. He knows his daughter well. A sink full of blood really means a small spattering. Still, he smiles at her with fondness. She has always reminded him of his favourite sister. My aunt Iris is in her sixties and lives near Toronto. She wears cat-eye glasses and smokes cigarettes out of those long "lady" holders, the tips always stained from her signature bright-tomato lipstick. She kissed Pierre Trudeau on the cheek once when he was prime minister, and she loves grabbing my dad's face in her hands and kissing him on the lips and then the cheek, just to leave a mark. She is so large, so full of life, that even my father cannot help but be coaxed out of his shell by her. Dad, a man of admittedly few needs, will tell the story one day, after Iris has passed, of how she scolded him when he and Mom visited and he used a towel she'd set out for my mother, rather than the one she'd set out for him.

One day when I'm older, I'll meet her and understand what everyone means when they mention the similarity between her and Mom. She is who I imagine my mother, in another life, would have been. But such a life is difficult when you are afraid of so much. Afraid to leave your hometown. Afraid to let your mind be known. Afraid to show much of yourself. Still, when my mother finds herself in a space where she's comfortable, I can almost see those cat-eye glasses atop her nose, a long cigarette holder perched in her fingers and that bright-red lipstick shining through. When I'm older, I'll feel guilty for not allowing her that version of a life. I'll feel guilty for representing something I don't think she ever planned for.

NOVEMBER 17, 1991
HOME VIDEO

Dad is lying on the floor on his stomach, drifting in and out of sleep, as my siblings and I run laps around him. He occasionally swats at our legs when we get too close to his head. It's Sunday afternoon and we're at Baba and Gida's house after church—our weekly tradition. Baba and Gida only attend mass at their Catholic church during holidays, whereas we, along with my paternal grandparents and the rest of Dad's family, attend a Mennonite church every Sunday.

Dad's arms are wrapped around his head and his glasses are resting on the floor by his side.

"Take your glasses, Paul," Baba's voice pokes from behind the camera. "Your glasses, Paul. Paul, your glasses!" She's persistent, like that woodpecker who still lives outside my parents' bedroom window. Although, if I were to ask my father, I imagine he'd say he prefers the sound of the bird.

He turns his face away from her. He's trying to have his afternoon meddachschlop *and he never appreciates anyone interrupting his nap.*

When Dad is finished sleeping, we'll return home so he can check in on the animals; every so often, a cow will break through the fencing on the southern corner of our small pasture. And once he's done on the farm, we'll drive the two miles of washboard gravel road to his parents' farm, like we do every Sunday.

I look at the camcorder, then to Dad on the carpeted floor. "Dad, your glasses," I say. "Your glasses!"

"Your glasses are gonna get stepped on, Paul." Baba is frustrated now. If he would only listen to her. She is a woman who will never rid herself of the belief that the people around her would do better if they only listened to her.

James kneels on the ground next to Dad's head. He smiles sweetly, grabs the glasses, and places them on top of the big mahogany television set. He's like this, James. Thoughtful. Always calling me "Baby Brittany," and making me feel like a true sister. Always including me in games—unless he and my cousin George are together and I can't keep up with them.

Mom is sitting on the brown recliner in the corner of the room, cross-stitching. "Sing for Baba," she says to us. "Show us one of your songs from Sunday School."

Gida, sitting on the couch, pipes in. "Come on be my party doll, come on be my party doll!" A self-taught fiddle, guitar, and tsymbaly player, he is also a natural singer. His smooth baritone voice has yet to become hoarse, has yet to grow quiet. Those will be the first signs to those around him that something is gravely wrong.

"That's not it!" I laugh.

"No?" He raises his brows, an exaggerated look of surprise widening his eyes. "Sing me one of yours then!"

"All my sins have been forgiven," James begins, standing next to me. He brings his face close to mine and contorts it, making me giggle. He holds his hands against his chest, nods, and we sing together: "My sins have been forgiven, I'm on my way to heaven . . ." These are clearly the only lyrics either of us remembers and we trail off.

James changes his tune, switching to a song we both know well. "Oh, the Lord saved me," he sings.

Marion has been sitting two feet from the TV set this entire time. Her lips start to move but her gaze remains fixed on the screen.

"I'm as happy as can be. My cup is full and running over." James gives my shoulders a squeeze and runs over to Gida, hopping onto his lap.

Our grandfather wraps him up in his arms. "Aye aye aye," Gida says. Always the musician, his voice has a soothing and melodic quality to it even when he's speaking. "What a group of singers."

James smiles big and proud before resting his head against Gida's shoulder.

It's a cold Friday in December 1991, two weeks before Christmas, and there's a palpable tension beaded into the air. Mom is fluttering around Baba and Gida's house with an anxious energy, and keeps checking and rechecking the contents of her purse. This past week, Dad has offered only one-word sentences and has seemed angry with us children. Baba is recording us but keeping her distance. I have been fussy all day and no one has thought to comfort me. No one has thought to explain to me what's happening.

"Well, what're ya waiting for?" Dad says to James. There are three little mounds of winter attire on the living room floor.

James zips himself into his parka and tosses each end of his scarf behind his shoulders. Mom has situated herself on the floor, amidst the mittens and the toques and the boots, and James, dutiful boy that he is, backs up toward her so she can tie the scarf beneath his hood.

My boot will not slide past my heel and I start to whimper, exasperated and angry now too. Mom yanks me toward her and pushes my foot into place.

"Nice boots, eh, Baba?" Mom asks, looking at the camera. "Bought them in the States even!"

Baba doesn't answer her. Instead, she speaks to James and Marion. "OK, say goodbye to Baba and Gida."

James runs over to Gida and squeezes his neck. Gida's cheeks are growing hollow and he's developed a harsh cough, although we do not yet know why. The common cold is common enough to not worry anyone. He wipes his eyes quickly and then pulls Marion in for a hug. The kids both kiss him, one by one, before Baba puts the camera down to hug them herself. She saves her tears for later, when no one else is around.

I'm still whimpering, the boot solution not having solved much of anything.

"Brit!" Dad yells. "Quiet already!"

I stop crying, and we're all quiet as we file out of the house. It's time for my brother and sister to go back home. *To their real home. To their real parents.* No one explains why or what this means. I'm not yet old enough to ask such questions. It is just how it is—how it will always be.

—

Within a month, two brothers and a sister will join our family. But my mother is quickly overwhelmed. She tells the social worker it's too much for her and they are gone after a week. Then, one week later, two younger sisters come to stay. Mom tells me from the beginning that Stephanie and Bailey are just going to be with us for a short while, but I'm not sure I understand what that really means. They leave after two months. Then there is Julie and Sarah—and after Julie and Sarah, there is Amanda and Noreen and Shayanne. Then there is Fred and Shanny. After them, I will have several more sisters, but I will never have another brother. In total, I will have twenty-one foster siblings before my seventh birthday. Every one of them will be Native.

When one of the mothers in the neighbourhood refuses to allow her daughter to play with us, the "kids from CFS"—Child and Family Services—I will come to recognize an obvious truth: we are the children people do not want around. Our lives are movable. Transferable. An inconvenience that requires a solution. When we don't fit, we're simply relocated. The lucky among us are returned to our first families, although I suppose the definition of "lucky" is debatable. And aren't I the luckiest of all? I'm adopted. I'm reminded of this again and again and again—until I begin to believe there is something inherently wrong with me for not feeling unendingly lucky. But I'm the one they say does not ever have to leave. And I cannot deny that that is very lucky indeed.

Chapter Four

Within weeks of developing that nagging cough that refuses to go away, Gida goes to the doctor. His scans show a body that looks like a Christmas tree draped with lights. The cancer in Gida's lungs spreads quickly, like a Pac-Man chomping its way through his body, from lymph node to organ and back again. He sees no point in quitting smoking, the damage already done, and, really, he's not wrong.

It is his fifty-sixth birthday, a cold Groundhog Day in 1992 with over ten inches of snow on the ground. Baba and Gida's house is filled with friends and family. Cigarette smoke and recordings of Gida's own polka music waft through the living room, where Gida has stationed himself. Baba hurries from the kitchen to the living room and back to the kitchen, filling every empty plate she can find with birthday cake and pouring Coke into any glass she passes—and dosing a few with a shot of whiskey, as she sees fit. If she keeps herself busy, perhaps she will be able to out-scurry her own emotions.

Julie and Sarah and I are huddled around the game Operation. None of us have the necessary fine-motor skills, and the little man buzzes obnoxiously every few seconds as our tweezers make contact with his metal insides. My sisters joined our family a few weeks ago and have become my eighth and ninth siblings. Julie is a year my senior and loves being an older sister. She's taken to calling me "Baby Brittany"—the same way James used to. Sarah and I are closer in age, only a few months separating us, and she has yet to refuse whenever I ask her to re-enact scenes from our favourite movie, *Problem Child 2*. Sometimes she's Trixie and other times she reluctantly agrees to be Junior. Always, we end our game by running out of the room, squealing as the make-believe toilet in the pretend bathroom is about to explode.

Gida opens the gifts on the coffee table while Baba records him. A bottle of whiskey, a new long-sleeve flannel and a deluxe cassette storage unit Mom found at the department store.

"Look at how many cassettes it can hold! You can fit over one hundred in there!" she says.

Gida tries to look impressed, his face illuminated by the warm light from the lamp beside him. *I will never be able to use this*, his eyes seem to say. Mom looks like she's about to cry.

"OK," Baba says, abruptly placing her camcorder on the coffee table close to Mom. "That's enough."

Gida passes away in the hospital four months from the day he is diagnosed with stage four metastatic lung cancer. The hospital in which my other grandfather will die in a few years, and then my grandmother, and the one where, a couple decades from now, I will care for my own patients.

JULY 19, 1992
HOME VIDEO

We're on a stage. My sisters Julie and Sarah stand to my right. They're dressed in lacy blue-and-white dresses. I'm wearing a pink-and-white dress that's almost as wide as I'm tall. With its tulle and frills, this dress would embarrass any Mennonite child, but Mom can't help herself. She will always say that her favourite part of being a mother is the fun she has in making us look cute. We try to be agreeable, even when she tackles the knots at the backs of our heads with her hair pick. We're like well-tended dolls.

To my left stands my cousin George. He's the cutest child in the family and even my mother cannot deny this. Auntie has dressed him in a grey suit jacket, a crisp white shirt, a black tie and black dress pants. His chubby cheeks look as though they're ready to burst.

Grandma, sitting at a table in the very centre of the room, looks special today. She's wearing a short-sleeved cream dress with a mauve-and-red-rose print.

The piano begins to play, and Mom, standing a few feet below us offstage, waves at us to start singing. My sisters look slightly terrified. I can't blame them. A room full of staring, solemn white faces is daunting, even for the experienced among us.

"Oh, be careful, little eyes, what you see." We're shy and the camcorder picks up Mom's voice more than any of ours. We shake our index fingers and point to our eyes. "Oh, be careful, little eyes, what you see! For God is up above"—we point to the sky, our voices rising—"and he's looking down with love." Our hands settle against our chests. "Oh, be careful, little eyes, what you see."

It's my paternal grandparents' fiftieth wedding anniversary and they've rented out a hall next to the local skating rink for the occasion. They married when my grandmother was twenty-one and my grandfather was thirty. After having ten biological children, they began fostering and adopting. Although Mennonites have a skepticism of the outside world, some feel connected to the idea that by opening their homes to foster children, they are opening their homes to God. "Whatever you do for the least of these . . ." Throughout my childhood, I will listen as adults say they felt called to raise "these children" and impart them with God's love. Raising us means serving him. I will never hear my grandmother speak about fostering or adopting in this way, however, and for this I'm grateful. In the end, my grandparents adopted three children and fostered 169 more, almost all of whom were Native. By the time they were finished adopting, my grandfather was well into his sixties—and several of his grandchildren were older than his youngest children. When I was adopted, many of my first cousins already had kids older than I was. Mennonite families can often be like this, like a garden that is so large and so full, it's difficult to appreciate what was planted first. Grandma, somehow, is both the sun and the soil. None of us would be together if it were not for her. When I'm older and she's gone and I ask Dad and one of my aunts why my grandparents chose to foster when, really, no one else around them was during that time, all they will say is that she just loved raising children. "I dunno," Dad will reply, shrugging. "Mom didn't talk about why. She just cared."

Mom often says she never thought of fostering before she married Dad. No one in her life growing up had ever done so. She enjoys fostering because it's the only way she can raise more children, she's told me.

Dad fosters in the hopes he and Mom can show my siblings some love and make them feel cared for during a scary time while they're away from their birth families. He's continuing on with a tradition that's important to his mother—of course, he will never say this in so many words.

Today is a day to be celebrated, yes, but we do not celebrate quite like other families do. There is no alcohol. There are no toasts, no emotional tributes to a well-weathered marriage. There are no tears of any sort. No hugging. No gifts. But there is prayer and there is order. There are fresh homemade buns with strawberry and rhubarb jam, and sweet pickles and coleslaw. There is a guitar and a microphone and an uncle who strums and aunties who sing. There are thanks given to God and, although there is little display of affection, there is love. It's here in the way my grandfather adjusts my grandmother's chair before she sits down, in the way he catches the napkin beside her plate before it falls to the floor. It's here in the way my grandmother lifts me onto her lap when we're done singing and the way Grandpa taps me on the shoulder so I might turn to look at him. He speaks mostly Low German and his English is fractured at best. When we do try to communicate, we're left staring at each other, holding out our empty palms and offering shy smiles in lieu of spoken words. It is enough. It has to be enough.

SEPTEMBER 20, 1992
HOME VIDEO

It's a Sunday afternoon and we're at Baba's house for lunch again. Mom has dressed Julie, Sarah and me in matching white crewneck sweaters adorned with kittens and sparkles. My sisters and I are standing in front of Baba's brass stand, the one on which she keeps photos and an assortment of crosses. She's begun to fill frames that previously held photos of her and Gida with photos of her and me. My arms are hugging my older sister's waist. Julie's hair is cut short. It resembles Baba's style, which is quite fashionable if you're a middle-aged white woman. Still, the cut could never hide how adorable Julie really is. Her hair is dark, black, like I'll always wish mine to be. Sarah wraps her arms around my neck. We're a train of hugs and we're utterly delighted by this. In this moment, we're happy. There's no denying it.

Chapter Five

It's shortly before my fourth birthday when my mother tells me the story of my adoption. It will become my strongest early memory—one I don't need to colour in by looking at old photos or home videos. A memory I will later recall with more specificity than Mom ever will.

It's a warm summer day and the mosquitoes are out in full force. The ceiling fan hums, rattling its arms above us and sending tiny dust bunnies floating through the air. Mom and I are sitting cross-legged on the faded blue comforter of her bed. A thread, thick like fishing line, is poking out from the comforter's stitching. I wrap it around my finger; it digs in the tighter I twist. We said goodbye to Julie and Sarah only a week ago. These goodbyes are becoming more difficult. I'm learning, though I can't yet put it into words, that my family will never have the permanence others seem to be offered.

To tell her story, Mom sets a few of my dolls out in front of us. She grabs one of the Barbies and one of the Kens. It's Dylan, actually, from *Beverly Hills 90210*, but without his earring. Dad was furious when Mom bought him for me as an early birthday gift. He ripped the doll from my hands and declared, face reddened and spit flying from the corners of his mouth, that no child of his would have a boy doll with a piercing. Mom shrugged half-heartedly without objection.

"Barbie and Dylan wanted to have a baby," Mom explains, "but they can't." Her face is serious. "But, Skipper . . ." She picks up the teenage doll and sets the couple aside. "She has a baby, but she can't take care of it. See?" Mom is prepared; Skipper is holding a tiny baby doll sucking on a tiny soother and wrapped in a tiny blanket. Mom takes it from Skipper's arms and brings it to Barbie and Dylan. "So, Skipper gives her baby to this mommy and daddy." Her perfectly pencilled brows sit high on her forehead. She loves telling a good story and I'm an entranced audience. "And that's how Mommy and Daddy got Brittany!"

I nod, elbows perched on my knees. Makes sense. One mother has a child she cannot care for and another wants a baby. It's that simple. It will forever be this simple to my mother and my father. It will cease feeling this simple to me the older I become, the more questions I have, the more siblings I gain and then lose. But for now, it all feels straightforward. This moment does not redefine my life or what I understand of my family. Without anyone having explained it to me, on some level I think I already knew. None of my siblings had been born to my parents. My cousins Wyatt and George weren't born to theirs. To be adopted, especially if you're Native, is such a norm in my family, it probably could have gone without saying. In the same way

I knew on some level I hadn't been born to my parents, I think I knew I was Native. My foster siblings, my foster cousins, my adopted cousins—we all were.

What does change is that I begin to imagine my birth mother. A snapshot of her forms in my mind that I'm unable to forget: a teenage girl with long, dark-brown hair and warm, olive skin like mine. *She's tanned, too,* I will think whenever I imagine her. "Tanned." It's what Mom calls the colour of my skin. My skin, it seems, is almost an extension of her own. Even though, no matter the minutes she spends in the sun, no matter the time I spend hiding under the trees, our shades will never come close to matching. In my daydream, my birth mother always sits on a mattress on the floor in an otherwise empty room. She holds her knees tight against her chest as a social worker leaves the room, carrying something in her arms. It's a baby and that baby is me. *That's my mother,* I will always think. A faceless young girl, alone, in the corner of a room somewhere. She will remain there in my mind even when I'm old enough to know what the inside of a hospital room looks like. When I'm old enough to know that hospital beds do not lie flat against the floor, and that women usually give birth with at least a doctor or nurse or midwife in the room. When I'm old enough to know that the story of my birth mother and the story of my beginning are more complicated than Skipper and Barbie and Dylan from *90210*.

Years later, I'll wonder: Where does this image of my birth mother come from? Did I catch something on TV during a Sunday afternoon at Baba's? Did I infer it from the stories I'd heard, and would continue to hear—from my parents, from people at church, from strangers—about unwanted children and damaged mothers and incapable fathers, all of whom were always Native? When a couple in our town was diagnosed with infertility or after a woman suffered a miscarriage, I would often hear: *Why would this happen? There are so many unwanted children out there.* And when the laws changed and it became more difficult for white families to adopt Native kids, so many white people around me asked why. *Why, when these kids are so unwanted, are they being denied a family? Why are people being denied their chance at raising children just because they're white and the kids are not?* These questions, these judgments, would loop themselves throughout my childhood like a song on repeat.

I would come to believe—how could I not—that all that separates those of us who are fostered and adopted from those who are kept with their families is the fact that we are Native and they are not. There's a dirty quality within us, and it's something that can never be washed out of our skin no matter how hard our parents scrub. No matter how hard we ourselves sometimes scrub.

It's an early Saturday morning when Dad tells me to run to the barn to choose a cat to bring inside. Since Mom's white cat, Nadja, died and Julie and Sarah left, the house has felt insufferably empty. I've recently forged friendships with three imaginary brothers, Coyhoy, Teetaw and Boots, but they're moody buddies at best and they don't help me feel any less alone when Mom turns off the lights at night. So when I ask for a companion, my parents don't protest.

One of the barn cats had kittens a few months ago and Dad says they're ready to be separated. Neither of my parents feel it's a good idea to bring the five of them indoors, so I settle for just one. I will always want to bring them all inside; over the years our photo albums will contain pictures of me, eyelids swollen and red, holding kittens my father has ordered me to return to the barn after I've snuck them inside.

I choose a grey, black and white-striped kitten with a white moustache and white paws that look like they've been dipped in milk. It's the cuddliest with me, but I can't help but feel guilty for not choosing the others. Dad picks up the kitten, flips it on its backside in mid-air, and looks between its legs, before declaring it's a girl. I use my T-shirt to create a hammock for her and carry her back to the house, holding her tight against my stomach.

We've had so many dogs on the farm, but most of them have come and gone faster than my siblings. It's a tough life for dogs in the country. A few months ago, my dog Ruby, whom I'd named after a puppy in a children's book, was shot by a neighbour when he found her in his chicken coop. Another of our dogs, Dakota, was shot in similar fashion only a year earlier.

I walk inside, pretending I'm pregnant, and show my baby to Mom, who giggles. We think on a name for a few minutes before Mom suggests Tabitha. I decide that the name is almost as beautiful as my new kitten. Tabitha quickly evolves into Tabby. When it's time for bed, I place her on my comforter and she claims stock in half my pillow. I wiggle my head next to hers, trying not to disturb her, before I fall asleep. I don't mention my imaginary brothers visiting me for weeks.

MAY 9, 1993
HOME VIDEO

"Ugh, yuck!" The camcorder whips down to Mom's right foot. She's just stepped in manure on her way to the barn. From a chicken? Cow? Horse? She never can tell—it's all disgusting to her, regardless. How she ended up a farmer's wife, no one knows, least of all her. The camera cuts out for a second, presumably for her to yell to Dad, who is yards away, out by the pigs, and who will ignore her as she runs back to the house to grab another pair of wicker sandals.

"OK," she huffs, back behind the camera and clearly annoyed. "Here are the chickens!" The camcorder zooms in on the coop beside the barn. Dad built it when they first moved in a decade ago and he's filled it with wild birds of all sorts: hens and quails and fowls clucking and chirping, ducks quiet and settled off to the side.

Mom whips the camcorder around again. She has never been sturdy with this thing, and my stomach will always do tiny flips whenever I watch her videos. "Oh, there's James," she says, zooming in on one of the chickens. "He was the first one Brittany named." The camera zooms in on another. "And that one's Marion." She lets out one of her signature high-pitched giggles. "We just wanted to say we miss you and hope you're happy."

She will turn this recording into a VHS tape and mail it to the kids' house in the city. Although it's been a year and a half since they lived with us, she remains in contact with them. They were her first children after me.

Chapter Six

JUNE 30, 1993

PHOTOGRAPH

It's my fourth birthday and Mom has invited some aunties and uncles and cousins to our house to celebrate. I'm sitting at the head of the table, where Dad otherwise always sits, with a colourful Care Bear cake Mom bought from Penner Foods perched in front of me. James stands to my left with his arm draped over my shoulder. His smile will always be the first thing I notice whenever I see a photo of him. Marion is smiling too, but only slightly—she has always been the shy one of us three. She's resting her chin on the table, eyes wide at the cake. She still struggles to finish each meal, and Dad still refuses to let her leave the table until her plate is clear—but just as Dad always has room for chips after dinner, she always has room for dessert.

Several of my dad's biological siblings are here. George is also here, along with his brother and their foster siblings and a few of our other cousins too. This photo is like so many other moments in my childhood: an entire family of white adults situated at the periphery of the room, and Native children at the centre. There is not a single white child here. And not a single Native adult.

My parents don't explain why James and Marion come to live with us again this summer. This is just how it is. We live the kinds of lives where we are with our families and then we are not and then we are back with them again. James and Marion and I are all part-Native. I don't understand why my brother and sister are returned to their biological families while I remain with Mom and Dad. It's just another in a string of unsolvable mysteries. Like how God is real but we cannot see him. Or how Jesus lived and died and then lived again. All these things—they just are. *And why do you have so many questions anyway,* Mom always wants to know.

James is a little different from how I remember him. He's less affectionate, less open. It's like a door to one of the playrooms in his heart has closed and he's grown up in the time we've spent apart.

He and Marion—who seems mostly the same to me, apart from her hair, which has grown longer—are sharing bunk beds in their old room again. Marion has the top bunk, as before. Mom dresses Marion and me as twins once again. James resumes wearing his favourite pair of coveralls, excited to see that they still fit him—although the skin of his ankles has begun to peek out. Dad is in a better mood when James is around, and our family feels more whole than it's felt for a while. It's almost like nothing has changed. Even though everything has changed. I've had ten other siblings since they were with us. And I'm older now. Smarter. I understand that they're not staying forever.

"Now I lay me down to sleep, I pray the Lord my soul to keep," I say, my *r*s more like *w*s, my fingers folded diligently over one another. I pray for all my siblings who've come and gone. For James and Marion's parents. For Grandma and Grandpa and George. For Baba. And I thank Jesus for Tabby, who still sleeps next to me every night.

I've begun fearing the day I'll be taken away. What I'm most afraid of is being separated from Tabby. I can't imagine falling asleep without her, waking up without her. I wonder, if I show Jesus how thankful I am for her, if he might make sure I don't ever have to leave. I drift off to sleep slowly, Tabby's head resting on my forearm.

A creak on the stairs wakes us up. I tell Tabby not to leave the bed, then I tiptoe toward my half-closed bedroom door. Mom is standing at the top of the stairs, across the hallway.

"He's doing it again," she whispers to Dad. Dad is leaning against their bedroom doorframe a few feet from her, rubbing the ginger stubble on his chin. His face looks concerned or irritated or tired. I can't quite make it out.

"Well, go get him," he says.

I can hear James downstairs in the kitchen, whimpering like he's hurt. It's not the first time this has happened since James and Marion moved back in with us. It's not even the first time this week.

"He's calling for her," Mom says.

"Well, go!" Dad says. Now he's annoyed—this I can tell.

These nightly wanderings were never something James did when he lived with us the first time. Now, when he's not sleepwalking and calling out for his mom, I hear him crying in his bed before I fall asleep. I don't understand what's happened.

I step back from my door and slide back into bed next to Tabby.

"You're such a good girl," I whisper. I fall back asleep once I hear Mom return to her bedroom after tucking James under his covers again. The house is quiet and we're all where we should be.

Our grey Honda Accord hums down the Trans-Canada Highway, the wheat fields long harvested, the sun blanketed by grey clouds, as we travel an hour and fifteen minutes to visit the home of James and Marion's parents in Winnipeg. Usually, my siblings visit their families without me while I spend the day at Baba's, but today is not a scheduled visitation day.

No matter the length of the drive, car rides always put me to sleep, and I awake at the sound of James slamming the car door shut. I rub my eyes and see that Marion is still beside me in the back seat. When I jump out of the vehicle, a November gust surrounds me, sharp and fresh.

Inside my siblings' two-storey townhouse, the air thickens—it's like wading through swamp water. James and Marion run out of sight into the kitchen; I hear a chair dragging against the linoleum floor, then a chip bag opening. The living room is dimly lit and the curtains are drawn. Cigarette smoke crawls slowly toward me, reminding me of being at Baba's. James and Marion's father is sitting in a recliner across from the television, ashtray on his knee. My parents and I visited here a few times after my siblings left, and, twice, their father drove out to our farm. He's always greeted me with a hearty "Heya, Brit, how are ya," but today is different. Today there is no greeting for any of us, not even his children.

Mom is silent, a rarity for her, as she seats herself on a couch near the recliner. Dad leans against the staircase, near my siblings' father. I always marvel at the difference in size between their father and mine. Their dad is at least six feet tall, with broad shoulders and shoulder-length brown hair. He always dresses in a beat-up flannel shirt that smells like smoke and gasoline. Dad is at least half a foot shorter, narrow from shoulders to hips, and smells like wood shavings. Although he's not a large man, I'm always surprised to see Dad looking small in comparison to anyone. He will never seem small to me.

"She had her boyfriend beat me up last night," their father says. "He came at me with a bat."

I understand that he's talking about James and Marion's mother. "Boyfriend" . . . I guess they're not together anymore. Maybe that's why my siblings have come to stay with us again?

I listen closely to every word he says to my parents, who seem to have forgotten that I'm in the room too. I inspect his face through the darkness and I can see a mixture of purple and red swelling beneath his gold-rimmed aviators. His upper lip is almost the same colour as the maroon lipliner Mom uses to overline her lips. He has cuts across his nose and across his right eye. The patchwork of tattoos on his forearms always reminds me of the quilts my grandmother sews, but the cuts and bruising on his arms are so dark I can barely see the designs today. He's the most battered human I have ever seen.

James calls my name from the kitchen. "We're going to the playground!" he yells. I look to the adults, who are still speaking, before I walk out to join my brother. James throws open the back door and we race to reach the big tire swing, which reminds me of the one my father has hung for us at home.

It's not long until James and Marion leave us again. I can't explain how I know that this time is final—they won't be back again. Somehow, I just know. I don't name any more chickens after them.

My imaginary brothers return and I explain to Baba how the scratches on my arms are *actually* from Teetaw and not Tabby. "We had a fight," I tell her. "He was a bad boy and he hurt me."

A few weeks later, I'm told that new siblings are coming soon. A brother and sister just in time for Christmas. A miracle, it must be. I'm so excited that every night after I'm tucked into bed, I ask Mom how many sleeps are left until they're with us.

I keep asking until the day they finally arrive, after which another line of questioning takes hold of my mind—one I've obsessed over before. "But when, Mom? When? When will it happen? When am I going to be taken away?" I become so preoccupied by it that Mom soon grows annoyed with me. Annoyed of endlessly having to reassure me—of explaining that *No, Brittany, you will not get taken,* and *Yes, Brittany, you are here to stay.* Eventually, she stops repeating herself. I do not stop asking.

Chapter Seven

"Smile for the camera!" I say to Fred whenever I sneak the camcorder away from Baba. I hardly need to, though—my brother is always smiling. His thin upper lip dissolves the moment he laughs. He has a big gap where four of his top front teeth should be, bookended by two silver caps that cover his incisors. Mom gave him an unflattering bowl cut the first week he and his half-sister, Shannon, arrived, and she's maintained it in the six months since. Although he's only six days younger than I am, I think of him as my little brother.

Shannon is two and a half years old. We've taken to calling her Shanny, which seems to suit her. My sister is sweet, her voice soft and quiet. She climbs onto Dad's lap at church and he lets her sit there the entire service. She laughs at almost anything our brother or I do and it makes me think that, certainly, I must be the funniest sister in the world. I can tell Mom is excited to have another little girl around. She's cut Shanny's hair in a style similar to Fred's—I will never understand her draw to this hairstyle.

Each day, Mom combs the top half of Shanny's hair into a ponytail so it sits like a little spout at the very centre of her head. I would hate it if Mom did my hair like this but Shanny seems to like it.

My siblings and I spend most mornings laughing and screaming as Nala, our new black Lab puppy, chases us around the yard, our bare feet slipping on the grass wet from morning dew. We spend our afternoons in our *gummistiefels*, scouring the ditches at the end of our long, tree-lined driveway for tadpoles. I'm careful to avoid the culverts, and make sure Fred and Shanny never get too close either. Even when the water dries up and we play in the ditches, I avoid those culverts. Baba has told me too many stories of children drowning when they get too close, the suction so powerful it can pull you under so you can never get out. The sun shines so hot some days we dress in nothing more than our bathing suits and rubber boots as we trek down to reach the water, fishing nets hung on our shoulders and jars in our hands. Nala nips at the backs of our legs and weaves between us as Mom traipses slowly behind, carrying a lawn chair in one hand and a tall cup of iced tea in the other.

On a day so hot the farm cats are hiding in the shade of the bales and the cows are huddling under the trees at the periphery of the pasture, Fred and I make a dash for the ditch. Shanny tries to keep up but falls behind and, shoulders drooped, waits for Mom to catch up to her. "Shanny fanny," Mom calls. "Want some iced tea?" She holds her cup out for my sister to take a sip.

"Freddie, over here!" I yell. I'm several inches into the water now and some has trickled over the tops of my boots, but I don't care. With his small fishing net held against his shoulder,

Fred sloshes over and crouches down to meet me.

"Look," I whisper, pointing a few feet in front of us. His eyes squint and his head draws in closer to mine. The water is murky and they're barely noticeable, blending in with the mud, but we can see a herd of tadpoles clustered together near the underside of a big rock. Fred's eyes widen. "There's a lot of 'em!" he says, and we reach for our nets. Shanny is sitting behind us on the gravel road with Mom, taking another sip from her iced tea.

"Now," I say, and our nets dive under the muddy water, gliding past each other, before we raise them high into the air.

"We get any?" Fred asks, bringing his net back down so he can look into it.

I inspect mine, counting with my fingers the small, slimy creatures wriggling around. "Four!" I say.

"I got chree!" Fred says, pronouncing the word in his own way. He points at his net and counts them again. "One, two, chree!"

My cheeks and shoulders feel the heat of the afternoon, my ears thrum-thrum-thrumming. I look over at my mother, her legs stretched out in front of her, her face aimed toward the sun. Her skin is shimmering from the baby oil she's applied and is starting to turn red.

On the walk back to the house, Fred does not stop looking at his jar. Maybe he never caught tadpoles wherever he lived before coming here. "Do you think they'll turn into frogs?" he asks.

"I dunno," I say. "My cousin George says they do." My tadpoles have only ever died.

Fred grins, looking back at his jar. "Yeah, I think they will."

—

In the evenings, we march to the bathroom, where Mom runs toothpaste across each of our toothbrushes. Sometimes, when Fred tries to spit his toothpaste into the basin, it spatters all over the counter and Shanny and I laugh so hard we both swallow ours. Once Mom wipes us and the counter down, we run to our rooms, waiting for her to tuck us in.

"Night, Freddie," I call out.

"Night, Brittany," he says.

"Night, Shanny," I say.

"Night, Britty," she says.

I find an easy comfort in this routine. Happy to fall asleep knowing that my brother and sister are in the room next door. When I'm older, I will wish that Baba had been here to document these moments. To document it all. So I would always be able to hear the sound of Fred's voice calling goodnight. So I would never forget Shanny snoring from the top bunk. The benign melodies in the night that soothe me to sleep.

AUGUST 24, 1994

HOME VIDEO

Years from now, I will not remember this moment. Like many of the memories Baba catches on film, it will feel like it happened to another child. A child I recognize is me but whose memories have vanished. It will feel as though parts of me have died.

Baba is behind the camcorder as I attempt to ride my new bike down her street. She is nervous because I'm not wearing a helmet or elbow and knee pads. But I'm being raised running on gravel roads with bare feet—toughened by having hydrogen peroxide poured over every wound. I do, however, appreciate the purple-and-white tassels Baba made Dad tie onto the ends of my handlebars. How beautiful, I think.

Dad is jogging behind me and gives me a push as he yells, "Now, Brit. Pedal!"

My little legs hustle and I manage to make it a few feet before I lose control. Suddenly, I'm barrelling toward the curb. Dad rushes to catch my tail-end and snags me before I topple onto the concrete. He says something to me but Baba's camcorder is too far away to pick up our words. I step off my bike and Dad—in a move so silly, so unusual, I would not believe it if Baba was not documenting this moment—saddles up and begins to pedal the bike himself. I run after him, chasing after those tassels, a look of abandon on my face.

Later that afternoon, Dad draws a hopscotch pattern on the driveway and teaches my siblings and me how to dance our way across the lime-green tiles. One foot. One foot. Two feet. One foot. Two feet. One foot. I pick it up easily, following behind him and mimicking his hops. Fred does not get it, no matter how hard he tries.

"It looks like he's doing the powwow," Mom says. She and Baba laugh loudly, out of sight behind the camera.

"Hey." My father turns his head sharply and the two women stop laughing.

Dad circles back and grabs Fred's hand in his. It's a moment of such tenderness it will make me want to cry whenever I replay this tape. Fred glances up at our father, then back down at his feet. They do it together. One. One. Two. One. Two. One. Dad is still holding his hand.

—

In the fall, nine months after Fred and Shanny arrive, I begin kindergarten and Fred begins daycare. Although Fred is the same age as me, he's not ready for school yet, and this makes sense to me without anyone explaining why. Decades from now, in medical school, I'll understand that he has so many of the physical hallmarks, the "syndromic features," of fetal alcohol spectrum disorder.

I enjoy going to school. I love learning how to read and don't even mind the hour-long bus ride. My parents had enrolled me in T-ball in the summer, and a few of the girls from my team are also in my class, one of whom, Kassie, will become a lifelong friend. Although I get nervous at the start of most days, unsure of what to expect when I get to school—a trait of mine that will never fully dissipate—I love making new friends and I enjoy learning. I listen intently to what the other kids say, and I pay attention to what makes them laugh, what makes them cry and what they do that makes the teacher upset—and I take note. I'm always taking notes.

One morning, Dad lets me bring a chicken to class for Show and Tell. I love hearing the other kids' laughter at the sight of the bird. I feel proud. In later years, I'll bring one of our barn cats born without a tail and a piglet we're bottle-feeding because it was the runt of the litter.

At the end of our days, Fred and I return home excited to exchange stories and entertain our family. "I ate my lunch!" Fred always happily declares. "I had flies today," he says one evening, and Dad looks confused. Mom smirks. *Fries,* she mouths. Fred loves his fries.

I am not aware of this as it's happening, but during this time, my parents are quietly trying to adopt my siblings. Dad makes it clear to Child and Family Services that this is what he and Mom want to do, and that it's clearly what's best for the children too. "The kids are happy here," he tells the social worker. It's already been determined that they will never be able to return to their biological parents and they need a permanent home. "Why not us?" he argues. What matters more than the love my parents have for them? What matters more than the happiness my siblings feel here? "They are at home here," he says. "It shouldn't be about race or culture or where they come from. What should matter is that they have a home."

Chapter Eight

Billboards surround the periphery of our town. One sign reminds entrants that Jesus is "the way, the truth, and the life." The Mennonite religion is the foundation upon which this community was built in 1874. The town is decidedly dry and will remain so until a referendum in 2013. (In the end, it will be revealed that the "ban" on alcohol had never actually been law to begin with.) You're never very far from a church around here.

It's another type of family, church. Not the kind of family where you're free to share your individuality, your heart. In my world, family is for holding a shared legacy and traditions. For gathering around a hearty meal and offering thanks to the Lord. For keeping secrets. It's for worshipping together through song and prayer, and it's for the hierarchy of responsibility, providing, and duty. Church is much of the same.

Our church is filled with rows of identical pews, worn and splintered in some parts, but sturdy nonetheless. Life is promised to contain discomfort and pain, so why should our seating be any different? Surely it means more if we praise the Lord even amidst our discomfort. In a couple of years, I will slide across one of the pews—really, I should know better—and a long sliver will pierce through my tights into the back of my left thigh. Mom will bring me to the church nursery in the upstairs loft, designed so mothers can still pay attention to the service while caring for their infants, where she will pull tweezers from her makeup bag. Still squeamish, she will ask another mother to help, and I won't whimper when the woman digs into my thigh with the tweezers for a minute before retrieving the sliver. I will return quietly to that same pew minutes later.

Sometimes, sitting in these pews—Fred beside me and Shanny asleep between Mom and Dad—I wonder if I'm psychic as I try to guess the next words that will come from the pastor's mouth. Sometimes, I convince myself that I am, and this becomes my little secret. I'll never mention my sinful thoughts to anyone.

Most of Dad's family attends this church. My grandparents switched to this congregation years ago when their old church refused to allow one of my uncles to attend Sunday School because he was Native. "Dad said, 'If you can't accept him, you can't accept us,'" my father tells me. Most of our services are held in English, apart from the hymns, which we sing in Low German. I know only a few basic words of that language—but this doesn't stop me from at least pretending that I'm singing along.

We spend our Sunday mornings here and I'm back at church again on Wednesday evenings for Awana club, where our evenings are filled with biblical-themed crafts and games and, like at Sunday School, we're quizzed on the verses we spent the previous week memorizing. Unlike at Sunday School, we're awarded badges here for our mothers to iron onto our bright-blue vests. Of all the four- and five-year-olds, my vest has the widest assortment of badges. I've even won a badge for having won the most badges. I'm proud of my vest. Of being a good girl. Good girls do not get taken away.

I'm five years old, and it's my second year attending clubs at church. Next year will be my last, after I become sick with headaches and stomach aches most Wednesday nights and Mom eventually stops trying to convince me to go. She's never been one to put up much of a fight against anything, and I'm not overly convinced she believes in the cause of Awana as much as she should. But I'm okay with this. The only times after that that I'll agree to go to clubs will be on the rare occasions my cousin George asks me to. Those are the only times I'll feel comfortable being there.

My cousin has been as much a staple in my life as my parents, as Baba, as Tabby. I feel safe in his presence, protected, like I once did with James. I have secretly taken to hoping that he and I are biologically related. Wishing for a connection between us that spans our respective adoptions—a connection older and deeper than our current family can provide. *What if he's my brother,* I think. *What if our birth moms are actually sisters?*

Like me, George has grown up with foster siblings. He also has an adopted older brother, but he's so much older than us that I don't really know him. I have so many older cousins, some as old as my parents, that I don't know most of them beyond their first names. On the weekends and in the summers, George and I and my siblings are often together. Both of our mothers married into the family, and they love getting together to share gossip, a pitcher of iced tea and a bag of Hickory Sticks. We spend most of our summers outside while our mothers sit in plastic lawn chairs by the back door, shaded by the trees. There are times when George, his foster siblings, Fred, Shanny and I are on the other side of the yard, building a city in the sandbox or calling out to the cows in the pasture, and our mothers' laughter travels through the trees like a galloping bull's bellow.

Mom loves little nicknames. Shanny-Fanny, Freddie the Farmer and, for me, Pooperdoo and Poopichka. She calls my cousin Georgie Porgie, and his mom likes this too. For a while, Fred thought that was George's actual name until finally I told him it wasn't. Still, it's catchy—I can't lie—and I'll often find myself murmuring, even when I am an adult: *Georgie Porgie, pudding and pie . . .* Auntie calls George and me "Bert and Ernie," and I don't even care that I'm the less likeable character—I'm just happy to be a part of our pair.

George's hands are dotted with warts, and it's because of this that I always avoid touching frogs, convinced if I do my fingers will look like his in the morning. Whenever I notice a frog hopping along the gravel of my driveway, I yell for George so he can scoop it in his palms and hold it for us to inspect. When we're done, he sets it free. This is George's way. He's afraid of very little. But because he's soft-spoken, especially around adults, people think he has little to say. When it's just the two of us, there's never more than a second of silence. We lose ourselves outside, under the evening sky fading to night, as the grass dampens and the crickets come out to play. This is our church. The puddles on the driveway our communion. The pebbles poking at the undersides of our feet, the skin refusing to break, our tiny prayers. We have been baptized by the ditch water, forever children of this land.

God seems more real to me here than he ever will when I'm sitting on those stiff benches. He's in the soft breeze that sweeps the baby hairs at the back of my neck, beaded with sweat from running. He's in the grass stuck to our knees. In the howls of our dogs when the sun goes down. He's in the feel of the tree bark, prickly against my finger pads as I try to climb after my cousin who's already yards above me. God is here. I can feel it. Even though this isn't what I was taught. It's not what my parents believe. *You can't be here,* I want to tell God. *This is not where they say you are.*

With time, my body learns to tighten whenever I walk into our church. My back stiffens and my muscles grow rigid. I will always wash my hands at least two times after touching the steel beams in the foyer, which leave an iron-y residue on my fingers. I especially detest the church basement, with its cold, damp air and overpowering smell of the grape juice used for communion, stored there in bulk. But I try to ignore my body. *God is here,* I remind myself. *God is here, and if I don't feel him, it can only be because my body is wrong.*

It's not the last time my body will feel this way. Unsafe. But it is the first. My memories from this time quickly become disjointed. Perhaps it has to do with my age, narrative memories being more difficult to string together when one's so young. Perhaps it has to do with what happened—a way for my mind to protect itself from the pain. That shearing, sharp pain. That burning, deep pain. I wish my body could forget the pain. Whatever the reason, I will never possess a full remembrance of what happens here. My memories are like overexposed photos, like a VHS tape with black and white lines flickering across the screen. I will press the buttons, I will turn the knobs, hastily twisting so the picture might become clearer. I will want to see what there is to see. At some point, I will want to remember it all, because if I cannot remember it, I cannot protect myself. I am left just as exposed as those overexposed photos, just as chaotic as that fuzzy screen. I will want to remember it so I can control it. So I can tell my body to just stop hurting. So I can tell my body to stop remembering in ways I do not want to remember.

At times, it feels like a cliché, a little Indigenous girl left vulnerable in a church basement, surrounded by white boys and men meant to, if not protect her, then at the very least not hurt her. But clichés are clichés for a reason, I suppose.

But at six years old, I understand none of this. What I know within my bones is that God, the seer of all things, remembers. He was there, after all. And, of course, He is blameless. A perfect father with only perfect love for the undeserving daughter whose birth mom never wanted her. For something like this to have happened, it can only mean there is something wrong with me. It can only mean I welcomed it. And for that, I do not know if I will ever be able to forgive myself.

Chapter Nine

Fred, Shanny and I are told that they will be moving to their new homes one week before they leave. Really, it will always feel like we were given only a few minutes to adjust to the news and nothing more. Despite my parents' efforts to adopt my siblings, they've found themselves in the crossfires of a heated political argument over the "best interests of the child." My parents believe that race is irrelevant—that a family's love for a child is the only thing that matters when adopting. However, the government, after centuries of intentionally placing Native kids in white homes in an effort to "take the Indian out of the child," has recently begun prioritizing placing Native children into Native homes instead of white ones. Fred, Shanny and I understand none of this. All we know is that after two years with our family, my siblings will be separated from us and also from each other. They will be adopted into two different Native families who live several hours north of our home. It does not seem to occur to anyone that the children in question have voices too.

Mennonites distance themselves from the government—a lack of trust in government institutions is deeply ingrained in the culture. Despite this, Mennonites generally won't question authority. Life is simpler this way. Godlier, in many ways. So, I'm surprised, years from now, when I learn that my father questioned Fred and Shanny's social worker and challenged Child and Family Services. In a most non-Mennonite fashion, he disagreed with their decision to remove the children from his care—and he made sure they knew this. He made it clear that he did not think it was in the best interests of Fred or Shanny. It comforts me, in adulthood, when I uncover this part of the story. A part of me will feel taken care of when I discover that my father fought for this version of our family.

I will also feel conflicted about this part of my life, and isn't that a funny thing? That I'll feel both proud of my father's actions to try to protect a version of our family that I loved while also feeling angry at him for not understanding the complexities that brought us together in the first place. That I'll feel thankful for the government's efforts while also angry at how they seem to continually get it wrong, time and time again. What might have come of each of our biological families, our cultures, our communities had no one wished to erase us? In my parents' home, I would never have the chance to live within my culture. But now, maybe my siblings would have the chance to live within theirs. At the same time, I will always be heartbroken that they were prevented from becoming a permanent part of my family. They were already family to me. I did not want to know life without them.

When I'm older, I'll wonder if feeling this conflicted makes me less Indigenous. Does it mean that I care less about our cultures, our peoples? Does it mean that I'm betraying myself—betraying a part of who I am? I wonder if it just makes me a girl who will always wish her siblings could have remained her siblings.

My brother and sister poke their arms through the straps of their backpacks the day they're set to move. I pack a backpack too, though I'll be returning home with mine. Tabby follows us downstairs and I stop to kneel and scratch the top of her head. My siblings' bedroom has been stripped of the life that filled it. The bunk beds are naked, the drawers lie bare. There are no toys on the floor, and Shanny's slippers have been packed away. My toothbrush stands alone in the holder in the bathroom, as does my Minnie Mouse lunch box in the kitchen cupboard. We have not even left yet and the house is already occupied by the ghosts of them. Still, Tabby will be here when I return and for that I'm grateful. Fred picks her up and squeezes her a little too tightly. A tiny squeak escapes her, but he doesn't seem to notice. Shanny kisses Tabby's head and Dad opens the door.

"I'll be back," I whisper.

Dad pulls up to the parking lot. From the back seat, the three of us eye the four new parents stepping out of their vehicles only feet away. We have never met these people before. We don't yet know who Fred will be going home with. We've yet to learn who Shanny will call "Mom" and "Dad."

Dad stands back, hands in the front pockets of his jeans. He smiles, offers a quick handshake, and the nine of us stand in silence for a moment. I look to my mother and I look to my father, inspecting their faces, trying to parse what they must be feeling. Mom starts talking too much—fast and jittery. *She's scared,* I think. *Embarrassed, maybe.* She acts like this whenever she wants someone to like her. I reach for her hand but as soon as I graze her fingers, they're gone. I wish for her to see me, to look down at me, maybe to rub my back. But I'm small, too small for her to notice me right now. Too quiet for her to remember me here.

It's as though my father has managed to take a step back from us all without moving his body. Like he's a balloon that's deflated, a plant that's withered. It feels like I've opened the door to a room where he's changing. *I should not be seeing this,* I think. *I don't know what to do with this version of my dad.*

Later, when we return home, Mom will pack his lunch for tomorrow and I'll peek at his lunch box. It reminds me of a toolkit and always contains more wood shavings than crumbs. Sometimes Mom will pack him thick slices of ham sandwiched with butter in a bun from Don's Bakery. Sometimes she'll make him bologna and Kraft Singles on white bread. Always, she'll line his lunch box with an entire row of oatmeal chocolate chip cookies. I peer into his lunch box nightly, checking to see if Mom has remembered the cookies, and I'll picture my father eating these cookies at work and for some reason it will always make me sad. I imagine him as a boy who has just lost his family, eating lunch on the playground by himself.

Now, watching my father shrink from Fred's and Shanny's new parents, I don't think to reach for his hand. He is not that kind of father and I am not that kind of daughter. I come to him with scraped knees. I do not come to him with this. Like Mom, I'm not sure he can see me right now.

As Mom talks and the adults listen, my siblings and I do not say a word. None of us are crying, but none of us are smiling, either. We're silent. Fred's new mother opens her arms to him and he looks up at Dad, who nods. "Go," he says, and Fred walks to his new parents.

"Let's get a picture," Mom says. "Do you want a picture? I can mail it to you. Let's get a picture. There's a good spot!" She points to the single tree standing in the lot. "Say cheese," she tells Fred and his parents, and she giggles. Next, she directs Shanny to stand next to her new parents in front of the tree.

"Come." Mom beckons me and Dad. "Our turn." She hands the camera over to Fred's new mom.

"Oh, come on," Dad says. I can tell he's not in the mood.

"Oh, Paul. It's just one." She looks at Fred's mom and smiles. "Just one."

Then Mom offers Fred's parents his album, and Shanny's parents hers. She's done this with each of my siblings. She starts a photo album once they arrive and gives it to their families when they leave. She makes sure to include pictures of Christmas and birthdays and Easter egg hunts. She records the gifts they received for Christmas and from whom. If there are any recent photos of them with their biological families, Mom always includes those too. She tries her best to document it all.

Fred's and Shanny's albums are the largest she will ever create. They are filled with two years' worth of our childhoods. Fred's and my shared birthday parties. Shanny's potty-training. Fred's first day at daycare. The time we went to the zoo, and the time we went to a farm and petted llamas. There are photos of us in the yard, by the ditch with the dog, playing on bales and milking goats. In one picture, Fred stands next to Dad in coveralls that used to belong to James, holding a pail filled with milk replacer they will add to water to feed the calves. In another, Shanny is nestled on our aunt's lap at a family gathering, her ponytail fountain sprouting beneath Auntie's chin.

These albums do not contain the sound of the grasshoppers and the cows mooing on nights when the air in the house becomes so stuffy both Dad and Fred have a hard time breathing. They do not contain every Saturday morning we've spent, for the last two years, cuddled on our parents' bed under their comforter, watching cartoons on their old television set, while Dad is outside and Mom is in the kitchen on the phone. They do not contain Dad yelling at Fred and me for talking loudly through the walls in our bedrooms late at night. They do not contain Fred saying he doesn't want to leave. They cannot hold any of this. But they are all we have.

—

AUGUST 1995
THREE PHOTOGRAPHS

One. Fred smiles, his capped incisors sparkling, as he stands in between his two new parents, who look a lot more like him than Mom and Dad do.

Two. Shanny smiles, standing between hers.

Three. I smile, standing in front of two people who were, moments ago, our parents. Now they are just mine.

My siblings and I will never see each other again.

These are the photos demarcating the start of our new lives—our next chapters. Lives that have, despite our young ages, already included too many "next chapters" to count.

Chapter Ten

I will only have sisters from now on. Some of them will stay for a few months and some will stay longer. One of my sisters will arrive when she's just shy of four years old and will insist on asking three questions of every stranger she meets: *What's your name? Where are you from? Who's your dad?* Mom will tie her hair in a ponytail on the top of her head like she did with Shanny, but that's where the similarities will end. She will be boisterous and funny, making Mom laugh even on the days when Baba has said something on the phone to hurt her feelings. She will follow her around the house like an undersized shadow, and sometimes Mom will dress herself and my sister in similar outfits—oversized polka-dot shirts and bike shorts, and each holding a cup of iced tea.

Another of my sisters will arrive when she's six and I'm almost seven. She will be standing on our driveway with her social worker when I return home from school one afternoon. She won't be able to look me in the eye until the social worker comments on our similar appearance and our long brown hair that reaches to our waists. We look so similar that people will think my parents found my biological sister. She will arrive with a pink-and-green backpack and a teddy bear held against her chest. She will leave a year and a half later with a photo album.

In the two years after Fred and Shanny leave, I will have seven more sisters who arrive and then leave, stay and then go. I won't be surprised when any of them depart, and I won't be sad in the way I once was.

When I'm nine, Mom will receive a phone call from CFS about a baby boy who's available for adoption. I will watch as Mom scribbles down his details. Daniel. Three months old. Failed hearing test. Brown eyes. I will jump up and down at the news and, for a moment, I will think my prayers and my letters to Santa have been answered. But the discussion between my parents will last no longer than an evening—Mom will decide she can't do the baby stage again. "It's not fair to you," she'll say to me. It won't matter how much I beg, how adamantly I promise that I will change every dirty diaper.

DECEMBER 1995
THREE PHOTOGRAPHS

One. We're all seated on a bench from oldest to youngest. There are six of us girls: my two siblings, three of my cousins and me. We're all holding matching stuffed cats with inflated bellies and marbles in them so it sounds like they're purring whenever they move. We're at a Christmas gathering with Dad's side of the family at the high school gym where my aunt and uncle work as janitors.

Two. The men have set up a volleyball net—not that anyone knows how to serve the ball properly. My dad and uncles peck at the ball like chickens, and every so often, one of them tries to spike it but completely misses and his body spins in mid-air. They look like young boys for a moment and this makes me feel happy in a way I can't quite describe.

Three. The men have also set up floor hockey nets for the boys. We girls remain on the sidelines, playing with our cats—but every so often, I saunter over to the other side of the gym to watch George. He runs after the ball quickly, like he does when we're catching toads on my driveway. He's the fastest cousin for his age but, sometimes, I beat him when we race. It's not anything I feel the need to brag about, but I do like reminding myself of it from time to time. Mostly, I love the way the wind feels in my hair when I run. I watch the other boy cousins chase him and I think to myself that I could keep up with them if I wanted to. For now, I would rather just watch.

It's another Sunday afternoon, and we're spending it at my grandparents' farm like we have every Sunday that's come before. Like the harvest, Sunday acts like the end of a season. It's our weekly November. Sundays are for church. They're for lunch at Baba's house, and *faspa* at Grandma and Grandpa's farm. Sundays are for hurried mornings trying to get out the door and lazy afternoons digesting the food and the day. They're for intense games of tag between cousins on my grandparents' tree-pocked acreage.

They're for prayer and giving thanks, for tired eyes at the end of the night, and Dad lifting my limp body from the middle seat of the van, asleep after the two-minute drive home. Sundays are for family.

It doesn't matter how often I visit my family on Sundays, I can always feel my body pulsing with both nervous energy and excitement before we even get to church in the morning. Dad seems to appreciate spending time at his parents', and we're often one of the first families to arrive. Within a few hours, there will be vehicles lining the backyard, the driveway and the road out front. The house my grandparents live in today is very different from the one in which Dad was raised. Not that he talks about it, but I pick up on the occasional reference to the old house from others. Mostly, everyone is concerned with the here and now; we do not like to look back on what was or what might have been.

We are not storytellers. We are singers. We are carpenters and we are farmers. We are hard workers and we are pious. We do not share our feelings and, if we are women, we do not share our opinions. We all have the same opinion. But we are allowed our own type of storytelling. Sometimes, Mom will repeat to my aunties something she heard from one of the ladies at church or something she observed. "Did you see what Kathy was wearing?" she might say, one brow arched. Or, "Did you hear about that family that always sits at the back of the church? What's their name? Friesen, I think. Well, did you hear how their boy grabbed the handle of a pot of boiling oil and it fell on him? Did you see his scars? They were in church this morning."

And one of my aunts, often George's mom, might chime in, "Oh, yeah, he's going to need surgery."

"No!" Mom will say with a gasp, her cheeks pale.

I am in constant search of story, of a narrative that feels whole and truthful and that helps me understand my family and my place in it. To make sense of my adoption and my many siblings and their disappearances, which feel an awful lot like death. Still, despite the lack of a Mennonite storytelling tradition, I'm able to piece together parts of my father's history. Dad and his many siblings were raised in a one-room house with no plumbing and an outdoor toilet. This was common in earlier Mennonite generations, but as far as I can tell, there aren't many from my father's generation that grew up with that little. He, of course, seems to think nothing of it. He shrugs if I ever ask him about it and says, "We had what we needed." Or he becomes immediately irritated with my question and shuts me down. "Well, I don't know," he'll say, huffing, and walk away. He doesn't like talking about any of it.

At some point, my grandfather and his sons built a new house on their property, one with indoor plumbing and a cash-and-carry downstairs, a bucket for a toilet that my dad and his siblings would carry outside and empty out by the barn. By the time I joined the family, there was a working toilet that flushed and a small black-and-white television with long antennae in my grandparents' bedroom. Dad never had a TV growing up—the *evil box*, they called it. I'm not sure what changed but at some point, they allowed the box inside. *The Price Is Right* apparently didn't seem so evil to my grandfather after all.

In a way, it's like we step into the past whenever we visit my grandparents. It's a simpler way of being. There are fewer distractions here, fewer toys. The only decorations in the house are colourful quilts my grandmother has patched and sewn together. There are no pictures. There are no gold-wrapped Werther's Originals and there are certainly no Kahlua-filled chocolates, like the ones Baba loves, in glass dishes on the coffee table. There is no coffee table at all—only the sturdy wood dining table that Grandpa built himself, large enough to seat twenty. There are few chairs at the table. Benches offer more seating and they have been sanded thoroughly, unlike the ones at church. No one smokes and there is never any alcohol in the cupboards.

My grandparents' home always smells like a mixture of warm yeast from the buns rising in the oven and softened cabbage from soup simmering in a huge stockpot on the stove. It smells like the wood shavings left on our grandfather's collar and the manure wafting in from the pasture. It is earthy and it is comforting and it is familiar. I will never grow tired of it. In a few years, once my grandfather's health begins to fail and my grandparents move into town, I will wish I had paid closer attention. I will wish I could capture it all in a Mason jar like the ones Fred and I used for catching tadpoles in the ditch.

Today, I'm sitting at the end of the dining table. My sister is napping in my grandparents' bedroom, after having interrogated as many of my cousins as possible. *What's your name? Where are you from? Who's your dad?* My pencil crayons are neatly arranged in front of me and I've opened my colouring book to where I left off at church this morning. Goofy's head needs to be filled in.

And his shirt and vest—what colour should his vest be? A dark forest green, I think.

"Hey, Brit, you gonna come outside?" George asks, some of our cousins trailing behind. "We're gonna play No Bears Out Tonight."

I'd prefer to finish Goofy's look. Some of the older cousins are outside and I tend to feel shy around them.

"Maybe after *faspa*," I say, and I go back to colouring in Goofy's left ear.

Minutes later, I hear Auntie calling George and the others inside. I tuck my colouring book and crayons away. The women have set the table. Grandma's buns are in a large bowl at the other end of the table, but I can still smell them. She's also made *schnetke*, biscuits with an unmistakably flaky outer shell and a dense, subtly sweet core. If not done right, the dough in the centre can sometimes come out a little gooey. If overdone, they're too dry and the middle becomes hard. My grandmother's are always perfect.

There's also an array of half-pint Mason jars filled with homemade jams on display. Raspberry jam and blueberry jam and strawberry jam and peach jam. Deep pinks and dark blues and bright reds and soft yellows colour the tabletop. Once we're done praying, I'll try to sneak my way to the front of the line so I can grab some of my favourite, the strawberry rhubarb, before the jar is empty.

The soup pot stays on the stove. Grandma has made *summa borscht*, with potatoes and dill from her garden and farmer sausage from a pig Dad recently butchered. There's a big tub of No Name sour cream next to the pot, which Dad and I will scoop out into our bowls. There are also a few jars of sweet pickles that Grandma has brought up from the basement, which I'll be skipping. I will always prefer Baba's sour or garlic pickles. There are also a few bowls filled with No Name ripple chips. And always (always, always, always) there are a few packages of No Name wagon wheel cookies. They are Grandpa's favourite and Grandma will continue to serve them for *faspa* even years after he's gone. It's a feast to feed the masses, and with more cousins than I will ever be able to count, some of whom show up only a few times a year, I will never understand how my grandmother is always able to provide enough without knowing how many of us she'll be feeding. I think of Jesus with the five loaves of bread and two fish. There is always enough.

I stay seated as everyone gathers. Some sit at the table, while others remain standing, their hands clasped behind their backs. The men wearing hats remove them and everyone bows their heads. Sometimes, I sneak a glance to see Mom peeking through a squinted eye. She likes to watch everyone with their eyes closed, spot if anyone picks their nose or scratches somewhere. I like watching just her. My grandfather says the prayer in Low German. I imagine he's saying something along the lines of *Our gracious heavenly Father, we give thanks . . .* Dad always prays in English when we're at home and he begins every prayer like that. Low German is not a delicate language. It's harsh, with abrupt stops and starts between words. But it will always feel like home to me, even though I can't understand it. My grandfather concludes his prayer with an amen and we're off to the races, which is, of course, to say that we slowly and quietly line up for our food.

Men and the youngest children stand at the front of the line. The women fill the plates of their children and wait until everyone else has passed until they fill their own. None of them ever complains. We're all fed, in the end. Then the women walk to their circle of chairs brought up from the basement. The men are already seated at theirs across the room. Most of us children settle at the table, and there is little, if any, talking. What is there to talk about when there's Grandma's food to be eaten?

I'm a slow eater—though not as slow as Marion once was. I don't think Dad could tolerate that. George and my other cousins wolf down their *schnetke* and soup so they can get back to their game. In between bites, I like to glance up at my family. The men sit with their heads mostly lowered, eating in silence. Occasionally, one of my uncles will say something in Low German and Grandpa, sitting in his recliner, will mutter a few words back. The women are a bit livelier. Mom can't help herself and shares a mildly inappropriate joke. George's mom has the loudest laugh, whereas Mom's is the highest pitched with a tiny snort at the end. Their circle always looks more fun than the men's.

I always feel like I'm on the outside, even when I'm on the inside. I have a Native aunt and uncles and cousins, but this doesn't stop members of our own family from making offhand comments about Natives being distrustful and lazy. Mom locks the doors when she sees a Native person while driving through downtown Winnipeg. No one seems to connect us—their Native relatives—to other Native people.

I'm also the only one in the family who's part-Native, which makes me feel even more different. "Part-Native" is a label that's really only used by my mother, and I'm not even sure I fully understand what she means by it. I'm not even sure if it's true that I'm the only one. "You don't even look Native," Mom tells me often. "Really, you don't!" What makes me not look Native, I wonder. My skin colour? My hair? My skin darkens like my cousins' in the summer, but it always eventually fades whiter than I wish it would. And my hair takes on a light reddish tone under the heat of the farmer's sun.

I will only ever want to look Native. I dress up as Pocahontas for Halloween when I'm seven years old, with a costume Mom convinces me is "just so cute." She's made it out of a burlap sack and she sticks a chicken feather straight out the back of my head—an outfit that will only ever make me feel humiliated when I look at the photo when I'm older. *I guess this is what "being Native" looks like,* I think, as I smile for the camera, feeling like a Native kid dressing up like a white kid who's dressing up like a Native kid for a night.

Peering over at my adopted cousins, at George, at my sister freshly woken from her nap, I think, *If I looked more like them, maybe I wouldn't be so scared that I don't belong.*

I just want to feel like I belong.

Chapter Eleven

I ate my flies, I rehearse silently. I'm sitting at the top of the staircase, Tabby warming my toes on the step below. *I ate my flies. I ate my flies.* I stop. I close my eyes and I repeat the words more slowly. *I. Ate. My. Flies.* But it doesn't feel right. It's more my voice than Freddie's. It's stopped sounding like my brother.

When Fred and Shanny were still living with us, Mom would sometimes take us to McDonald's and we'd spend the afternoon playing in the ball pit. I still remember the way those balls left my fingers feeling greasy. I still remember the stale smell of that play structure, the scent of fries and cheese and unchanged diapers. Why can I not remember the sound of my brother's voice? Something feels desperately wrong, like a piece of my brain is malfunctioning. *I can't remember the sound of my brother's voice.*

It's been months now since Fred and Shanny left. A few new sisters have come and gone, but it's not the same. Every night I imagine Fred's voice—a ritual that grounds me. I've returned, time and again, to the VHS tapes of my brother and my sister and me. Anything to transport me back to the times when we were family.

If I can no longer remember the exact sound of his voice, does this mean he's also forgotten the sound of mine? Has he forgotten what I look like? Has he forgotten me completely? Everyone seems to forget me—I feel almost certain of this. First, my birth mother. Then James and Marion. Julie and Sarah. And now Fred and Shanny.

I never think of my birth father when I think of the people who have forgotten me. Maybe this is because, from the beginning, he has only been included in my story through his absence. In the words the social worker shared with Mom when he first called to tell her about me: "The birth father denied being the father." In the story Mom told me about my adoption, when she set the dolls in front of me on her bed; there was only a Skipper doll to represent where I'd come from. There was no mention of a father. My father, it seemed, had forgotten about me before I was even born.

When I'm in between siblings and our family is just me, Mom, Dad, Tabby and the rest of the animals outside, it's lonely and quiet. With the windows cracked open, I can hear the breeze rustling the trees in the bush and the dogs playing out by the barn. The days are slow and my world feels like it has expanded in the most uncomfortable way—so big I could get lost and not know how to find my way back. I spend much of my time playing with my Barbie dolls and the toy horse trailer Baba bought me for my birthday, as Tabby chews on plastic high heels. Other days, I sit on the floor in the TV room with either a VHS home video or Bugs Bunny on the screen in the background while I write stories about Melvis Parsley, a character I invented who's an Elvis Presley wannabe who can't quite get people to show up to his performances. *That poor, poor Melvis*, I think to myself, *he tries so hard*. Sometimes I like to sit at my parents' old typewriter and write stories about an old woman and her old husband and their constant bickering.

Dad is often outside and Mom is typically on the phone with one of my aunts or a friend. She holds the cordless between her shoulder and ear while she cross-stitches or paints folk art. She loves to decorate our house with her designs: intricate stitched dresses and portraits of woodland creatures on tiny sleds. She uses a toothbrush to splatter flecks of white and gold snowfall behind the animals; I love running my fingers across the little ridges once they've dried.

In the late afternoons and evenings, I sometimes walk to the ditch and throw rocks into the reeded water. Our black Lab loves to run in after the pebbles and return with small boulders that look nothing like what I tossed in. I never catch tadpoles when I'm by myself. Other times, my dogs and I walk through the bush and I pretend that I'm searching for hidden clues—or lost in a forest, trying to find my way home. Or on a quest to find my long-lost sister who was taken when we were children. My dogs run ahead of me and zip around the trees as I crouch low, picking up dirt and inspecting it. *Yes*, I think, *I'm getting close*.

At the dinner table, Mom, Dad and I sit at our usual spots—Dad at the head of the table. He begins every meal by leading us in prayer, then for the rest of the dinner Mom does most of the talking. She is always the one doing most of the talking. Sometimes I add a thought or two, but it feels like Mom and Dad struggle to listen. Dad sometimes grunts at my contributions, and sometimes scolds me if I seem too excited for the dinner table. Sometimes, I can't help but feel like our family is incomplete. Like there are other people sitting at the table with us but I can't see them. I can't hear them but I can feel them.

"When are they coming?"

"You're ours," Mom says, but without much conviction. She's long been annoyed by this question and how often I ask it.

But my fears have only grown stronger the past few years—more specific and tangible the older I get. I want to know. I want to know exactly when I'll be taken away. I want to be prepared. I want to have time with Tabby before we're separated. I need to make sure I know precisely where my stuffed cat and her kittens are at all times, even in the middle of the night—especially in the middle of the night—just in case they come for me then. I want to know whether I'll be allowed to pack a big garbage bag with my things or if I'll only be permitted a backpack. I need to know.

"How much time will I have to get ready?" I ask. *Please, just tell me so I can be ready. I'm not ready to leave. I just want to be ready.*

"You're adopted," Mom says. Again she says this.

"If they take me away, how long until I can come back?"

"They won't. You're *ours*, Brittany."

You're ours. You're ours. You're ours. I almost believe her. Her words enter but they do not settle. Sometimes they're enough that I stop asking for a few days. Sometimes they're not, and I dream of hiding places in the house, spots I've used when my cousins and siblings and I have played Hide and Seek. There's a hole covered with plywood in the closet of the bedroom formerly used by my siblings. It's dingy and dark and I'm sure I've seen mice in there before, but I've decided it's the best hiding spot in the house. Another option is the barn. Or in the woods, where one of our dogs went to die a few years ago—Dad says dogs will do that when they're ready to go—but I don't like the idea of hiding out there.

I know I can see something Mom can't. Something she and Dad are unwilling to acknowledge. Sometimes, we are just taken away. There is no rhyme and there is no reason. Sometimes, like George once told me, it's just our time.

A breeze stirs the bush and the trees and makes them whisper. I'm seven years old and George is eight. We're waiting for the sun to dim, for the fireflies to start dancing. The mosquitoes are quiet this year and my skin is grateful. We're surrounded by tall birch and evergreens and maples and poplars on my parents' five-acre farm. Soon, stars will begin to decorate the sky. They'll sprout like the freckles across Dad's face and neck and arms in summer. I'll never have freckles—my skin does not do such things—but I'll forever be entranced by the way those tiny brown spots emerge out of nowhere and then fade with the heat as summer comes to a close.

I shut my eyes, inhaling the night. The scent of dirt mixes with the pine and birchbark and manure from the cows in the pasture. The breeze carries the faint, sweet smell of the purple lilacs behind us, and it settles softly in the centre of my chest. The crickets are beginning to chirp, and the coyotes that are hiding in Dad's cousin's wheat field across the road have already started singing. Being afraid of the coyotes never occurs to us. "They're more afraid of you than you are of them," Dad says. He must be right because I never see them.

My foster sister has just left and our house is empty again. Two more sisters will join us next month and none of us know yet that they will be the last. I grip the top of my Mason jar loosely and look at George. Tabby is just behind me, chasing flies in the grass. I can see her white paws flickering as she swats into the night air. My two Labradors run back and forth between George and me. Our parents are inside playing canasta and drinking instant decaf coffee and RC Cola. Our bellies are full of watermelon, of Auntie's fresh-made *roll kuchen* and Mom's lemon meringue pie.

George has already caught three bugs to my zero. That's always how it is between us. I spend most of my time in my head, trying to notice it all, take it all in, document whatever I can document—while George is running and leaping and trapping. He's always the one doing the work. Catching the toads. Climbing the trees. Convincing me that it's a smart idea to army-crawl under an electric fence in the rain while he hoists the wire off the ground with a branch. It never occurred to me to be angry with him when the branch snapped and the wire left that big, red mark across my back for weeks after. I knew the risks, after all. After playing numerous rounds of "who can keep their finger on the electric fence the longest" on our grandparents' farm, my body remembers the sting of those fences all too well. (I had long suspected one of our cousins of cheating at that game. His finger would hover just above the wire, whereas George and I planted ours firmly against it. Somehow, we still managed to outlast him, which is why I never made a fuss over it. *Let him have it*, I figured.)

A glint catches my eye and I drop my Mason jar to the ground, lunging with my bare hands. I like doing it this way. Feeling the electricity buzzing in my palms, like a far milder version of that wire. Then prying my thumbs open to see flashes of light and life. I glance at George, his eyes and teeth illuminated against the backdrop of his skin and the darker night around him. I won't be able to keep this one—it's too much of a hassle if you don't trap the firefly in the jar right away—but I don't care. It's enough to know I've caught it myself.

It's hours later and we're heading inside for the night. George has five fireflies in his jar and I have two, although I caught a few more and released them. The dogs plop themselves onto the small front porch Dad built just this past summer. Dad lets the dogs come inside overnight in the winter sometimes, when it's so cold that not even he wants to go outside to stock the woodstove. Otherwise, they're in the barn, warmed by hay and heat lamps. Tabby saunters past them, following George and me inside.

"So, did you catch some?" Auntie is the only one to ask about our hunting trip.

"Yep," George answers. "We caught a few." He places his Mason jar on the kitchen counter. I open Dad's toolbox on the floor in the entrance and hand over a small nail. George starts piercing holes in the lid of his jar before he takes mine and does the same.

I see that there are a few *roll kuchen* left and I grab one and take a bite. *Schnetke* are year-round. *Roll kuchen* are only made in summer, and I eat them every chance I get. Auntie doesn't put as much salt on hers as Mom does, but still, I delight in the way the light, crusty deep-fried pastries fall apart in my mouth.

My uncle and Dad subtly nod at one another, which signals the conclusion of the night. Auntie and Mom chat over each other as they pack up the food and clear the dishes, and George and I siphon whatever scraps we're able to from the disappearing dishes. Hunting for fireflies always works up an appetite.

Dad turns on the eleven o'clock CBC news as Mom and George's parents walk to the entrance.

"Here ya go." George hands his jar to me, shrugging. "You can keep 'em."

I knew he would do this. It's perhaps part of the reason I'm never too concerned about trapping many of my own.

"Thanks," I say, and George smiles before he follows his parents out the door.

I grab our captured fireflies and call Tabby. She obediently follows me up to my room, where I place both jars on my nightstand, next to my Pocahontas AM/FM radio. I know they'll look like ordinary bugs in the morning, but for now they're lightning in a bottle, reminders of the stars outside. Reminders that what seems unimpressive in the day can carry a bit of magic into the night, when all that has changed is the light around us.

I lie on my bed, staring up at the glow-in-the-dark stars and planets Sticky-Tacked to my ceiling. Mom hauled Dad's ladder upstairs a few weeks ago and spent hours peeling those plastic stars from their packaging and pasting them above my bed. She started in one corner and slowly made her way across the room until the sun lowered into the fields and she developed a headache and had to stop. I look at the perfect Little Dipper laid out just above me, the shooting stars, Jupiter and Mars and the many moons painted like those in the sky outside. My eyelids start to droop as the fan whirs up above and those stars fade into hundreds of tiny fireflies.

George falls asleep in his bed tonight, as I do in mine. We do not know this yet, but they will come for him in one week. Child and Family Services will come to take George away. Even though he is adopted. Even though he is ours.

It's just his time.

Chapter Twelve

I can't say why everyone is so quiet. I can't say why I say nothing. My parents and a few of my aunts and uncles and I stand at the end of the narrow driveway of the townhouse George can no longer call home. No one is sure where George is calling home tonight. I don't know the details and I don't know how or why it happened, but I do know that CFS came for him earlier today. My movements feel slow and detached, my tongue heavy. I feel like I'm carrying a backpack stuffed full of rocks from the ditch.

Over the next few days, I try to listen in on Mom's phone calls with Auntie. At night, I sneak into the hallway and stand outside my parents' bedroom door. I want to know where George is. I want to know when he might come home. Their room is quiet, as it so often is.

After about two weeks of tiptoeing my way from my room to theirs, I finally overhear something.

"Talk to Naomi today?" Dad asks.

There's a pause. "She says she'll be seeing George on Friday."

"Good."

Mom sighs. Another pause. "Did you talk to Pete?" she asks.

No answer, but I assume Dad nods because Mom asks, "And?"

"I'm going to their house tomorrow when the social worker is there," he says.

"Oh."

There's no sound for a while except for the faint noise of the eleven o'clock news and Lloyd Robertson's voice, and I know my parents have fallen asleep. I peek through the crack in their door to see their two bodies, backs turned to each other, the light from the television set flickering against their headboard.

George's father will go to jail in the coming months, but while he awaits his sentencing, Dad insists he live with us in what used to be the playroom downstairs. My parents have also decided to stop fostering children—a decision they seem to land at hastily.

"It was time," Dad says, when I ask why.

"It just got too hard," Mom replies.

It will be only me and my mother and my father from this day forward. And my uncle, for a time.

Living with the knowledge that George may never come home feels like hot, unrelenting pain. It's worse than missing any of my siblings. Every morning, I wake up and sit in front of my dresser, my arms wrapped tightly around my knees, unable to open a drawer to pick an outfit, confused about why I feel so heavy. Tabby is always tucked patiently beside me.

What's wrong with me? I wonder.

There is so much wrong with me, a voice answers.

I never again ask my mother when they're coming for me, even though it remains my deepest fear. Instead, in a testament to the way my father has raised me, I focus my attention on how to prevent it from happening. I will do everything I can to not let this become a part of my story—again. I will measure what I say like Mom carefully portions milk and flour when she follows Grandma's recipe for *roll kuchen*. I will be careful about what I allow others to see and what I share. I will divulge no secrets, even when I'm hurt. I will make note of each and every rule and I will know what's expected of me. I will remember all that I need to remember and I will try to forget all that I can forget. Because I know that no one likes a child who doesn't do what's expected of her. No one likes a child who knows too much. And no one likes a child who forgets too little. Least of all if she's a girl.

When Uncle comes to live with us, I begin spending most weekends and a few evenings a week at Baba's house. Other than being away from Tabby, I don't mind. If I'm honest, I enjoy spending time with Baba more than I do anyone else, apart from my cat.

I'm in her living room, lying on her couch and watching the Saturday programing on CBC, when I hear the back door open.

"Brit!" Baba calls from the entrance. "Come help me with the groceries."

When I walk into the kitchen, she has already placed the paper grocery bags on the counter and is opening the cupboard above the sink where she stocks her cigarettes. She settles a cigarette between her lips, lights it and inhales. She motions to a bag with pizza pops in it and I know to put them in the freezer.

"Well," she says. "You won't believe what happened at the stop sign on Main by Don's Bakery." She inhales again. There is no one else in my life like Baba. Barely bigger than I am, she still insists on lifting me up off the ground whenever she sees me. Years ago, Gida bought her a license plate cover that reads "Tiny but powerful," and she will always insist that good things come in small packages. Like her and me, and "like dynamite," she always says with a wink.

"I stopped at the sign when two young guys were at the sidewalk." She folds her arms against her chest, her cigarette held loosely between her index and middle finger, her nails painted their classic shade of dusty mauve.

I hop up on the countertop and sit with my legs dangling off the edge. It's where I sit in the mornings when Baba cooks breakfast on the stove and we listen to the funeral announcements—her favourite.

"Well, I say . . ." She draws on her cigarette again. "Those two little shits walked across the street and gave me the finger!"

"What?" I ask. "What'd you do?" I can picture my Baba, eyes barely grazing the steering wheel of her grey Pontiac Parisienne, approaching the intersection too hot. I wouldn't be surprised if she came close to hitting those guys and hadn't even noticed.

"I didn't do anything!" She gestures like she's swatting at a bug and her cigarette almost flies from her fingers. "But you know what I did after that?"

"What?"

"I gave them the finger right back! And I said, 'Hey, fuck you too, buddies!'"

"Baba!" I laugh. I'm only mildly surprised. There is no way I'm making mention of this to Dad when I go home on Sunday.

"Ah, to hell with it." She points her chin at one of the bags. "The ice cream is melting. Put it away."

I jump off the counter and do as I am told.

"Now, what should we have for lunch? You want a grilled cheese?"

JANUARY 1997
PHOTOGRAPH

Baba does not have to tell me to smile with my teeth showing. I am almost impermissibly happy today. George and I are standing side by side in Baba's kitchen, my left arm around his shoulders, his right arm around mine. (Baba has babysat the two of us ever since we were babies, even though she has no familial connection to George. She has never been his grandmother, but he will always call her Baba all the same. He won't become aware of the fact that the two of them aren't actually related until he's a teenager.)

It's already been six months since George and his older brother were taken away. When George first left, he lived with a foster family in Winnipeg. Thankfully, he has now moved to a foster family in town, and it's become easier to see him.

I've agreed to go to church clubs with George tonight for "Twin Night." I've been avoiding clubs for over a year already, but for George, I'll return. I will happily claim the title of his twin, even if it means being back in that church basement. We're both dressed in bright-red long-sleeved crewnecks, mine tucked in, his left out. I wear a blue baseball cap whereas a black one sits atop George's head. His jeans are plain; mine have pockets speckled with yellow and red and purple jewelled flowers that feel too girly for me, but they're the only ones I own. To complete our look, we both wear thick, black-rimmed eyeglasses from the dollar store that distort our vision and make our eyes look twice as large. I don't know what George has done with his real glasses, but I can't imagine he can see very well tonight.

Now that he's with his new foster family, George has been able to return to his old school on the other side of town. His new foster sister is a girl in my class, and I want to cry whenever I see her at school. She doesn't know how lucky she is, I think. They better be treating him okay. I have never been an aggressive child but I want to hit this girl whenever she laughs, whenever she looks happy. Sometimes, when we're supposed to be reading during class, I imagine what it would be like to run to her house after school, to grab George and take him home with me. I can't understand why he isn't living with us, why my mother and father have not chosen to foster him. Why did they take in Uncle and not George?

Tonight, and for now, we are lucky. Tonight, George is here and we are together and I do not have to wonder what he is doing or if he is safe. Tonight, I feel safer too.

—

There is no greater sin in Baba's book, apart from an unwashed resealable plastic bag, than sleeping in past 7 a.m. on a day off. Her mornings begin at least two hours earlier than mine, with a cigarette and a cup of steaming English Breakfast tea, as she catches up with her diary. Sometimes she records what I said in my sleep the night before. Other times, she makes a list of everyone who died the previous week and the times and locations of their viewings and funeral services. She notes the weather. She recalls anything amusing that happened at her job at the dollar store. She purchases a diary at the start of every new year and, on particularly busy years, she has to buy another one by June.

My mornings often begin with Baba instructing me to go to the bathroom, where she has neatly laid out a bar of soap, a fresh washcloth, a toothbrush and toothpaste. "You need to wash your face every day." She feels strongly about this. I usually roll my eyes at her, before doing exactly as she says.

Mom rarely washes her face at the end of the night, let alone encourages me to do so. I'm the one to remind myself to brush my teeth at home. At Baba's house, everything is laid out for me. I know what time we'll go to bed and what time she'll wake me up. I know what the options are for breakfast and I know what card game we'll play after supper. I'm grateful for the order of things.

My lunches are grilled cheese sandwiches made with Kraft Singles, along with a side of sour pickles and a glass of Coke. I like taking a bite of my sandwich and then of a pickle, just to taste and feel the conflicting flavours and temperatures. I eat at the coffee table, my lunch in front of me and a handful of twenty-five-cent peel-away lottery tickets beside my plate, while Baba sits in her pink velvet rocker and watches TV. Sometimes we splurge and she buys the scratch cards that cost a dollar twenty-five, but I never have as much luck with those.

Our supper is mashed potatoes and sour cream and breaded pork cutlets. Sometimes, Baba boils potato perogies she's made herself and serves them with fried onions and thinly sliced ham. Around eleven, after I've completed my nighttime routine during which I've washed my face yet again, we crawl under the covers, Baba on the left and me on the right. She tells me she loves me in Ukrainian and I say it back. She clicks off her bedside lamp and I turn onto my stomach. Because she knows me so well, she doesn't close her eyes, knowing that I rarely go to bed without asking her to tell me a story. I love the one about the time when she was a child and she coveted a pair of black shoes so badly she lied to her mother and said they fit when they were at least two sizes too small. "They made my toes bleed. But it didn't stop me from wearing 'em!"

After a story, she rubs my back, an act so comforting I can't fall asleep at her house without it. On the rare occasion where she falls asleep before I do, I wake her up. "Baba," I whine. "You stopped rubbing." Then I feel her hand making circles on my back again.

The more time I spend at Baba's, the less she records what we do. The camera and camcorder are put away and it becomes just me and her.

I'm spoiled at Baba's house. I know this. I can be selfish here. When I return home, my parents are annoyed by the "bratty" attitude I've developed after just a weekend away. I'm spoiled—and yet often I feel like I don't have enough. I wish I wanted and needed less.

Such a lucky child, so many remind me. *To be unwanted and then adopted, how lucky. To be raised by someone who doesn't have to love you but chooses to love you—how special.* Any time someone says this to me, the image of my birth mother flashes in my mind. Faceless and alone. In an empty room.

"Adopted children are always Native," a lady at church with no children will one day say to me, "and we never knew any well-behaved ones. But if we knew they could be like you, we would've adopted."

Grateful, I remind myself. *I need to be grateful and happy. I need to be a good girl.* These are the labels I must wear like the badges I used to get at church clubs. *What is there to feel other than gratitude?*

Chapter Thirteen

George moves back home with his mother shortly before I turn nine—after almost two years away. My uncle is out of prison and had been living with my grandparents until he was able to return home too. *George will not be taken away again,* I tell myself. *He's here. He's here and he doesn't have to go back. It was just his time, but now his time is done.* I'm starting to think maybe I won't be taken away either. I am nothing if not well-behaved—my emotions are tied to a leash I hold taut. I've learned to control what I can control. I've learned to make myself unseen. You cannot take what you do not see.

I prayed myself to sleep for a week straight when I learned George would be coming home. Finally, our family would be whole again. Or as whole as it ever had been. I counted down the days until he returned, and I was no longer filled with an ugly distaste for his foster sister whenever I saw her at school. *He's not yours anymore,* I thought. *Soon he'll be home and in his own bed and having his own cereal in the morning.* Auntie never bought anything with a brand name and I could always taste the difference between theirs and the cereal Baba bought—but still, it was *his* cereal in *his* home.

Now that he's here, the air feels thicker between George and me, and the silences draw longer. George is a different boy than he was before he was taken. It feels like he always has something to say but never says it. Like he has lived an entire lifetime that I know nothing about. We still have fun when we're together—we still laugh—but not like we used to. Not the kind of laughs that make us clutch our aching stomachs. And we've stopped looking each other fully in the eye. His eyes are almost black, so dark you almost think you can see a star or two in them. But I just can't look at him and I'm not sure why. It doesn't feel like it used to and it makes me want to cry. Though I don't.

Dad has changed, too, although it's difficult to say what's caused it. His anger has always had a finicky trigger. Sometimes it's predictably set off by my complaining or whining. By a disobedient horse outside. By my siblings and I running around Baba's house on a Sunday afternoon after church while he's trying to take his *meddachschlop* on the living room floor. Other times, his anger explodes without warning.

For as long as I can remember, I've both loved and feared him. He can be rageful and kind. Patient and irritable. Protective and accusatory. I try to avoid him while also trying to make him proud. He sees the world in the simplest terms, yet he's utterly complex to me. Sometimes, he feels more like an idea than an actual person, but I can't say why.

He helped coach my softball team for a few years despite not even knowing how to throw the ball. Some Sunday afternoons, he would bring his glove and mine to Baba's and we would play catch in her backyard before he abruptly stopped throwing and went inside without a word. *I guess we're done,* I'd think to myself. And we were, but still, I cherished those moments.

Dad walks around the house and yard now with his shoulders drooped more than they ever have been. It feels like he has fought a battle and lost, but I'm confused by what battle this might have been. Has he changed because my parents have stopped fostering children? Because his brother was in jail? Grandpa has also been sick recently, so Grandpa and Grandma sold the farm and moved to a small house in town. Grandpa's in the hospital now, too unwell to come home, hacking up and spitting gunk from his lungs into a small Styrofoam cup near his bed. Sometimes, I peer into the cup and notice how much it reminds me of black tar and I think of the patched asphalt on the street in front of Baba's house. How that dark goo sizzles in the heat and feels soft against my toes when I run barefoot outside.

Dad has less to say at the dinner table, not that he ever had a whole lot to say before, and he kicks at the dogs or the cats whenever they cross his path. I don't go to him to pull my loose teeth anymore. There is even more that is unsaid now. So much that lurks between me and George, between me and my father, while my mother seems unbothered by it all. I feel like I'm constantly searching for something. Someone to explain what has happened. Someone to explain what is happening. Why it is happening.

Instead, all I have are the glow-in-the-dark stars stuck to my ceiling, blurred by my fan whirring above me, and Tabby beside me as I hold on to her a little bit tighter. But, still, I know that it's more than other kids have.

It doesn't take long for Grandpa to die. Although I never had an actual conversation with my grandfather, I miss him. I miss the farm and I miss the smell of their old kitchen and I miss that red glider swing Grandpa built years ago. Grandma has continued hosting Sunday *faspas* in their new house, which is a fraction of the size of their old one—not that it was very large either—so all of us kids sit on the floor, wherever we can find the space to eat, before we run outside to play under the sole tree in the backyard. It's not the same but it's still something.

I begin developing headaches in the fourth grade. I frequently return home from school with a vice around my temples. Sometimes, the pain throbs and my body heaves and I throw up to relieve the pressure. I find comfort in Tabby, who stays by my side.

After a few months of missed recesses and my teacher calling my parents to share her concern, I'm brought to the doctor. This is a rarity—going to the hospital feels a bit like a luxury to my parents, rather than a necessity. The only other time Mom brought me to the hospital, apart from when I'd gone in to get vaccinations, was over Christmas break a few years before, when my forty-one-degree temperature had been running for four days. I'd had to leave halfway through our family gathering, which wasn't too much of a loss, I suppose, since I'd spent the entire evening in and out of consciousness in Grandpa's recliner.

"It's stress," the doctor says at my appointment for my headaches. He and my parents conclude that I'm placing too much pressure on myself at school. I admit that I feel anxious in the moments before the teacher starts the timer for our Mental Math Minutes, but apart from this, I haven't found school particularly difficult. But if the doctor says it's stress, it's stress.

Dad is a firm believer in "sucking it up." "You just have to relax," he says in the car on our way home. As we pull into the driveway, I vow to keep my headaches to myself.

I'm also in the fourth grade when I begin a ritual I share with no one but Tabby. Mom is downstairs in the kitchen and Dad is outside when I tiptoe into their bedroom to rummage through their drawers. There's something specific I'm hoping to find: the worn manila envelope that contains all the details of my adoption. I found it during an earlier raid of Mom's room and have looked at it again since, though she sometimes changes where she keeps it. I like to think she doesn't mean to hide it, but I'm not sure that's true. Maybe she just doesn't think it matters to me? This information feels like it's mine, though, so I don't feel guilty for stealing it for a portion of the afternoon. Reading these papers, scouring them for evidence of where it is that I come from, who it is that I belong to—this is just for me.

Today, the envelope sits in the top drawer of her chest. It's in the same spot where she keeps my twelve-inch ponytail from my first haircut last year and my old palate expansion appliance. I can still feel the ridges on my tongue where the expander dug so deep it bled. I told my orthodontist, but he never seemed to care, so eventually I stopped mentioning it. When he removed the appliance, he saw the scars on my tongue and asked me why I'd never said anything. I shrugged and told him I wasn't sure.

I smoothly pull out the envelope from the drawer after noting its exact placement, so I can ensure it looks undisturbed when I return it. Tabby is waiting in the hall for me and leads me back to my bedroom, as though she knows exactly what our plan is today. I close the door halfway so I can hear if Mom is coming up the stairs. Tabby jumps onto the bed and watches as I sit on the floor and lean against my bed frame.

I begin the careful process of pulling each document out of the envelope, one by one. It doesn't matter how often I do this—it will always feel like I'm on the cusp of some sort of revelation, as though I'm seconds away from discovering a detail from my past that will forever change my future.

First, there are the yellow sticky notes. I imagine Mom had placed a pad of them next to the telephone precisely for calls as urgent as this one. *Little girl, 8 lbs, 11 oz. Brown eyes, brown hair, red dot in eye,* one says. *Part native,* another one says. Next, I pull out the card from my foster mother. *Congratulations to the Happy Parents* is printed above a drawing of a rocking chair. "Dear new parents," she'd written inside the card. "Congratulations! You have a gorgeous baby girl whom we have had the privilege of caring for. She likes to be wrapped in a couple of blankets. She'll fuss if too cold."

Next is a document from my social worker. "We know you will be pleased to know that Brittany is legally your child," he writes. "Your child's birth certificate will be forwarded to you in the near future."

There are other items too. Legal documents. Vital statistics application forms. I place each sheet on top of the previous one, sure to keep them in the same order. Finally, I reach what I've come for. It's a two-page document provided by my social worker. "This is in response to our agreement to provide you with the background medical information on your daughter."

I scour these pages, sentence by sentence, word by word. I read and reread every single detail, every single letter, until there's no new information to be found. A familiar image of my birth mother flashes in my mind. She's in that hospital room again, sitting in the corner on a mattress on the floor. She's by herself. She has no face but her hair is dark, curling at the edges like mine does. A social worker is walking away from her and a baby is in her arms. I do not recognize myself, but I know that I'm that baby.

The social worker has written out information from my hospital medical records. He has recorded my weight, my Apgar scores, the time of my birth, my normal physical exam. I follow the words closely, my soul praying for something, anything, that I might have missed before. The language is detached. Formal. The social worker is not talking about "my" mother, but "the" mother. I am not "her" baby, but "the" baby. He writes that "the birth mother" has dark-brown curly hair and hazel eyes.

"The relationship between the birth parents is terminated," he writes, "and the birth mother feels some bitterness toward the birth father who has refused to see or talk to her since he found out she was pregnant. At times, he denied being the father." *Unwanted,* a familiar voice whispers. *Forgotten.*

Tabby sighs behind me as she takes a long, drawn-out stretch. She seems to know that this exercise—what will become our weekly ritual, one I will repeat and repeat in the hopes of somehow, miraculously, learning something new—is coming to a close.

"I hope that the above is of assistance to you as you help your child understand her birth family."

There's one paragraph at the end of the document that's my very favourite. Every time I read it, it wraps itself around me like the quilt that Baba covers me with whenever I'm sick and Mom drops me off at her house so she can take care of me. I will return to these papers again and again and again over the years, simply to read this one paragraph:

"The birth mother would like the new parents to tell the child that she had the child's best interests at heart and thought about the adoption a great deal. The birth mother would like the child to know that she thought adoption was best. She would like the child to know that she was and always will be loved."

That is the end of all that I have to find. I place all the pieces back into the envelope.

I'm resting in the back of the van, my eyes closed. I'm eleven years old. Mom, Baba and I have just been to Zellers. I made Baba laugh by trying on wedged heels several sizes too big for me. "Strut, Brit," she called, and I pretended I was walking down a runway, like I do when I'm at her house wearing her high heels.

When we reach Baba's house, I open my eyes just enough to see Baba open the passenger door and grab the plastic bags between her and Mom. She looks back at me in the middle, then steps outside the vehicle. I'm asleep by the time Mom backs out of the driveway.

The light—that light—is blinding. My eyes are open again, but it's so bright everything looks white. And it's loud—screeching tires, breaking glass and my mother yelling, "Shit, no, shit, no, shit, no!" It's a collision of so many things at once. It feels like a shattering, like my world and my body are being torn into a million different fragments. We're spinning and my head is thrown back with force—the energy travels from my neck all the way to my stomach. I close my eyes and wait for the spinning to stop.

I open my eyes. There's smoke and dust and glass and the smell of burnt rubber. I close my eyes. A high-pitched ringing feels like a stake plunged into my ears. I want it to stop. *Please God make it stop.*

I open my eyes and Mom is moving now. She's whimpering like a puppy as she tries to push herself from the driver's seat. The door will not open, so she wriggles her body through the misshapen window frame. I close my eyes. The van has stopped spinning, but my body won't. *Please God make it stop.*

I open my eyes and Mom is outside the van. There's a bang on the door and then everything goes quiet. I'm alone. My awareness suddenly shifts to my left leg. I'm hanging limp off the long bench seat, suspended by my lap belt—and my knee, my knee, it's burning hot and cold at the same time. *Please God make it stop.* I close my eyes.

I open my eyes and there are sirens screaming and there is a gnawing and shrieking sound that reverberates through the entire vehicle. It is the loudest noise I have ever heard in my life. It sounds like Dad's table saw, only louder, fiercer. I can feel a shiver like an electric current pulse up and down my whole body. I close my eyes.

I open my eyes and I'm on the ground. A voice I don't recognize is shouting words at me. *But what is he saying? Nothing makes sense.* I close my eyes.

I open my eyes and I'm still on the ground. That voice is still calling out directions and words I can't string together. I just want to get up and leave. "Don't cut off my leg!" I scream. It is still there. I did not lose it yet. I scream this again at the voice and try to push myself away from him. *God, please don't cut off my leg.* I close my eyes. *I just want to go home. Just let me go home.*

PART TWO

Chapter Fourteen

This day and night will always feel blurred. They will feel like snapshots, flashes from a mind that cannot, or maybe doesn't want to, remember. That's what happens with concussions, I will learn. It's also what happens when terror threatens to overtake your entire world. I'd never been in an accident like this before, but the feeling—that feeling of having no control over my body, no control over what might happen to me—was uncomfortably familiar.

I fluctuate in and out of consciousness as the ambulance speeds along the highway and down the streets of my small town. I'm strapped to a stretcher, the hands of the paramedic no longer having to do the work of restraining me. Dad will later tell me that he was sitting in the corner of the ambulance, but his presence never becomes a part of my memory of this night. My leg, bent at an alarming angle, has been stabilized with two orthopaedic slabs. My neck is in a stiff collar. I want to move, but there is too much holding me down. My body feels like a volcano in the aftermath of an eruption, sizzling from the heat, only small amounts of lava oozing out now.

I'm carted down the hallway of our local hospital on the stretcher. The fluorescent lights buzz overhead, and as I'm wheeled along they zipper together into one long string of light. I'm ushered into a room with a curtain. A cascade of voices talk over one another. "Let's set up two large-bore IVs." "Did someone call for an X-ray?" Everyone is speaking around me. But no one is speaking to me. My confusion feels more exhausting than the pain. A bright light shines into my left eye. Then my right. "Can you feel this?" a voice asks. I feel something slide against my toes. "Yes," I answer. I can feel it. I can feel my leg.

Someone has pulled out scissors and they're cutting down my pantlegs. They cut off my shirt and place little stickers across my chest. I don't need a bra yet, but I'm still embarrassed. I feel hands all across my body. On my arms and my chest and my feet and *down there.* My body feels like it belongs to me even less than it did only moments ago.

"You're going to feel a little poke," a voice says. "We're just putting something inside to help you pee." I feel a light prickling sensation as something slides inside me. "Another poke," a new voice says, and then I feel a jab like a bee sting to my inner elbow.

I realize I'm in the same room where, a few years earlier, Mom had to have her scalp stitched. She'd collapsed right after I wiped out on my bike. I'd been flying down a gravel road at a campground we were staying at when I turned too fast around a corner and my wheels spun out from under me. The lifeguard had tried to wash out what she could, but my left leg looked like raw ground beef, and she'd told Mom and Dad to take me to the hospital. I was just thankful Dad hadn't suggested the hydrogen peroxide.

At the hospital, I allowed my mother to hold my hand, more for her sake than my own. "You're gonna be okay, Brit," Mom said. I couldn't help rolling my eyes. I was embarrassed I'd fallen off my bike, but I was even more embarrassed by her show of emotion. She squeezed my hand as she looked down at my leg and then back at me. Then her irises rolled up and her body fell hard and limp upon the hospital floor. Nurses and a doctor came rushing into the room and hoisted her onto a stretcher. Minutes later, I walked myself out to the waiting area, my leg freshly bandaged, where Dad and I waited for Mom to be treated. Her wails echoed through the halls. I knew I'd eventually feel sympathy for my mother, and that I'd help care for her when we got home, making sure she had water and ibuprofen and an ice pack, but I couldn't help but feel frustrated in the moment.

"Brittany." My mind jolts back to the present moment—to the sound of yet another voice I don't recognize. "Did you hear what I just said?"

I try to shake my head, but it doesn't move. "No," I say.

"You broke your leg, dear." There is a woman attached to this voice and she's standing at my right side, leaning over the guardrail of the stretcher. I look down, my neck still immobilized, and notice that she's holding my hand with both of hers. Her touch is comforting. She loosens her grip on my hand, but I squeeze hers tighter. I don't want her to leave.

Dad is standing at the edge of the room, speaking to a doctor with salt-and-pepper hair. Dad's hands are in his pockets and his face is solemn. My father is a serious man, but I've never seen him look so serious.

The lady tells me they're going to have to take us to Winnipeg. She has to let go of my hand, she says. She can't come with me. I don't know if Mom is alive and I want to ask her, but she's already gone—my stretcher whisked out of the room before I can get the words out.

I still don't know what happened, not really. But I know that somehow, in the span of seconds, my body became not my body anymore. I have felt this before—sort of. I was five and I was six and I was alone and my body was not my body. But that was different. That was a lifetime ago. And I've been good since then.

I want to belong to me again. I make myself a silent vow. I know enough to know that I'm the only one who can keep me safe. It's not so much words as it is a feeling deep within me, a bubbling from my core, travelling through my organs and into my bones to become a promise, a truth that will guide me in the days and weeks and months to come. I will never betray myself in this way again. I will not be weak. I'll resist the temptation to allow others to ever see my insides. When I'm scared or hurt, I will not cry and I will not scream. I will decide what others can see and who is allowed in. I will be the one in control.

NOVEMBER 1, 2000
TWO PHOTOGRAPHS

One. Our maroon caravan sits in the impound lot. Dad wants to inspect it and has come to take photographs of the evidence. I imagine him placing his hand on the driver's door, running it along the caved-in window, making sure to not cut himself on any of the broken glass. Later, he'll remark on how tiny the hole in the glass was that Mom slipped out of. How there was milk replacer for the calves all over the interior, the maroon seats dusted beige. I wonder if he thought of his daughter as he looked at the broken bucket seat in the middle, if he wondered what my body looked like as the firefighters pulled it out of the van. If he had any emotions upon seeing the wreckage, he mentions it to no one.

Two. One half of the blue car driven by the impaired driver sits next to its other half. The engine was completely severed from the rest of the vehicle. They say the driver was still behind the wheel, trying to start his engine with his car in a ditch, when the ambulances arrived. That's how impaired he was. His adult son was apparently beside him with fractured ribs and who knows what else. The driver, Dad was told, had little more than a scratch.

Chapter Fifteen

"Wiggle your toes for me." Another voice I don't recognize.

It's been fourteen hours since the accident and I'm lying in a bed, surrounded by strangers. My eyelids are heavy and it feels like there are tiny flecks of sand beneath them, scratching at my eyes every time I try to open them.

The voice speaks again, asking me if I can move my toes. I glance toward my feet and see a man with thick grey hair, slightly dishevelled, wearing a long white coat. He has kind eyes.

"Can you feel this?" he asks, lightly touching my left big toe.

"Yes."

"Now, can you wiggle them?"

I suppose I do as I'm told because he replies with a "good" and a nod to the three younger people standing next to him at the foot of my bed. The three of them appear a little frightened, and I can't tell if their expressions are directed toward me.

Baba is standing next to my bed, leaning against the railing, and Dad is sitting in a big chair with fraying seams. Mom isn't here—I still don't know if she's alive. I want to ask but my brain feels unfamiliarly fuzzy and I don't know how to get out the words. They both have worried looks on their faces, which makes me feel like I'm a wounded bird that's been found outside and that everyone is too afraid to touch.

My body has never ached in this way before. It's as though a concrete roller has driven over me and flattened me against the bed. Just lifting the arm that's propped up on a pillow takes a surprising amount of effort. It's like my brain and muscles have lost their connection to each other. A machine beeps loudly and I'm immediately reminded of the headache pulsing across my temples.

"Hold on, you kinked a line." A nurse sighs as she pulls at the tubing coming out of my right elbow. It's one of many lines and tubes and catheters coming out of my body like tentacles. They are either feeding me or draining me—I have no idea what's doing what. There's even a tube coming out of my left nostril, taped against my cheek. This isn't the first time a nurse has appeared to be exasperated with me. I want to apologize, but I feel like I'll throw up if I try to speak.

My throat hurts as a whisper escapes. "I have to pee." I'm embarrassed that of all the words, these are the ones I choose to say.

"Yup," the nurse says, peeking below the bed. "You are."

"Oh." I will forever hate Foley catheters.

It's as though the accident has given others, so many others, the right to poke at me and stick things into me and scold me without warning or explanation. I wish I had the freedom to be angry, to bite back, to tell them to stop touching me, to stop touching my body in places I don't want to be touched. But they are the doctors and the nurses and I am the patient, and Baba has taught me better than to complain. Dad and church have taught me better than to believe I have any sort of say in matters like this. To be angry is to be engaging with sin and I already have too much going against me. I can't afford to feel anger beneath the gaze of God.

"Brit . . ." Baba's voice is slow and her eyes soft. No one has ever uttered my name as gently as she does in this moment. "Do you remember what happened last night?"

What kind of a question is this? I wonder. It's probably the dumbest thing she's ever asked me. Of course I know what happened.

"I jumped off your roof," I say, rolling my eyes.

For as long as I can remember, I've always pictured myself breaking a bone in this way. *It makes sense that it finally happened,* I think, as morphine runs through my IV.

It's Sunday evening, twenty-four hours after the accident. Baba is the one who's explained everything to me. She started by telling me that Mom is still alive and in another part of the hospital. She told me about the crash, the memory of which flashes back in sharp slivers.

I haven't eaten all day in preparation for surgery on my leg. But I've just learned they won't be operating on me today after all. They bring me supper but I can't eat. The painkillers and whatever else is flowing in my IV lines seem to be doing their job, lulling me in and out of consciousness, but when I'm awake, I feel nauseous and irritated. My body wants no one and nothing near it.

—

It's Monday morning and the nurse tells me again that I won't be able to eat as they prepare me for surgery. "We have to pin your leg in place," one of the doctors says. "You broke the biggest bone in your body and it needs help in order to heal properly." Again I eat nothing and drink nothing all day, but I'm not hungry anyway. The combination of the hospital food and the headaches and the morphine, along with Baba's incessant attempts to feed me, completely siphon any appetite I might have had. And I don't like to eat when I'm scared. I don't like to eat when I don't know what's going on around me. I must stand guard. I must watch, like a farm cat caught in a thunderstorm, looking for the driest, safest place under which she can shelter.

It's Tuesday morning and today they have assured Baba and me that I'll be having the surgery. Dad is—well, I don't know exactly where he is, but I think he must be with Mom. I'm visited by a couple of my aunts from Dad's side this morning. They're in my room for no longer than five minutes before Baba, shamelessly and without apology, throws them out. "You think Brittany needs to hear about your arthritis in your hip? Get the hell outta here!" The woman may be small, but she has always known how to make her voice heard. *Small but mighty, you and me, girl,* she always reminds me.

This is the most nauseated I've felt all week. I float in and out throughout the day, feeling like I can never quite land anywhere.

I'm in my hospital room, Baba by my side, when the surgeon explains that the procedure should not take long at all, and that I can see Baba later in the day if everything goes well—which they expect it will. Despite this, Baba asks each of the doctors and the nurses three times over how they think the surgery will go. I assure her I'm fine and she doesn't need to worry so much, but she still repeatedly tells me that everything will be okay.

I'm in the elevator now. I'm being wheeled to the operating room, which is on another floor of the hospital. The movement makes my nausea worse and I close my eyes.

I'm in the operating room and there are too many faces hidden by masks I don't care to peek behind. I float out of the room, out of my body, again.

I'm in the recovery room and a baby is screaming in the bay next to mine. The crying is so relentless that my first words to Baba are "Just make it stop." Soon, the grey-haired doctor with the kind eyes arrives to speak to Baba. I remember now that he sang to me before the surgery, as the anesthesia began to pull me under. "It went well," I hear him say. He looks calm and confident—this is just a regular day for him. Just another broken bone, another set of hammers and screws and metal plates and nails for him to use so he can put people back together again. Despite his reassurance, Baba still looks panicked. The worry in her eyes, the way her eyebrows pinch in the middle and her shoulders tense and crawl up her neck—she will carry this look for weeks.

I'm finally back in my hospital room. No crowd of masked faces, no elevators, no screaming baby. I didn't think I'd miss this stiff bed and these plain walls as much as I have the last few hours.

But here it's quiet. Here, the door is closed and Baba and I are alone. I am home—sort of.

Baba wheels me over to see Mom the day after my surgery. My mother's left ankle is hoisted in a sling above her bed—her entire leg is bruised and swollen. She has a broken hip and pelvis, but the doctors have told her it's the ankle that will be the most difficult to heal. Her eyes are bare of their usual black eyeliner and her lips are tiny and shapeless. Her brows are unlined and I can barely see the sparse hairs scattered above her eyes. Seeing Mom like this feels somewhat disorienting.

My father is leaning against the windowsill as I say hello to my mother. Mom immediately begins to cry. I know this is unkind, and I scold myself for thinking it, but she reminds me of a toddler whenever she cries. Her upper lip quivers and her eyes get wide with tears. She has this way of always making me want to run to her and hold her, reassure her that everything is going to be all right, as I rub her back and shush her to sleep. It will always feel like this between the two of us. I will always feel responsible for taking care of her. But my wheelchair prevents me from leaning over to comfort her and I'm grateful for the barrier. I don't feel like sharing my body with anyone right now.

Dad and Baba are letting us have our moment. It's a moment I haven't asked for. It's too laden with emotions and tears and something that feels like, but isn't quite, love. My fingers reach for the back of my head, searching for those tiny pieces of glass that have been prodding my scalp. Every day I find new scabs there and I've taken to picking them and making them bleed. I haven't been able to bathe yet and my skin and hair are coated in a tacky powder—the milk replacer for the calves. (The van also held big bags of candy Mom bought at Zellers earlier that day, and our visitors keep telling us how there are gummy worms all over the highway now.) My skin begins to prickle and I feel like I want to leave my body.

I close my eyes. It's so swift, so efficient, I almost don't realize it's happening. My body is my body, I know this, but suddenly it feels distant. Detached. And I feel safe. Protected. No one around me notices a thing, but I notice. I can feel it. It's like there's a protective film that covers me, a layer no one can see, but I can sense. My hands are my hands, of course, but they are also not my hands. My body is my body, but, also, it is not. Any emotions that might be here feel removed, as though I've managed to divorce myself from them, and I can breathe a little easier. The weight of me feels lighter, the noise that surrounds me muffled.

"I thought you were dead!" My mother is sobbing now. "They told me you lived, but I kept saying, 'You're lying to me! I know she's dead. She's dead—I just know it!'"

I can't understand why Dad doesn't reprimand her. I wish that he would. If I were crying, he would tell me to suck it up, or some variation of the same, and I would be grateful for the reminder. But for some reason he's never been this way with Mom. I'm the strong one, the tough one, like him, so perhaps he expects more from me. He got into a car accident once too, early in my parents' marriage, long before I came around. Dad was driving down a country road a few miles south of home. He approached an intersection, his side without a stop sign, when another driver approached from the other side, ignoring their stop sign. Dad walked a mile and a half with a fractured leg, cracked in almost the same spot where I broke mine, to the nearest house to call for help. By the time the ambulance arrived, the young passenger of the other vehicle had died. She was a young foster girl, I heard Mom say once, and no one had buckled her in. I could never forget that part of the story.

Mom pulls me by the shoulders, closer to her, and I have to push my body up out of my wheelchair to meet her embrace. I don't know what to say. I will let her hold my hand for as long as she needs, I decide. We are mother and daughter, after all. And I know this is the kind thing to do.

"You're having a dream, Brit!"

Baba's face is inches from my own. She's gripping my shoulders, and I'm sitting upright in bed. Out the window, I can see an indigo prairie sky with a few of its stars poking through. It must be the middle of the night. I don't know where I am. I'm dizzy and I think I might throw up. My chest is heaving along with the fast fluttering of my heart. *The hospital, I'm in the hospital.*

"You're having a dream!" Baba shouts again. "You. Are. Having. A. Dream!" Her hands grip my shoulders tighter.

I don't understand why she's being so aggressive. "Baba! Leave me alone!" I shout right back at her—I have never shouted at her before—and push her hands off my body with more force than I mean to. I feel a wave of shame wash over me. "I'm fine," I say with finality. "Let me sleep."

This exchange will become a ritual of sorts—one we'll repeat several times a night while I'm in the hospital. Over and over, I'll scream in my sleep, and she'll wake me from the nightmares. It will continue when I'm released and living with Baba too—trying to rest on the couch in her living room as she slumbers near me in her pink rocking chair. And then, when I'm home, I'll go through it by myself for weeks—waking up in a panic, out of breath, unaware of my surroundings. My heart racing, lights flashing in my eyes. I will feel like there's an electric current pulsing through my limbs and my chest. Over time, I'll learn to slow my breathing by placing one of my hands firmly against my sternum. It's a practice I will mention to no one. Who would I tell, anyway?

NOVEMBER 3, 2000
PHOTOGRAPH

It's the day before I'm to be discharged from the hospital. I'm sitting on the toilet for the first time since being hospitalized. My left leg, which is in a cast from my ankle all the way up to my hip, is propped up on a trash can so I can position myself somewhat properly on the toilet. The nurse has just removed my Foley catheter and instructed me to pee, otherwise it'll have to be reinserted.

Although Baba takes out her camera much less often these days, she has kept it in her purse since I've been in the hospital. Snapping the occasional photo of friends who visit, of her sister, my aunt, my teacher, who brings me a box full of cards from my classmates.

"Smile, Brit," she says.

I'm in no mood for smiling. I'm in no mood for pictures of myself peeing. Yes, I know how much she loves me. And, yes, I know I'm a "bad granddaughter." The nurses, according to Baba, have already said as much. She walked past the nurses' desk the other night and overheard them talking, she tells me. "'Can you believe the way she treats her grandmother?' That's what they said, Brit. Even the nurses are noticing how you're treating me."

I know I need to be kinder to Baba—to not become annoyed when she tries to make me eat or when she wants to take my photo. But despite this I have no tolerance today for her "smile with your teeth showing!" So, I don't smile.

This is one of the only times I don't obey my grandmother. She takes the photo anyway.

"If looks could kill," Mom will say, laughing, when she sees this photo for the first time.

Chapter Sixteen

I spend weeks living at Baba's house, just me and her, though sometimes Dad joins us for dinner. Mom spends the next five weeks in the hospital. Midway through, she's transferred from Winnipeg to the hospital in our town. What I find most difficult about living at Baba's house is being away from Tabby. She has just had kittens and can't be separated from them for too long—and there's no way Baba would want a whole litter in the house.

I can tell taking care of me and cooking for Dad and travelling back and forth to the hospital to visit Mom is taking its toll on Baba. She's shorter with me, quippier. Comments she'd usually keep to herself are much quicker to be shared. She tells me on more than one occasion that I'm eating too much. When I left the hospital, I weighed sixty-two pounds, including my cast, which stretches from my ankle to my hip. I *have* been eating chips more than anything else lately, but almost everything apart from plain chips makes me feel nauseous. I don't say anything in reply to her, though, and I don't say anything when I overhear her telling Mom that I'm getting too fat. I hide my face under the blanket that night to conceal my crying. I didn't realize until the tears came how badly her words stung.

He's yelling. He's yelling and his words are coming sharp and hot like the iron rod he uses to poke at the logs in the woodstove. That brown, rusted piece of metal turns bright red, crimson. It's the same shade as his face in this moment. He has never been an articulate man, but he makes up for it with the forcefulness with which he screams. He makes up for it with the specificity of his insults and his apparently fervent belief in their truth.

I think he's ashamed of this part of himself. Not the shouting and not the unkindness, but his lack of education. I can feel it in the way he explodes at my mother whenever she makes a joke at his misspelling of a simple word, like forgetting the "w" in the word "wrong" or writing "rite" for both "write" and "right." I can feel his shame whenever I look at his handwriting, which is only ever in capital letters. I think he must not know the rules—he must not know when capitalization is necessary.

I should have known better. This is what my mother always says to me whenever I'm on the receiving end of one of his raging outbursts. "Brit, you shouldn't have. You know better." *Brit, you shouldn't have spoken. Brit, you shouldn't have asked. Brit, you shouldn't have breathed.* Though sometimes these words aren't necessary because they're so obvious; in these cases, she just looks at me, rolls her eyes and walks away.

Sometimes, she pretends nothing is happening and she can't hear the words he's calling me—*fool, no class, smart ass.* Sometimes, she steps aside and bobs her head in agreement. Until the yelling drags on—then she grows tired and returns to pretending it's not happening. Sometimes, I'm genuinely confused by his anger, because I said nothing and did nothing. Rather, something *she* said seemed to make him angry with me. Sometimes, it feels like she offers me up as bait, and I cannot understand why.

There are times when I feel sad for my dad. I can tell he's hurt when my mother prods at his intelligence and I can tell that there's a part of him that wishes his life held more. A better-paying job, maybe. More respect, perhaps. He's craving something, I think he's hurting too . . . but I'm not sure of anything beyond that.

I don't feel for him right now, though. In this moment, I feel for neither of my parents. The three of us are sitting in the truck we were able to afford once we received a small sum after the accident. We're parked in Baba's driveway and Dad is yelling. Mom is looking ahead into the black sky contrasted by falling snow. My broken leg in its cast is stuck on a small pillow on the console between the two of them. Moments ago, we were all at Baba's house, where Mom and I have been living while Dad goes back and forth between Baba's house and ours. (He has the cows and pigs to feed each day and needs to chop wood for the outdoor stove so our pipes don't freeze.) The stairs at our house are too difficult for Mom now that she can't walk unassisted. Since living at Baba's, Mom has started eating a lot more, and the weight gain has made it harder for her to use her crutches. "Baba pisses me off," she told me, "and I can't say anything. So, I eat."

As we prepared to leave Baba's earlier to go to a gathering at a local restaurant with Mom's friend and her family, Mom almost fell from her chair when she tried to get up. Dad laughed and grabbed one of her crutches to mimic her clumsiness. At first, she laughed, as though she were in on the joke, and Mom's friend and her husband laughed too. Mom's told me I should do this if kids ever make fun of me—"It ends quicker that way." But the joke kept going and Dad kept laughing. I stood awkwardly, waiting for it to end. Mom fixed her gaze at the ground and began to cry. "Sometimes you can be such an asshole," she said. The room went silent. That was our cue to leave. I hopped toward the door. Whereas Mom appreciates her wheelchair and seems to enjoy being pushed around and cared for by others, I avoid my wheelchair at all costs. I hate the bulkiness of the thing and I hate relying on others to manoeuvre me around.

Now we're in the truck and my father's voice is cutting as he tells my mother how disrespectful she is. How unacceptable it is for a woman to speak to a man like that, and how no woman in his house will *ever* speak to him like that again, does she understand? He is the head of this house. He demands respect and how dare she not give it to him. Her eyes are still directed ahead of her and tears are falling hard down her cheeks. I know not to insert myself here. I stop myself from telling my father that I didn't think he was treating her with respect either. I stop myself from telling him that I don't think he's being very fair. I know what will happen if I do. I know, because we have been here so many times before.

I'm usually my mother's protector in moments like this and, really, I don't mind. I'm stronger than her. It only makes sense.

Often, when Dad starts yelling, I'll say something to redirect his anger at me instead and, always, Mom is appreciative. Sometimes, she stands behind me, which cues me to speak up. Really, I'm not sure what started first. Did she start using me for protection or did I insert myself, and she welcomed it? I don't think it much matters, anyway. It is my job, all the same. But it is not my job tonight. I'm angry with her and I do not step in for her. She should have known better.

A short drive later, we're at the restaurant and Mom pulls out her photo album of the accident. She entertains her friend's family with photos of the crash scene, of her bruised body, of her legs and arms held by slings attached to the ceiling. She tells them she climbed out of the window on the driver's side and hobbled with a broken pelvis and hip over to the sliding van door and tried, but was unable, to open it. How she then, terrified of an explosion, staggered a couple of yards away from the vehicle. Everyone laughs at her somehow thinking a few yards would save her from the blast.

She shows them the photo of me in my hospital bed, shades of purple under my eyes, and the one Baba snapped of me peeing for the first time after my catheter was removed. "If looks could kill!" she says again, and my gaze shifts to my fingernails. I've been picking them a lot more recently and the corner of my thumbnail is starting to bleed. I wish she wouldn't show this album. I've looked at it when I'm by myself, still confused about how I could have forgotten so much of the crash. Every so often, nightmares still wake me and I wonder, if I could just remember everything that happened, if I were able to catalogue it in my mind, if I could then let it go. Maybe the nightmares would never come back. Regardless, Mom's retelling of this night does not help.

Someone proclaims that surely angels must have been watching over us. Another, in disbelief, says how ironic it is that the drunk driver barely had a scratch on him, and isn't that just the way things go. Dad shakes his head at the question of whether charges have been laid yet. Months from now, we'll go to court and the driver will not show up, and we'll go to court again and the driver will not show up again. Eventually, Dad will tell me that the man has been deported. Singapore, or maybe Vietnam, he thinks.

The conversation has gotten off-track now and Mom knows she needs to recapture everyone's attention. Her story is not over yet. "And then . . ." She builds suspense as she flips to the back of the album. This is her favourite part in her routine, I can tell. "There are these!" From a pocket on the last page, she slowly pulls out a plastic Ziploc bag holding three nails, each one at least five inches long, and sharp enough to break skin. She holds them out to the room. Someone takes a photo of Mom doing this and, later, she puts that shot in the album too.

"Those were in Brit's leg?" someone asks.

"Yep," Mom answers with nonchalance, despite the fact that it's taken her two months to build up the capacity to look at these nails without gagging. I'm in the corner while all of this unfolds, my head bowed, having moved on to pick and pull at another cuticle, wondering why my mother left me in a vehicle she was convinced would explode.

When I ask her about this years from now, she'll tell me that's not what she did. "Uh, did you dream that?" she'll ask. "I think you made that up."

"You're right," I'll say, and I'll question why I thought I heard her say such a thing in the first place.

Sometimes I get the sense that my father lives in a sort of cage. I feel it in the way he keeps everyone at arm's length. I feel it in the way his spine is always stiff. I don't know what it's like for him to be inside this cage, but I know what happens when his rage breaks through and I know what it looks like when it tears apart everything in its vicinity. I know what follows in the days afterward. I know what will follow after this.

Tonight, when we get home from the restaurant, he won't say a word. He won't speak to either of us for a day or two or three. He won't look at me but he will eat what Mom and Baba put on the table, and he'll fall asleep watching the eleven o'clock news. We will live with the ghost of him for days until he re-emerges, acting as though nothing has happened at all.

I picture him grabbing the pieces of the metal on the ground, the remnants of his cage, and opening his toolbox to reconstruct his sturdy home. He only ever does this in silence. I'm never sure if he's punishing us for something we've done or if he's punishing himself. It will only ever feel like punishment to me.

Chapter Seventeen

It's six in the morning when Dad enters my room at Baba's house and sits at the foot of my bed. Mom and I are living back home again, for the most part, but I still spend most weekends and some weekdays at Baba's, especially now that we've all been going back and forth to the hospital so often to visit Grandma. Baba's house is only a two-minute drive from there, so sometimes on late nights, Dad sleeps in the stiff cot across from my bed after visiting his mother, like he did in the early days after the accident.

Grandma has been sick for months now. Everyone thought she would die before Christmas and, certainly, there were some nights her death seemed seconds away. *Not without my baby*. Her words were a little slurred but we knew what she was saying. She would not die before my youngest uncle came home to see her. So, she kept hanging on. Even when she saw angels in the corner, ready to take her, she refused to go. My uncle was still in another province for work. To see my grandmother fight to survive simply to see her youngest son, who also happens to be

Native and adopted like me, sent ripples into the earth beneath my feet. She was displaying her love, her fierce kind of love, in front of us all, and refusing to hide. I felt held in our family in a way I hadn't before.

My grandmother is a soft woman, but she has never been physically affectionate. Women of her era and background simply are not. She has never been the type to rub my back or embrace me with kisses. At the end of our Sunday *faspas*, I stand in line behind my cousins and wait my turn to quickly hug her goodbye. It's not that she's cold, but rather, that Mennonite grandparents and children (and parents and children, for that matter) maintain a certain distance from each other. Love does not need to be displayed in order for it to exist. But when someone is dying, veils are sometimes withdrawn.

I will spend years after Grandma's death asking myself questions about her. What kind of mother was she? What kind of woman? Why did she foster and adopt so many children when no one else around her was doing the same? I always saw her as a bit of an archetype: a Mennonite woman who spent her life submissive and soft, modest and intentionally unnoticed. But I think she possessed a type of strength I never recognized at the time. A type that emboldened her to shoo death away with her hand more than once. To say, *Not today, Jesus. Not without my son.* Hers was a strength, I will realize, that is quiet and calm. Is this a kind of strength I can carry with me, I will wonder, even though I carry no part of this woman in my bones or DNA? Is this the kind of strength that I *want* to carry with me?

I'm lying on my side in bed when Dad taps me on the shin. I'm not as easily startled when I'm awoken anymore, although this has taken quite some time. I look at my father's face, and I already know what he's about to say.

"Grandma died," he says.

"Oh." I don't show my sadness to my father. I never show my sadness. I'm twelve, after all. "Right. Okay. Thanks." I lie my head back on my pillow and turn to face the wall. I pretend I'm already asleep by the time he leaves my room a minute later. Is this strength? I'm not sure, but it feels like the closest thing to it.

I keep my eyes closed when I hear Baba clinking some pans in the kitchen. I imagine she has convinced Dad to have some breakfast before he leaves. It's morning, and he's been up all night and *you know, you really need to eat anyway, I mean come on.* Food has always been a form of medicine for both of my grandmothers.

I picture Grandma in her hospital bed only a few days ago. She had always been plump, so I wasn't used to her hollow cheeks and the way her clavicles jutted through the pinned shoulder seams on her hospital gown. I had never seen my grandmother with her hair undone. Her hair was whiter than the snow falling outside and reached all the way to her tailbone. It reminded me of silk, like shimmering strands of a spiderweb. It looked naked and untouched. I was standing beside Dad, who was standing beside his mother. He was washing her back. A nurse surely would have done this for him, but given the fact that he was there, he would have considered it incomprehensible and inappropriate to ask a nurse to do such a thing. Grandma looked unfamiliar and not just because of her hair. No. She looked different because she was being taken care of. And, maybe, I was so close to her death that, for the first time, I could actually see her.

Lately, I've developed a peculiar appreciation for a well-structured obituary. On Saturdays, I hop up on the counter across from Baba and her radio, in the nook she still calls "Gida's spot," as she begins her morning ritual. She prepares her tea, lights her cigarette, then turns the radio dial, and the familiar voice comes on: "And now, for this morning's funeral announcements." Baba's cigarette hangs lightly from her mouth as she writes down the details of the deaths of people she knew in her diary. Sometimes, she mutters, "Ah, I thought he already died." Other times, she'll share stories about the deceased. *You know, Brit, he was my second cousin—my baba and his baba were sisters—and when I was a teenager and went to dances where Gida played in the band, I'd see this cousin dancing with Anne Topnik who was not his wife. I tell you, didn't Gida and I have something to talk about on the drive home!*

It's clear to me what makes a good obituary. It's about the story. The details are important, of course. No one wants to forget a child or spouse or parent. But it's about more than that, I think. I want to know about the person's life. I want to know what kind of a person they were. With honesty and kindness, but without sentiment. That feels important.

JANUARY 31, 2002

OBITUARY

Peacefully with her family by her side, Tina, age 80 years, passed away on January 31, 2002 at the Bethesda Hospital.

Her memory will be cherished by her family and those who had the pleasure of knowing her. "SAFE IN THE ARMS OF JESUS."

She is survived by eight sons, three daughters, thirty-three grandchildren, thirty-four great-grandchildren, four step-grandchildren, fourteen step-great-grandchildren, three sisters, six brothers, many friends and family.

She was predeceased by her husband, her parents, two brothers, one son, one daughter, one daughter-in-law, two grandchildren, two great-grandchildren.

In lieu of flowers, donations may be made to Union Gospel Mission.

I'm sitting in the fourth pew, next to Mom and Dad. I don't think there's anyone in this entire church to whom I'm not related in some way. On my other side sits George, who's as quiet and contained as I am, and his parents. Baba is here too, at the back of the church, because she always liked Grandma. They were obviously different and, in some ways, worlds apart, but they respected one another. Baba may not understand my father's family, but she never criticizes them. She would have had something to say had Dad forbidden me from wearing pants and getting my ears pierced, like some Mennonites; but Mom loves earrings so much

I think she would've pierced my ears in secret, if she needed to. Also, this is the funeral of someone Baba knew, and she generally makes an appearance at things like this.

I can tell Dad is nervous as he walks down the aisle and up to the pulpit. He'll be speaking in front of the entire congregation and he has never been one to make any sort of speech. I'm caught off guard by how much he looks like Grandma in the way he walks. It will be this way from now on: I will notice details about him that are similar to her—things I've never noticed before. Like the way he answers the phone with a slow, two-toned, almost sing-song "Hello," or the way he always says goodbye with a "Yup, bye" in the same two notes. His neck is stout and his eyes are small and grey-blue like hers. His hair was an orangey-red until he went bald in his early thirties, and I wonder if hers was too before it turned white.

My stomach somersaults when I see Dad's eyes gloss and his upper lip quiver at the pulpit. He takes a second to steady himself before he speaks. "If you hear rocks tumbling up here, don't worry. It's just my knees knocking because I'm a little nervous." The congregation laughs and I see his shoulders loosen.

He tells the story of when, weeks earlier, he had taken his mother's dentures, cleaned them, brushed them, and reapplied the bond before putting them back in her mouth. She began spitting and sputtering and gagging, and no one could understand a word she was trying to say. Someone ran to grab a nurse, certain she must have been having some sort of stroke or heart attack or something. "Turns out," Dad tells the congregation, "I put her dentures in upside down." The crowd laughs again. Dad's eyes glisten a little and I no longer see my father standing behind the pulpit. I see a child who has just lost his mother. A little boy with red hair and suspenders and a bleached collared shirt and hand-me-down shoes, ready for church—but untethered, alone. By the time he makes his way back down the aisle and sits beside my mother, he is my father once again.

Our family is never the same after the loss of my grandmother. She was the warm light around whom everyone and everything gathered. She was the centre of us, our nucleus. We stop getting together as a family. We stop having Sunday *faspa*s and Christmas gatherings. Cousins will get married, babies will be born, but our family will grow ever more distant. The fissures that have always been present will splinter. We will become a family of memories.

This last semester, George and I have attended the same junior high, but our nods and smiles have been barely perceptible when we've passed each other in the halls. We grew less close after he was taken away, but after Grandma dies, we become more like strangers. Every time we purse our lips at each other in a way that acknowledges the shared history between us, I feel a deadened part of me awaken once again, only to wither within seconds. Tiny deaths, I suppose.

The loss of his mother creates a shift in Dad I didn't anticipate. How does a child predict such things? The answer is, of course, that a child cannot predict such things. But I've made a life of predicting things, of observing the tones with which words are spoken and the way body language shifts in the people around me.

I've learned to fill in the gaps when not much is said. The change in Dad manifests as unpredictable waves of rage. Days will go by where he doesn't speak to me or to my mother. He spends most nights sleeping on the couch downstairs or, when he can't sleep, woodworking in the barn or in the shop he eventually builds for himself. He will never sleep through a full night again. His anger will be released upon the horses and the dogs and the cows and, less frequently, the cats—and I will hate myself for not stepping in to protect them. But I already step in between him and my mother, and she has come to rely on me like a reflex. The three of us are strangers passing in the night, and in the day we forget how to be family. Though sometimes, I don't know if we've ever really known how to be a family.

Chapter Eighteen

There are barbed vines in my stomach, crawling and twisting themselves around each other. It's a pain I've never felt before, achy but sharp, like the stab of a paring knife. I'm thirteen years old, at home by myself on summer break, when I first notice the blood on the toilet paper. The sight itself doesn't shock me. I've seen so many cows and horses give birth that blood has never been a hang-up for me. An image sparks in my mind like a burst of lightning: a memory of myself at five or six years old, burying a pair of panties deep in the bathroom trash can because they were flecked with blood. But as fast as the image pops up, it's gone.

I swing open the cabinet under the sink and look for Mom's tampons. Although the idea of sticking something into myself doesn't feel very appealing, I figure it's cleaner than the alternative. Last year, one of my friends stained her pants at school and had to wear a sweatshirt tied around her waist for the rest of the day. I pull out the box and open the instruction pamphlet to an image of a woman with her knee bent up. Is her leg on the counter?

The toilet? When I was younger, I could bend my legs over my head and behind my neck. It almost seems like I need that kind of flexibility now. I rip the wrapper and slide out the applicator. I'm struck by its size, how it's so much bigger than it seems like it needs to be. Already I am aching for yesterday, when all of this was still some theoretical possibility in my distant future.

Within days, I run through Mom's tampon supply and her big bottle of ibuprofen. I realize I'm going to have to tell my mother I got my period. I can't think of any way around it—I don't want to spend my birthday money on tampons.

I find my mother in her bedroom, pressing a flat powder puff onto her cheeks, and decide to get straight to the point. "Mom, can you buy more tampons? I got my period."

"You got your period?" she squeaks.

"Yeah," I say, too nauseous to entertain any sentimentality. "Can you buy more pads and tampons? But, like, not the big ones that you usually buy?"

Later, I hear her crying on the phone with Baba: "My baby's a woman!" She's clearly touched by my entrance into womanhood, but I just feel annoyed. I had secretly hoped I would be one of those girls who didn't get their period until they were sixteen, but no luck.

I read somewhere that periods come every twenty-eight days, so I make a mental note of the first day I start bleeding. Exactly twenty-eight days later, I stick a tampon in—isn't that what I'm supposed to do? When I mention it to a friend, she laughs.

"You don't need to wear a tampon if you don't have your period. Don't you know that?"

"Oh, yeah, I mean, I know that," I say. "I'm, like, pretty sure I basically just got it anyway."

I did not know that. Embarrassed, I sneak off to the bathroom between classes and take the tampon out, wincing a little as the dry cotton scratches against my skin. Before I drop it in the dispenser, I flush the toilet to avoid being overheard by the girl in the opposite stall. It doesn't occur to me that she might be doing the same thing.

With each period, my cramps worsen—my body protesting more and more. Some days I feel so sweaty and nauseous I can barely stand. My lower stomach seems to pulse with white-hot fire. I think of animals in labour, of their primal cries. When the pain gets too intense, I call Mom to pick me up from school and drop me off at Baba's. Though she's long past needing them herself, Baba keeps her bathroom cupboard stocked with pads—and has even taken the time to ask me which products I like best. When I'm at Baba's, I raid her supply, swallow ibuprofen, and rest a bag of frozen peas against my forehead, allowing the pain to crash over me in waves. Once, when I'm feeling too weak to even stand, I lean over the side of the toilet and vomit directly onto Baba's floor. I mop it up later and never tell anyone what happened.

The thought of complaining never crosses my mind—we're not a family that complains about pain. Mom is the exception to this rule, of course, and her pain is afforded a level of theatricality that borders on hysteria.

"It hurts, it hurts!" she squeals when she cuts her finger slicing watermelon. "I can see the bone!"

I run her finger under cold water before carefully inspecting it. "No, Mom, that's just your skin, I don't see bone."

When it comes to my own pain, neither she nor Baba will suggest I see a doctor. It never occurs to me to even ask.

Chapter Nineteen

I'm attending eighth grade in a mostly white junior high school in a mostly white town, which, in recent years, has been expanding at one of the fastest rates in the country. To be a girl in this school, in this town and in my family feels like walking into church already knowing where I'll be told to sit and finding my way there before the usher utters a word. It feels like the race has already been mapped out for me, the finish line determined, and all I must do is walk across it as I watch the boys run on an entirely different track. To be a girl is to aspire to marriage and childbearing above all else, and maybe a job as a receptionist. Be fruitful, we are told. To be a girl is to be held by others, to be possessed by anyone but oneself.

I was ten years old the first time a boy asked me to give him something I didn't quite understand. I was walking home with a friend after school when a group of white boys on bicycles began circling us. My friend quickly broke out but I felt stuck, dizzied by the bodies whipping around.

"Hey," one boy called out to me. "How much do you get paid?"

"What?"

"Per hour? How much do you get paid per hour?"

"I don't know what you're talking about." I took a step forward but he stopped right in front of me, blocking my path.

"For blow jobs." He couldn't suppress his smile. "That's what you do, isn't it?" The other boys all laughed. I could see my friend in my periphery, just as confused as I was, but laughing alongside the boys.

"Whatever," I said and I pushed past him. I would never forgive myself if I cried.

My friend caught up with me by the time I reached the stop sign at the end of the street and we walked the three blocks to her house in silence.

Mom started laughing before I could even finish my story when I got home later that night. I suppose you can only be known by the initials "B. J." for so long before boys start forming ideas. She never told Dad.

I didn't know if I'd ever been given another name. Mom and Dad chose Brittany when they met me, and my foster parents had referred to me for the first two weeks of my life as "baby girl." If my birth mother had named me, that information wasn't mine to have. In second grade, I'd spent the entire year asking my mother if I could change my name to Crystal. I liked the sound of it and the way it brought to mind opalescent glass and stones and diamonds. Instead, I was B. J., for my first and middle names. It's hard to change a name, even when it attracts unfortunate attention. By the time I reached junior high, my moniker preceded me, garnering me a reputation I had never earned and certainly did not appreciate.

I walk into Baba's house and the smell of her cigarettes drifting into the entrance from the living room brings me back into my body. I've just returned from an evening with my boyfriend, although I don't really like calling him that. I'd always hoped boyfriends would be soft, caring. He is neither.

I met him when I was in the seventh grade and he was in eighth. I went out with his friend for a few months until he broke up with me on his birthday. He had asked for a blow job. It's what he expected. I didn't want to. He dumped me. On the same phone call, he asked if I'd like to go out with his friend instead. I said no and hung up. Months later, the friend asked me himself in person. I'm not sure if I felt flattered or just thankful that a boy seemed to like me, but I said yes. I think I'll always regret saying yes.

He's nice enough at first, although he really seems to like making fun of me in front of his friends. The whole first week, we only kiss, but I'm pretty sure I overhear him telling them we've done way more than that. With my nickname and the reputation it's given me, I guess his story's believable. Sometimes he says that because I said no to his friend, I should say yes to him. Like he deserves the piece of me—and more—I've already denied to someone else. I will come to wish I'd broken up with him earlier. I don't know why I didn't. If I'm honest, maybe I don't think I deserve to be treated any better than this.

Baba calls to me as I go to grab myself a can of Coke from the fridge. She's sitting in her pink chair when I walk into the living room and she waves me over to give her a kiss on the cheek. "Mom's gonna be here in twenty minutes," she tells me. I sit down on the couch—CBC news flickering on the TV in front of us. *Twenty minutes,* I think. *Twenty minutes.*

I will tell no one what happened tonight for another ten years. I will tell no one about how I was trapped in a vehicle with two older white boys, one of them my boyfriend and the other his older brother who's in high school. *I never should have joined them at the indoor pool,* I scold myself. *What was I thinking?* I will make no mention of the tiny jolt I felt in my chest when his brother locked the car doors or of his eyes squinting into narrow slits in the rear-view mirror when he told me he would not let me leave unless I did what he said. Looking back on it, I will wish I had screamed. I will wish I had thrown something—hit them, hurled my body, anything. But I'd vowed to myself after the accident that I would never let the chaos inside of me reveal itself again. And I wasn't sure fighting would help much anyway. Still, I will question myself and judge myself for not having fought at all.

Instead, I sat there calmly, as though nothing and no one could bother me. I felt overpowered, but I didn't want to show this to them. I knew they could sense my hesitation, but I didn't want them to feel my fear. I turned inward and allowed my mind to cushion itself. I let them do what they did, and I didn't make a sound. By the time I left the vehicle, I felt like roadkill, or like a bloodied deer with a broken hind leg, hobbling back into the woods.

Mom picks me up from Baba's and we drive home in silence. In the bathroom, I wash my face, staring at hands I know are mine but do not feel like mine, as Tabby waits by the door. I stare at myself in the mirror, inspecting the contours of my thirteen-year-old face. I've never known from whom this face descended, but tonight, I don't know to whom it belongs. I'm everybody's girl and I'm nobody's girl.

It's a cold November night and the woodstove has broken down once again. I grab Tabby and I hold her close against my body, feeling the warmth of her wet nose against my neck. "I just wanted it to stop," I whisper to her before I fall asleep. And she reminds me, in her way, that it already has.

I'm not a particularly sympathetic character, I learn, but I don't understand why. My teacher gathers my class, grade 8-B, one morning, to hold an impromptu, closed-door meeting. One of our classmates is anorexic, she tells us, and has become dangerously thin. She'll be going into treatment and she won't be returning to class for the rest of the year. She and her family would like us to understand how much she needs our prayers.

An hour later, I'm crying in the upstairs girls' bathroom while my best friend, Michaela, who's in another class, tries to console me. My teacher walks in to find us huddled in the back stall. "Girls," she says, rushing over to us. "She's going to be okay. Don't worry, girls. She's getting treatment."

I blink back my tears as my friend shoots my teacher an incredulous look.

"That's not why I'm crying," I tell her.

"Oh, B. J., did you have sex, honey?" There's a knowing look on her face. It seems to say, *I knew this would happen to you.*

I'm speechless. My friend looks as though she might throw fists, and a small part of me wishes she would.

"No," I say. "I . . . I've been making myself throw up."

It's the first I've spoken about this to anyone. I've been forcing myself to vomit since that night with the boys. I've come to hate my body—watching it expel its contents feels apt. A further emptying, of sorts, of a body that already feels empty. Vomiting feels like a type of punishment, like I'm giving my body what I think it deserves. But it's also such a thunderbolt to my senses that it brings me back to myself, back to a body that can feel again. It doesn't make me feel good, but it makes me feel real.

My teacher takes a step back. "Well," she says, "today is not about you. It's about your classmate."

Rumours begin to spread about me. They are not kind. Everyone around me seems to have a better idea than I do about the type of girl I am. I can see it in the way some of the boys' mothers look at me—I can see in their eyes that they're afraid I might hurt their sons. I can feel them examining my body from my head down to my feet, and up again. When I see a boy from my class at the arena and say hi, I swear his mom puts her arm around him and guides him in another direction. My male classmates tell me they aren't supposed to spend time with me—then they follow me to class. These moms don't want me to taint their precious boys.

I don't know how I got here, to this place of being so distrusted by women, white women I don't even know. Whose sons are the ones making jokes about my body and my name. Whose sons are the ones slapping my butt as I walk past them in the hallway—the ones asking for "favours" in the boys' dressing room after school. These are the children whose mothers are trying to protect them. From me.

DECEMBER 24, 2002
PHOTOGRAPH

I'm sitting on the floor in our living room. Beside our Christmas tree, beside Tabby, whose white paws are perched on my lap. It's like she knows, like she always knows, that I need her close. My parents are on the couch across from me and Dad is asleep. Mom is watching a Christmas movie. Baba is behind the camera, telling me to smile. I smile but I don't show my teeth. I've had braces for the last six months, after having spent a year sleeping with headgear hooked into my back molars and strapped behind my head. I've never been more thankful than when the orthodontist said I didn't have to wear it at school.

It's Christmas Eve and I've just had a fight on the phone with the boy who's no longer my boyfriend, but for some reason won't leave me alone. I broke up with him shortly after that night in his brother's vehicle, and since then he and some other kids at school have decided I'm a slut. I feel like I can't argue with them. If I wasn't a slut, I wouldn't have been in that vehicle in the first place. What happened wouldn't have happened.

My skin is pale and the discolouration around my eyes has become darker. In years to come, whenever anyone sees this photo, they'll tell me that I don't even look like myself. I know, I'll say, because they're right.

As soon as this photo is taken, Baba will get up and pour us both a cup of tea. I can't say I love the taste of tea yet, but I do enjoy the way she makes it for me. Then Baba will sit down, cover her legs with a blanket and tell me to come closer, so Tabby and I can lean against her chair.

The cycles of binging and purging continue for months. I don't consider myself to have an eating disorder—that all feels too dramatic. Besides, the vomiting has never been so much about the eating and controlling of food for me. If I'm able to hurt myself first, anything else that's to follow surely will hurt me less. If I beat others to it, I'm protecting myself in some way. But after reading about bulimia nervosa, I suspect I have at least an element of it. Still, I don't like thinking of myself with any sort of label—and I hate the idea that others might think they know anything about me based on a diagnosis alone.

I go see my guidance counsellor one day during my lunch hour. She's a middle-aged Christian woman who reminds me of Dr. Phil's wife, Robin, with the haircut of Joyce Meyer. I first started visiting her after I told my friend about my throwing up, and I've been coming back to her ever since. I think I just like having someone to talk to, someone who seems like she cares. She's warm and it feels comforting to be in her presence. I decide to ask for her advice. I don't enjoy making myself throw up and it's not like I want to keep doing it forever. She gives me all the handouts she has on bulimia and some worksheets on cognitive behavioural therapy. I take them home, hide them in the base of my nightstand and finish them within the week. I'm always a good student, and I appreciate anything that gives even the semblance it's listening to me, even if it's just a list of written questions. Eventually, my guidance counsellor gives me an ultimatum: I must tell my mother about my bulimia by the end of the next week or she will do it for me.

"Ew," Mom says. Her face twists. "Why?"

"I don't know," I say.

"But you don't even like those long tongue thingies they use at the doctor's for throat swabs, remember?"

I look down at the corners of my nails to see them nearly scabbed over from my picking. I want to tell her it feels like punishment in the way others have punished my body. I want to tell her that if I'm the one causing myself the pain, then it all feels more manageable, lighter. If I'm the one injuring myself, I leave little room for others to do the same. I want to tell her that what I want from her is to be held. To have my back rubbed the way Baba used to when I'd fall asleep next to her. To be told I'm loved. To be told I'm okay. To be told that she, not I, has always been the lucky one.

My gaze lifts from my fingers and back to her and the reality of our situation dawns on me. She's the one who's hurting. She's the one upset by having to see herself as a mother with a bulimic daughter. She's the one whose self-worth is being called into question. I have to care for my mother now. She never asked for this.

I push myself off the living room floor and walk over to the green couch she saved up for and is so very proud of. I sit beside her and put my hand on her back. She doesn't look at me, but I can see her eyes welling up.

"We can't tell Dad," she says. "He'll get too angry."

I nod. She starts to cry. I can tell what she's thinking. "You're a good mom," I reassure her, rubbing her back.

"No, I'm not," she says. "What kind of mother lets her daughter do this?"

"It's not your fault. It's my fault, Mom. I'm sorry. I'm the one who's making myself throw up. I'm the one doing it. Not you, Mom. It's not your fault."

"Are you going to do it anymore, though?"

"No," I lie. "I've already stopped."

I'm fourteen when it happens again. It's the same time of year with the same boy. I want to say I'm that same poor girl, but I'm beginning to grow a little tired of hating myself. I've never managed to get away from him, given that we go to the same school and see each other in the hallways nearly every day. I guess I don't think I deserve much better, either. So I let him back in. I let him call me and sometimes I call him back. I don't argue when he says cruel things to me and I don't fight back when his friends make fun of me. I laugh or I pretend that I don't hear their words. *What's the point?* I think.

There are hockey tryouts in town, and my friends and I are tipsy. Earlier, we stole some liquor from Michaela's father's cabinet. It's the first time we've ever done something like this together, although each of us has been drunk before. *At least it's better than raspberry Sour Puss,* I think as I gulp down my vodka and 7 Up. Still, this isn't so much an act of rebellion as it is an act of curiosity. It's just something to do on a Saturday night before watching some hockey. Later, I'll suppose the fact that I was drunk made it easier for him to blame me for what happened.

It's cold out and he and I are alone on the frozen grass outside the arena. It doesn't hurt like it did the first time. I'm conscious enough to notice this much. I'm floating in and out, and part of this is the alcohol and part of it is because I know how to detach from my body already. This will help me remember less too. I've always had a good memory for phone numbers and birthdays and Mental Math Minutes. My memory is something I've learned to hide from others. Nobody likes a girl who remembers too much. And if I can't forget, at least I can pretend to forget. I have learned to pretend to forget so much already.

Chapter Twenty

"Dad thinks you're having sex," Mom says one night before bed. I'm fourteen years old.

My brain stutters for a few seconds before registering what she just said.

"Wh—okay . . ." I try to grasp onto a single thought. Nothing comes.

Dad and I haven't really spoken much in the nearly two years since Grandma died. There have been entire weeks where we haven't said a single word to each other. When he does speak, it's often some loud, angry outburst, which means he definitely won't be speaking for another few days.

Mom is different. She talks as I'm doing my homework and she talks while we're at the dinner table when she's home in time from her job as a cashier at the grocery store and she talks when we're in the middle of a church service. She could have a conversation with a corpse, I'm convinced. That is, if she weren't terrified of things like that. At the start of every spring and the end of every fall, Baba takes me to Gida's grave to clean up the flowers. If Mom ever comes along, which is increasingly rare, she refuses to leave the vehicle. The look of disapproval on Baba's face almost matches the one she wears when she talks about Mom getting baptized as a Mennonite. Mom hates cemeteries. Her biggest fear is that a hand will reach out from one of the graves, grab her ankle, and pull her down with it. People think she's joking, but she's completely serious.

"He thinks you're having sex," she repeats herself. "He told me yesterday." She doesn't seem angry and she doesn't seem disappointed, just . . . like she's wanting information. Like she's an older sister trying to figure out how to play this situation, wanting to know as much as she can before taking sides. "He was looking at your messages on MSN Messenger and he thinks you're having sex."

I'm confused. I'm not having sex and I'm not talking about sex on MSN. We just got dial-up that we share with our neighbour down the road, and half the time our internet doesn't even work. When I'm on there, my friends and I mostly talk about which movies we want to watch this weekend and at whose house we're going to watch them, and let's make sure to get popcorn with extra butter and Chunky Monkey ice cream from 7-Eleven that we'll finish before we even start the movie. I'm not saying we're totally innocent—I mean, last weekend we found a Myspace page outlining how to conduct a séance and we tried to do one ourselves. We didn't have the proper tools, so we put my friend's mom's candles in the middle of our circle while we repeated the chants out loud. But Dad couldn't possibly know about this.

"Well, I'm not," I say. I wish I didn't sound so defensive because I can tell by the look on her face that she doesn't believe me.

"He thinks you are. And you should've seen him—he was mad! You even made him cry, B. J."

I feel so embarrassed I can't look at my father for days after this. Why is he snooping in the first place? I didn't expect this of him. I've never seen Dad cry, and to think that something like this brought him to tears—I don't know what to do with this information.

Church has always been clear on sex before marriage: it's a sin that carries consequences that reverberate through the generations. I once heard a pastor tell the entire congregation that his children and grandchildren were living with generational sin because he and his wife had had sex before they got married. Later in that same sermon, and this part was the hardest for me to hear, he said, "Some women tell me, 'Well, I don't really like sex all that much,' and I have one thing that I say to them. It's not about you!" People chuckled and I shrank in my chair.

Despite our church and family's stance on premarital sex, Mom has repeatedly told me since I was a young girl that if I ever got pregnant as a teenager, she and Dad would make me keep the baby. It's always felt like something she's prepared for, as if she and Dad had had this conversation before they even adopted me. I wonder if she thinks I'll follow in the footsteps of my birth mom. I've heard her say the same thing to her friends before, too. "We've always said, if Brit had a baby, we wouldn't let her give it up. We'd keep it and raise it." What am I doing, what have I done, that she keeps bringing this up? Every time she says it, it feels like

I'm supposed to be grateful—grateful that she won't let what happened to me happen to my make-believe child. Mostly, I just feel confused. But I reason most moms wouldn't support a daughter who got pregnant—some would even kick their daughter out of the house—and I know I'm lucky.

It doesn't occur to me to tell my parents what happened to me last year or earlier this fall. I can only imagine how angry Dad would be, how disgusted Mom would be. Years ago, one of my cousins accused someone of touching her and he ended up going to jail—but she was also taken by Child and Family Services, and I haven't seen her since. I don't even know where she went—Winnipeg, I assume. All either of my parents said about it was that she was lying. Another of my relatives had accused her father of touching her when I was much younger. The case went to court and everyone thought he was going to go to prison—until she told everyone she'd lied, and the case was dropped. "These girls just want to destroy their families," Dad said. "She made the whole thing up."

One time I asked Mom if she really thought our cousin had lied. Why she would go through everything—the police, the court system, all of it—if it wasn't true? Mom shrugged. "Well, you know, some girls just do. They just want the attention, so they think, 'Huh, I'm gonna get him back,' because their dad pissed 'em off or something."

I still think my cousin was telling the truth, but I'm not sure it was worth it.

Sometimes, I hate the look of my bare skin. I get out of the bath and dry myself with a towel and I just can't help but hate it, hate my skin, hate my body. It feels distant, like it's covered in cling wrap and I can't properly feel the water or towel against it. Sometimes, I think someone could press a lit cigarette onto my forearm and I wouldn't even flinch. I don't like thinking like that, though, because I know kids who've had that happen to them. One of my foster sisters had scars on her arms from her dad doing that to her. That's one thing I know my parents would never do. And, that's the thing, isn't it? No matter what, there's always someone who has it worse than you do, always someone who's felt more pain than you have. So, it's hard for me to know what should be causing me pain and what shouldn't. This is part of why I try my best to keep it all in.

Sometimes, I feel so hidden, I wonder if anyone will ever see me. I think I could die in my sleep or in another car accident and, apart from Baba, no one would be that sad.

We take health class in grade nine, where we learn about abstinence. That's the only kind of sex education that matters, we've been taught. Everyone at school still thinks of me as a slut, although I think that's starting to change. My boyfriend, who's not really my boyfriend—or at least, sometimes he says he is and other times, when he's into another girl, he says we're not really together and what's wrong with me anyway—is in the tenth grade and not at my school anymore. I can't say I mind the distance.

We also learn about depression in health class. How it's not even sadness so much as immobility, a darkness that creeps over someone and infects their entire life. I think of Dad. I wonder if that's what he has, but I'll never ask him. I can only imagine how angry he'd be if I did. So many of the symptoms we were taught about seem like what he's had the last few years. Except for the anger—our teacher doesn't really mention that. I wonder what's so wrong with me that my mere presence seems to cause him so much rage. Some nights, these questions play like a relentless loop in my head: Why does my father hate me so much? What was so wrong with me that not even my birth mom wanted me? What was so wrong with me that my birth father couldn't even admit he was my father? Why can't I do anything right?

Chapter Twenty-One

I'm late again. Some mornings, like today, when the snow isn't piled too high, I grab my parka and call out a "Bye, Bob!"—my nickname for Baba—before I dash through her backyard and her neighbour's to meet my parents at church. I'm perpetually running ten minutes late. We changed churches around the time of our accident a few years ago, and our new church is a three-minute walk (or thirty-second sprint) from Baba's house. Mom said she wanted to go to a church with more children my age, but there are actually fewer kids my age here. I refuse to go to youth group—I'm not interested in making friends at church, if I'm honest. I feel like church kids don't get me. Mom really likes it here, though, and Dad doesn't say how he feels either way.

This church is more modern than our last, and I imagine that's what Mom likes about it. The pews in the middle aisles have cushions and the ones on the side are lacquered well—no splinters to be found. There's a band with drums and a bass guitar, and their songs are catchier. This church is more flexible, more evangelical.

Mom loves that the pastor can keep her attention during his sermons and, certainly, he's an animated storyteller. Still, some things have not changed—once the pastor opens his sermon, Dad's head bows into his hands, his chin nestling in his palms and his elbows on his knees, and he doesn't move again until the closing prayer. Sometimes, I catch his head looking heavy and know he's asleep, and sometimes his body jolts itself awake—but I make no mention of this to anyone. None of Dad's family attends this church, and I miss seeing my cousins, especially George, in the foyer when I walk in, even if we wouldn't say much to each other. It was one of the few points of contact we still had.

I made sure to thoroughly blow dry my hair last night so not even a strand was damp this morning. Sometimes, my parents call Baba before they leave for church to ask if I'll be ready in time for them to pick me up. Last weekend, I didn't leave myself enough time, and my hair wasn't even half dried by the time my parents pulled up on the driveway. Dad was livid at the sight of me. Mom looked straight ahead as my father yelled, calling me lazy and classless, before demanding that I get out of the car. Before I was able to shut the door he shouted after me that next time I'd better have some flippin' respect. I was not going to make that mistake again.

When I arrive at church, the worship leader is instructing everyone to stand, which is lucky. I scurry along the back of the room and up to my parents' pew. The whites of Mom's eyes are reddened this morning and her eyeliner appears smudged.

"Are you okay?" I mouth to her. She nods curtly and keeps her eyes on the screen at the front of the room, where lyrics are projected for all to follow. I always hate it when the worship leader doesn't line the sheet up properly and the words are slanted for the entire song. I want to march right up there and straighten it out for her but, of course, I wouldn't dare. As long as I'm not the one singing, I like church music. It reminds me of the times we stuffed ourselves into my grandparents' living room, most of us sitting on the floor, and sang along as one of my uncles played the guitar. Or when Grandma was in her final hours at the hospital and everyone gathered in the family room off to the side to hear my uncle play his guitar. The melodies echoed throughout the hospital and no one seemed to mind.

After the service, we're sitting at Baba's kitchen table when Mom breaks down with little warning. They don't know what happened, she tells me. They don't know exactly when it happened, either. Dad found her on Friday night, when I was already at Baba's house for the weekend. Tabby, unresponsive and stiff on the floor next to her favourite rocking chair.

My face grows hot and my eyes begin to burn. There's a ringing in my ears so sharp it's painful. I feel the urge to scream, to burst into tears, to hit myself in the face, something—anything—just to make them see me. Instead, I stare at my plate.

"Two days ago?" I ask. "This happened two days ago and you didn't call?"

Mom keeps crying and Dad shrugs. "What did you want us to do?" he asks.

I push my chair away from the table, stand up, and walk determinedly to the bathroom. I will not let them see me cry. I lock the bathroom door and slide down the wall until I'm sitting, my knees against my chest. I drop my head into my knees and the tears come hard. The tension in my shoulders releases. These are the silent kind of sobs, the kind that feel so painful, there's no noise that can do them justice. My mind flashes to Marion and James and Fred and Shanny and George and the others. So many others. It flashes to a few months ago, when the boy hurt me once again, and how Tabby was there for me afterward. Tabby was always there for me—the first time he hurt me and the second. When Fred and Shanny left and when George was taken away and when he came back. After the accident and when I began hurting myself. She'd wait outside the bathroom for me. It feels like there is an implosion within me and I can't contain it.

I'm not sure how much time passes before Baba's voice calls through the door, sympathetic but firm. "Brit, that's enough."

I push myself up and walk to the mirror above the sink. I hate the look of my face when I've been crying. I hate the way the skin around my eyes turns a little purple and gets swollen. I hate the redness around my nose and the blotchiness of my skin. Worst of all, I hate knowing others can see I'm in pain simply by looking at my face. I run my hands under the cold water until the feeling in my fingers starts to disappear. I press my cool fingers against my eyes, willing the physical display of my pain to go away.

Baba is back at the table when I sit down a few minutes later. Mom has eaten nothing more off her plate; Dad is reaching for another helping of mashed potatoes.

A thought dawns on me and I'm shocked to realize I'm only thinking of it now. "What did you do with her body?"

—

My brain never mistook a shadow for Fred, a creak on the stairs for James. But I see Tabby around the house for weeks after she dies. In the corner of the kitchen, the refrigerator light illuminating her white paws. I grab some water and close the door and she's gone again. I awake in the middle of the night to go to the bathroom and see her sitting like a loaf of bread in the corner of the hallway. I pass her on the step, the second from the top of the staircase, where she often waited to meet me. Where we once sat together, Tabby warming my feet, as I forgot the sound of my brother's voice. I try not to think of her body in the stove, in flames and then ash, converted to heating our house for the night.

I close my eyes and I see my father tossing her in with one hand before I had the chance to say goodbye, the flames engulfing her. I shake my head, willing the images loose from my mind. This house is already filled with too many ghosts I do not wish or know how to acknowledge.

My bedroom holds an emptiness now. Tabby used to return to it, night after night after night after night, to sleep by my side. She's the only one who has always been here with me. And now she's gone. But the ghost of her gives me comfort, like she is reminding me—like she has always reminded me—that I'm not entirely alone.

"There is new life to be found here," the pastor says from the pulpit, holding up a book called *The Purpose Driven Life.*

It's been over a month since Tabby died. Christmas came and went, and we're in a new year, 2004. I've been hoping the turn of the calendar will dislodge the part of my brain that feels stuck. I can't move past Tabby's death. I miss her and I feel more alone than I've ever felt before. The only times I can manage to eat enough is when I'm at Baba's house on the weekends, and only because Baba forces me to. It's as though my body is repulsed by the thought of having to digest anything more than my grief. The upside, perhaps, is I've mostly stopped throwing up. I can't bring myself to do it anymore, like my body's paralyzed in the absence of Tabby, and the thought of not having her to return to when I'm done makes me that much sadder. My body feels like it has nothing to offer, not even in penance or punishment. *She was just a cat,* I remind myself. But those words feel like a betrayal of my experience. A betrayal of her.

I sat alone on the couch on Christmas day, watching reruns of *Joanie Loves Chachi* while my parents and Baba entertained one of Mom's cousins from out of town. Joanie and Chachi sat by the fire, one scarf wrapped around their two necks, as Chachi's stepfather told the story of when he was alone as a child on Christmas. He stared into his neighbours' window, watching as they sang Christmas carols and drank eggnog. A family, he said, that's what he would have someday. My eyes stung, but I refused to let the tears come. I wanted a family too.

"You can find your purpose in life!" our pastor exclaims. "Your purpose, your mission, your reason for being here!"

A reason for being, I think. I desperately want someone to tell me why I'm here. Why my life looks the way it does. If I can make sense of it all—my adoption, the losses I'm scared to even acknowledge as losses because I'm not sure they're mine to acknowledge (after all, shouldn't I be simply be grateful to be here?), the disconnection from my body and my family and my parents' culture. Often, I've wondered: Did my parents really want *me*? Or did they simply want a child? Or is that just parenthood? No one can choose their children. Not really, anyway. No one can choose their parents, either. I just wish—and I feel ashamed for this thought, too—that my parents weren't glorified for wanting the unwantable child. If I could make sense of my story, find a reason for it, maybe I'd find a sense of belonging too. Maybe this book could give me that. It's literally written into the title, after all.

I walk to the office near the back of the church after the service. I have money saved up in my chequing account, an account Baba opened for me on my first birthday and into which she happily deposited one hundred dollars. I've been working as a server for a local catering company on the weekends. I tell my mother I'll withdraw twenty dollars and pay her back after the service if she can lend me the cash now to purchase the book. I feel a lightness in my chest—a pang of something unfamiliar but recognizable. I almost don't want to acknowledge it, lest it slip away from me before I have the chance to hold the book in my hands. I feel hope.

Chapter Twenty-Two

It's the spring of 2004. I'm standing behind the pulpit, three hundred white, hopeful faces staring back at me. I look down at the neatly folded looseleaf in my hands and inhale. I can already sense my body detaching from the innermost part of me. Or, perhaps, the innermost part of me is detaching itself from my body. I tell the congregation I'm adopted, although anyone who knows my parents already knows this fact. There's never any mistaking me for their biological child. I tell them I was raised by my parents, who joined this church a few years ago. I look over at the pastor, who's sitting in the front row, and notice he's smiling. There's a joke he's told more than once up here about us "lucky" adopted children, and I wonder if he's thinking of it now. A bully picks on another kid for being adopted, and the adopted child replies, "So what? My parents chose me. Yours were stuck with you!" The congregation laughs whenever he tells this joke, and Mom always looks at me and mouths, "See?" I never laugh. There's a boy in my class who, as an intended insult, accuses other kids of being adopted.

"I'm adopted," I've said to him, unblinking. It didn't seem to change anything. I don't think this would work on him either.

I glance back at my looseleaf again. I share a few vague details about my accident and how God was there for me and my mother. This is my "testimony," a supposedly intimate retelling of my story, meant to be replete with details about my life in an effort to display God's faithfulness. The farther a person has fallen, the higher she can lift his holy name. Our scars, his healing. Our pain, his glory.

When I first sat down to write my testimony a few weeks ago, I thought about how I might make my story sentimental and captivating, something that could really glorify God. That's what makes a good baptism testimony, if you ask anyone. But approaching it in this way felt like a betrayal to myself. I don't share intimate parts of who I am with even those closest to me. I certainly can't do so in a room filled with so many strangers. And although I still want desperately to belong with the people I am told are my people, I can't go against who I am. So instead I share the bare minimum, and the rest I hold in for myself.

Like the host body that rejects a donated kidney, I can't seem to fully accept this donated culture. *But maybe,* I think to myself, *my baptism will solve that.* Maybe the water and the power of the pastor's prayer will fix whatever it is inside of me that's always prevented me from feeling like I belong. Maybe this, what I'm about to do, is the answer to it all.

I look up from my script and back at the faces staring at me. It's like I can hear their thoughts. *Saved girl,* some of their faces say to me. *Lucky girl,* others say. These are the looks I've received all my life and I recognize them easily.

—

I was sitting in the pastor's office when I decided I would get baptized. Mennonites aren't baptized as babies. The rite is reserved for those who are old enough to pledge their faith to Jesus and offer their testimony before the congregation. I've always known I would get baptized one day, but wasn't sure when. Mom was baptized when she first started attending church with Dad, which, of course, pissed off Baba and which, of course, still pisses her off to this day. "I mean, come on," she always says. "She was baptized as a baby—why would she need to be baptized again? It's insulting!" But Baba tells me she will happily be there to watch me get baptized.

The book I bought from the church library, the book I was so hopeful would offer me purpose and meaning like its title and the pastor both promised, was no help in the end. I dutifully read its pages. I meditated upon the words. I tried to remind myself that this life really is not about me, like the book said—that life is a test and a responsibility. I already felt so much responsibility—to take care of my mother in the ways she could not take care of me, to be the adopted child my parents expected of me, to be well-mannered and never too emotional. I felt the responsibility of managing my father's increasing emotional volatility—to step in between my parents whenever that volatility expressed itself as rage. I just wanted God to see how hard I was trying. And to make the sadness go away. I could handle the rest of it, but the sadness felt too strong most days. I'm not sure the book was written for a girl like me.

And so I asked Mom to take me to the pastor one evening. She'd noticed I'd been quieter than usual, and it had become a chore for her to encourage me to attend my indoor softball practices. She let me skip most evenings and I instead spent them lying in bed or on the couch with *Friends* reruns playing in the background until it was time for me to go to sleep. Years from now, I will learn from my mother that my father went to visit the pastor during this time too. When I ask her why he went, she will say, "I dunno. I think he was depressed or something." And that will be the end of it.

I met with the pastor in his office on a cold Wednesday night in the middle of February. I sat opposite him as he swayed side to side, back and forth, in his black leather office chair. There was no rhythm to his movements and I wondered what kind of motor was driving him. The thought of having either of my parents there with me had never occurred to me, or, I suppose, to my mother. Dad didn't know I was here—Mom thought telling him would make him too angry.

I shared with the pastor that I had been feeling desperately sad lately, although I told him I couldn't pinpoint why.

"I just want to be happy," I said. "I just want to know the meaning to . . . it. Why we're here. Why I'm here, I guess." I didn't mention wanting to know why I'd been adopted, why my first family hadn't seemed to want me, why none of my siblings ever seemed to stay.

He leaned his body forward. His brown hair parted on the side and swept across his forehead—I imagined he'd found a hairstyle he liked several decades ago and hadn't thought twice about it since. He pressed his fingers into a triangle and this reminded me of when my siblings and I used to fold ours together and recite, "Here is the church and here is the steeple." Then the pastor pushed himself out of his chair and toward an easel at the back of his office.

HELL. He wrote the word in big, red letters at the top left of the easel's white poster paper. HEAVEN. Big black letters on the right side. He drew a line in the middle of the page, separating the two—I could tell this wasn't the first time he'd done this. Beneath HELL, he wrote "sadness" and "depression" and "anger" and "jealousy." Beneath HEAVEN, he wrote "joy" and "laughter" and "purpose" and "meaning." He paused for effect, looking back at me meaningfully. Then he wrote JESUS across the line in the middle.

"You said you've been feeling sad and depressed," he said.

I nodded.

"Now, the only way out of those feelings and into finding meaning and purpose . . ." He used his black marker to point back at the board. "Jesus. It's Jesus."

I felt confused. My problem wasn't one of disbelief. I'd been a devoted Mennonite my whole life.

"And the only way to fully know Jesus," the pastor said, "is through committing your life to him. Baptism."

If baptism could wash our sins away, perhaps it could also wash my pain away.

I decided it was worth a shot.

I was lying in bed a week after meeting with the pastor, no happier, with no greater understanding of why I seemed to be suffering, when Mom entered my room trying to coax me into attending softball practice. "If you go, you'll feel better," she said, sitting at the foot of my bed. It was a line she'd tried once or twice before. Sometimes I would go just to see her smile, but I couldn't say practice ever really left me feeling much better. I shook my head and closed my eyes.

Suddenly, I felt Mom's body stiffen, and the air in my bedroom seemed to cool a few degrees.

"What's going on?" Dad's voice was loud and it was strong.

"Brit doesn't want to go to practice tonight," Mom said.

Silence hung in the air.

Dad looked at me and back at Mom. "Why not?"

I didn't know what to say. I didn't have the energy to explain how I'd been feeling or for any sort of one-way fight.

"Well, she's been really sad lately, and so she went to see the pastor last week and . . ."

Dad's face seemed to pulse red-hot. I knew Mom hadn't meant to let slip that I'd seen the pastor, that she'd only revealed it in her nervousness, but I still felt betrayed.

What followed was screaming and yelling. A boisterous combination of "This is my house" and "I'm the head of this household" and "Nothing happens without me knowing about it." I guess Mom had been right—Dad was angry—but I hadn't expected him to be *this* angry.

"Tough," he said finally. "You're going to softball." And as he left the room, his voice called out back to me, "And you're going to stop moping around and start feeling better. Whatever happens, sometimes we just have to get over it."

—

The water in the tub is colder than I expected it to be, and the feel of it against my bare feet sends little currents up my legs and along my spine. I take one step, then another, and begin to shiver. I feel the eyes of every single person in the congregation on me as my lower body is submerged. This baptismal water, this holy water, feels as icy as the water in the ditch felt as it seeped into my boots when Fred and I hunted for tadpoles. This water looks just as brown and murky too. The pastor places his hand on my back, like we rehearsed earlier in the week, and I criss-cross my arms, my right over my left, to lie across my chest. But when he grabs hold of my wrists, it feels tighter than we practised. I feel held but not in a comforting way. It reminds me of the moment your Ferris wheel car begins to lift off the ground and you realize the only way off the ride is to wait until it stops. I'm at the mercy of the one who is controlling the wheel.

"Brittany," the pastor announces, his voice booming, "upon confession of your faith, I baptize you in the name of the father, the son and the holy spirit." I close my eyes, bracing myself for what's to come. The rest of my body is plunged beneath the chilly water, the pastor's forceful hand against my chest. All sounds muffle themselves and, for a moment, my body feels as though it's floating in a sort of limbo. This is a moment that will separate all that happened before and all that is to come. It's the moment I'm supposed to be declared anew.

I open my eyes and see the muddled outline of the pastor's body in the water next to mine and the lights blurring above me. I want to take some of the water in my mouth, to swallow some of it, but I don't. I close my eyes again, and I'm five years old. Fred splashes me and the two of us laugh. My brother and I plunge our

Mason jars deep into the stream before we pull out our jars to show each other who, of the two of us, has caught the most tadpoles.

My body is tugged back out from under the water and I open my eyes to a room full of church members clapping. Everyone is so proud. I can feel it in the air and in their smiles and in the way the pastor proclaims that I'm a new believer under God. Mom and Dad and Baba and my softball coach and some of my aunts and uncles—they are all so happy for me. But I can't suppress the feeling that I'm a fraud. I thought the water would cleanse me of the sense I don't belong here.

I step out of the tub, wrap myself with a towel that's handed to me and walk myself down to the basement to change. As I wipe the tub water from my eyes and blink the remnants of my baptism away, a tiny crack forms in my heart. I didn't know it was possible for me to feel even less like I'm meant to be here. I think of the ditch water and how it felt no different against my skin than the holy water. I have to wonder if there really was something in that ditch worth remembering. My brother and the way his capped teeth glinted as he smiled wide at the sight of the tadpoles in our jars. The lightness in our steps as we walked back to the house side by side, our feet squeaking and starting to prune in our rubber boots. Our two jars on the ledge of the kitchen window, the sunlight streaming through them, as Fred and I excitedly planned for tomorrow. We would maybe keep them for a day or two before releasing them back into the water. Catching them was never really the point.

Chapter Twenty-Three

The sun is sending bright streams of light through the blinds in my bedroom, and the old woodpecker is hammering away at one of the trees just outside. I nestle my nose against the fur of the grey-and-white kitten sleeping beside me. I scratch his head and he wraps his paws around his face as he sighs. I picked Jimmy up from a neighbour's farm a few days ago and he has fallen asleep on my chest every night since. It's nice to not feel so alone in this house anymore. His purrs fill in the spaces where the silence hung heavy before.

I push myself up from bed and walk to the bathroom. I rub my eyes and I stare at my reflection in the mirror. My hair has started curling again. It went from curly to straight a few years ago—and then, it was as though I fell asleep one night and woke up the next morning with waves and kinks I didn't recognize. I think of my government documents. "The birth mother has curly, dark-brown hair." I move my face toward the mirror, inspecting it closer. Along with changes in my body, about which I'm developing more and more anxiety, my face is morphing too. I still have a tiny scar on the bridge of my nose from a scratched chicken pock, but the rest of my face is abandoning its childlike qualities. I'm starting to look more like a woman. My cheeks are hollowing out and my eyes look like they tell more of a story than they did before— but maybe I'm the only one who sees what they're trying to say. My eyebrows have finally begun to fill in since my disastrous year-long affair with tweezers. Mom is annoyed that I don't dress my face with makeup, but I like leaving it bare. I like seeing what there is to find in my naked face. I like wondering about the ways in which I might look like *her.* I can't help but think of my birth mother, especially today, on my fifteenth birthday.

Back in my bedroom, I open the top drawer of my nightstand. There, I've stored a photo of Tabby wearing a baby-blue cardigan meant for a doll and sitting in my lap. I'm not looking at the camera and I'm smiling in a way that looks like it's coming from somewhere deep within. Beneath the photo sits the Adventure Bible I was given at our old church when I turned seven. I started reading it diligently that year, highlighting the places that felt significant, or at least felt like they should feel significant. And beneath my bible sits my new diary. I've strategically placed items above it to alert me if it's been tampered with. A few years ago, Mom spent an entire day crying after she listened in on one of my phone calls and heard me mention the sweater I'd received for Christmas was in a different colour than I'd asked for. I suspect she still listens in on my calls from time to time, because I sometimes hear a subtle click on the other end. And I threw my last diary in the woodstove after I suspected she'd been reading it. I'm not sure she knows I have this one.

I flip through the pages I've already scrawled in since I received the book as a gift from a friend a few weeks ago. So many questions. But there are no answers. I've never had any answers for my questions. I'll spend the coming days and weeks and months filling in the rest of the diary. Then I'll buy another one and fill it. And another one after that. I'll write about how nervous I am for my upcoming exams—how upset I am with myself for making "careless mistakes" on my calculus homework. I'll draft detailed study plans so I can refer to them on a nightly basis. I'll write and I'll pray and I'll question and, secretly, I'll cry. I'll plead with God to please just remember me. I'll wonder if my birth mother ever remembers me, if anyone in my family remembers me, especially on a day like today.

It's a few weeks later and I'm at the Children's Hospital in Winnipeg for my biannual follow-up with an orthopedic surgeon. There's a two-centimetre discrepancy in the length of my legs, on account of having fractured the growth plate in my femur during the accident. I suppose I'm lucky I've grown very little since the age of eleven.

I smile at the grey-haired surgeon when he enters the exam room. I still remember the kindness in his eyes when I woke up after the accident and the way he sang me to sleep as the anesthesia settled in.

"Look at your joints," he says, prodding at my kneecaps. "Noodles! They're like wet spaghetti." He jostles my left kneecap, then my right, and stretches the ligaments of my ankles, commenting on my hyper-flexibility. He asks about school and softball and the animals on our farm, and he jokes about my apparent affinity for breaking and spraining the lower joints of my body.

"Jump off the table and walk to the door on your tiptoes," he instructs. I follow dutifully, returning on my heels before he has the chance to remind me to do so. I know the drill by now.

He spends ten minutes with me, maybe even less, but it makes the hour-long drives into the city and back, plus the hour-long visit to Walmart on our way home, worth it for me. *This,* I think to myself, *this is the kind of person I want to be. This is what I want to do.* I want to become a doctor. I want to make other people feel seen in the ways I feel seen here, if even for a few minutes.

Standing through the doorway with his hand on the door handle, the surgeon turns to look at my mother, then back at me, and finally at her again. Before he closes the door, he says something he will not remember and I will never forget: "Her personality will carry her far in life." Mom laughs awkwardly and I smile politely. But inside, I'm beaming. It's one of the kindest things someone has said to me. *I definitely want to become a doctor,* I think.

Chapter Twenty-Four

DECEMBER 24, 2004
PHOTOGRAPH

Baba and I are sitting on the floor. Jimmy, of course, is in my arms. His fur has grown long and full, reminding me of a bobcat's; he leaves little tufts all around the house. He has fallen asleep with me every night since I first brought him home and he follows me everywhere I go, including into the bathroom. If I ever close the door on him, he sticks his paws underneath and scratches until I let him in. He sits on my lap when I study, and when he wants more attention, he crawls onto my textbooks.

Baba and I both look happy in this photograph. There is more life in my face now, and the dark shadows under my eyes have disappeared. Mom has dressed the tree perfectly, and the small room feels cozy and warm. This is the closest I've felt to being whole since Tabby died.

—

I'm already running late. I never give myself enough time. Every night before bed, I tell myself tomorrow will be different, and every morning, I wake up and think, "Ah, it's enough." It isn't. I bring the space heater into the bathroom and set it up so it'll be directed at me when I'm finished my shower. Then I climb in and turn on the water so it rains on top of me. It's warm for about five seconds before the heat disappears and it's as cold as the snow outside on the ground. I howl before I turn the shower off, my hair half wet, goosebumps pocking my entire body. "Not again," I mutter as I grab my towel and wrap it around my shoulders so tightly it squeezes them.

Both the furnace and the hot water tank are kept going by the woodstove outside. It's been breaking down a lot this winter—more than it ever has before—which means we're not infrequently left without heat and warm water. Sometimes, I'm aware it's happened and can prepare—washing my hair at Baba's on the weekends or, if I really need it, boiling water in big pots on the stove to add to my bath. But that takes so long that usually I prefer to just go another day without bathing. Other times, I get tricked. The house is cold when I wake up, but the water's still warm when I turn on the tap at the sink, lulling me into a false sense of heated security. On days like these, I get into the shower thinking I'll have enough time to at least shampoo my hair before I abruptly realize otherwise.

I stand in front of the heater for a few minutes, knowing I'm only making myself even later for school, but my muscles are too stiff to carry me through the house when it's this cold. This heater is heaven. On frigid nights, my parents let me bring it up to my room, where I point it directly at my face, the only part of my body I sleep with exposed. I also wear two pairs of socks, sweatpants, a long-sleeved shirt and a hoodie, and hide myself and Jimmy under a comforter and a quilt. Mom will often come into my room on nights like these to tuck my blankets under my feet, and I feel like a baby again, swaddled.

Once I've finally raced upstairs and gotten dressed, my face washed with icy water, my hair still wet and still dirty, I pick out one of the head scarves Baba let me borrow. It's navy with red and white flowers on it, and it's my favourite of hers. I stand in front of my bedroom mirror and comb my hair so it sits in a bun at the back of my head. I wrap the scarf first around my head and then a few times around the bun, then I tie it at the bottom and hide the knot. I've been doing this a lot lately. My friends think it's a fashion statement of sorts, like when I wear other pieces of Baba's clothing, and I don't correct them.

Baba has always had the best closet of anyone I know. Since I was a little kid, I've loved going through her closet and pulling out one box after another of her high heels, excited for the day they'd fit me. They're still a size too big and, considering I've stopped growing, I don't think I'll ever fit into them. Instead, I take tissue and stuff it into the toes so my feet are snug, and this mostly works. Baba also lets me wear some of her sweaters and shirts, and she loves telling people my favourite store to shop at is "Baba's Closet." Next year, in the high school yearbook, I'll be voted "Best Shoes in the School" and I'll be photographed next to a guy friend, the two of us lying on the floor and surrounded by his shoes and Baba's.

I adjust my scarf one more time, making sure it's even, when I hear the bus coming down the road. "Shit!" I yell, before running down the stairs. *Not again.*

It's when I'm in the eleventh grade that becoming a physician starts to feel like a real possibility to me, even though I still have no idea how to go about accomplishing that. No one I know has ever gone to university, and it's not like my parents have any answers. All I know is that if I study and get the best grades I possibly can, I'll have a better chance. I've been drafting four-week study plans and have already mapped out my final year of high school so I can take as many university courses as possible. One of them costs three hundred dollars, and I've made sure I'll have enough for it with the money I've made as a catering server.

I spend every single lunch hour in the library. I overheard some of my classmates making fun of me when I was walking past the cafeteria the other day, and it just seemed so odd to me. I'm studying in the hope of becoming a doctor—what's there to make fun of? I know there are other ways to spend my time—God knows Mom reminds me of this—but they don't interest me. I've refused to date since cutting contact with that boy, and I still have never gone to a high school party. I'd rather spend my nights with Jimmy at home, even without any heating, or the occasional Friday or Saturday laughing at infomercials late into the night at my friend Shayli's house, binging on tacos and her mom's spicy bean dip.

I've been getting nineties in every class, and one of my teachers comments on how proud my parents must be. But my parents have no idea how well I'm doing in school, and it's not because I'm secretive about it. Mom sees how often I'm studying and it seems to make her nervous. She still asks me why I'm not wearing makeup and also why I don't have a boyfriend. It may seem surprising that my parents want me to date, but young women in my world should already be on the road toward marriage. There will be many girls in my graduating class who marry by the time they are twenty and many more who will have their third child before I even start my career.

Still, with all of this studying and all of my dreams of one day living in an apartment where the heat never shuts off, I fall asleep most nights—and this part is maybe what I'm most ashamed of—crying myself to sleep. I'm doing everything right and others seem to think I'm gifted. Lucky, they say. "You've been raised so well," adults now tell me. But I don't feel gifted or lucky. And why weren't they saying this a few years ago? When it felt like the same people were calling me a slut? I don't feel like I've changed who I am. I've always tried to treat people kindly, and I still care more than I wish I would about, well, most things. The only thing that's changed is how others see me. So then why can't I see myself? Why do I feel so much pain, pleading with God, asking him to tell me what's wrong with me? Begging my invisible father to want me, to see me, to notice me. Sometimes, I think a loving God would be so much easier to believe in if he were a grandmother.

Chapter Twenty-Five

AUGUST 2005
PHOTOGRAPH

The basketball is in mid-air, a foot or two from the rim. A second after the photo is taken, the ball makes a swish as it falls straight through the hoop. A boy, three years younger than me, from a reserve three and a half hours away, stands a few feet in front of me. He lunges after the ball and tosses it back to me. This is our third game of twenty-one today.

Although I've just met this boy, I'm quite fond of him. One of the first things he said to me was a question. "Hey, are you a half-breed?"

I laughed. I hadn't heard that word in years, but the tone he used when he said the word was different from the one used by people in my town. "Yeah, I guess so."

"Oh, yeah, yeah. I thought so. You look it."

I smiled. "Thanks."

There's an ease to our conversations, and we're almost always laughing. He's funny and says things before he thinks them through, and his accent reminds me of my brother Fred's. His smile reminds me a little of his too, though without the silver-capped incisors.

Once this game is over, we'll play another. And then another and another until the lunch bell rings and we run to line up with our respective cabins.

It's my first of two weeks as a volunteer camp counsellor and, aside from the expectation that counsellors wake up an hour and a half earlier than the campers to spend time in prayer and devotion, I'm mostly enjoying myself. I've never been a morning person, and although we're in the thick of the boreal forest in Northern Ontario, and in the early-morning hours when all else is quiet I can hear the birds singing and the breeze whistling through the evergreens, I have not been converted. I traipse into the dining hall each morning still rubbing my eyes and patting down my hair, minutes before the staff meeting begins. I grab some apple cider powder and hot water and sit next to my friend Shana before the camp director instructs us all to bow our heads in prayer. It still doesn't make sense to me to bow my head, and so I choose not to.

I met Shana when we played softball against each other in elementary school, and again when we played on the same team in the ninth grade. She lived a town over and had always gone to school there, but our schools merged in the tenth grade. She has pale skin with freckles and bright-red hair I often remind her I'm jealous of. She's grown up hating her hair, and I want her to know it's beautiful. She, in turn, tells me she loves my skin colour and hair, which feels nice. She's Mennonite, but she's different from so many of the girls I've grown up with. She has what we will one day come to laughingly call a "resting Mennonite face," which is to say she looks a combination of solemn and angry, but she's neither of these things. She is full of fire and grit. We call each other late at night before exams to make sure we're understanding the material, only to end the calls realizing we spent twenty minutes talking about the exam and the rest of the hour laughing at who knows what. In some of our classes, we finish our work early and then chat for the rest of the class, until sometimes our teachers come to us and say something like, "Listen, girls, there's not much I can say because you're at the top of the class, but could you at least pretend you're working? Or talk a little quieter?" For whatever reason, Shana finds me hilarious, and making her laugh when she least expects it has become one of my favourite pastimes. I never feel judged when I'm with her.

Shana's the one who told me about this camp. It's being hosted by her Mennonite church, for children from the Wabaseemoong Independent Nations. I didn't know her church and I didn't know the other counsellors—and it will be years before I'll understand the complicated history between churches and First Nations reserves—but I knew I wanted to spend two weeks with other Native kids, so I asked her if I could join.

It's been years since I've been close to my Native cousins, aunts and uncles. Sometimes, when I'm sad and lonely, I remember when George and I chased each other in our grandparents' yard. When we swung ourselves high on Grandpa's old red canopy swing until we couldn't suppress our laughter. I feel like a girl who has lost two families. Some days, in between school and studying and work, I find a few minutes to slide an old home video into the VCR, just so I can remember what it felt like to have siblings and cousins. To be surrounded by family.

I have an hour of free time right now, before dinner. Some counsellors are reading their bibles, while others are playing guitar and singing worship songs into the trees. I walk into the kitchen and grab the phone receiver off the wall, then I wrap myself around the corner.

"Hello?" Mom says.

I can barely utter a hello back before tears start falling down my face.

"Brit? Is that you?"

"Yes, it's me."

"What's wrong? Who died?" This is always her first question whenever she receives an unexpected phone call.

"I don't understand these people. They're not like me. I didn't think this would be so hard," I say, surprised by my own vulnerability.

I'm surrounded by Mennonites, but they're not like my family. The girls don't dress as conservatively, but they're still conservative in the way they think. I overhear one boy telling another how he talked with his sister about whether her tight pants were appropriate for school, and they'd decided as a family that, no, they were not. These Mennonites are mostly soft-spoken and they're kind, but they're also sheltered and naive. I don't understand this type of separateness. Although Grandma only ever wore conservative dresses and Grandpa spoke little English, I never felt my family was much cut off from what I understood to be the wider world.

I suppose, with so many of us adopted into the family, we remained more tethered to the rest of society and aware of how our lives were influenced by outside forces like the welfare system. These Mennonites speak of the Native kids at camp with affection, but also with an undeniable otherness. My two worlds, my identities, my cultures, are colliding, and I have no idea how to piece them together.

Mom reminds me I only have a few days left at camp, and she's sure it'll get better.

The next morning, I'm one of the last volunteers to arrive at our staff meeting. I grab some apple cider and sit down at an empty spot at one of the tables just before everyone bows their heads in prayer. When the director asks if anyone would like to share this morning, a male volunteer raises his hand.

"God spoke to me yesterday and it really hit me," he says. "I was playing basketball with one of the kids and it was such a good reminder." He pauses, his eyes wide and serious. "We need to be intentional." Heads all around me nod in agreement. "I played basketball with this boy and I shared with him about Jesus and I shared some stories from the Bible and we had a really good discussion about it."

I know Jonathon, the boy he's talking about, and I also know that Jonny (because that's what everyone who knows him calls him) was likely hoping his conversation with the counsellor would win him an extra item at tuck that afternoon. *Do you even know Jonny's name?* I want to shout at him. *Do you know that he's the only boy in a family full of girls? That most of the time, his parents are gone, and because he's the baby of the family, one of his four older sisters takes care of him? Do you know that another one of his sisters, the only one to ever call him Jonathon, might have impulsively punched you for the things you're saying about him now?* Instead, I sit quietly, my thumb never leaving the edge of my mug and my cider growing cold.

What is it to be Native—or part-Native? This question doesn't leave me during the two weeks I spend at camp, and it pokes at the back of my mind after I return. Do I need to look Native to be considered Native? Do I need to have been raised by Native parents?

I don't think a lot about the other side of my biological family, my birth father's side. Because my government documents say my birth father never wanted me, and because it's clear the decision to give me up was my birth mother's, I guess I still think of myself as having come from only her, and I often find myself forgetting about him as easily as he forgot about me. I know my father was white, or at least that's what the papers say, and I know that's a part of me too, but I don't know what to do with that.

I've always felt more connected with being Native. I just have. But sometimes, I wonder if I also want to feel more connected to the Native part of me because that's the part of me I don't share with my adoptive parents. I've always struggled to feel like I belong with my parents. I've struggled to feel seen and heard by them. When I had siblings, it always felt like it was them and me, plus my parents. It never felt like my parents and me, plus my siblings. The siblings and cousins I loved, and who loved me, all shared this similarity with me: we were all adopted and Native. And when it feels like Mom is trying to take this from me, telling me I "don't even look that Native," it feels like she's trying to shear off some of my skin, like Grandpa used to do with the wool from his sheep. It makes me want to hold on to it even tighter.

Being Native means one thing to me and a different thing within my family and another thing within my town and another thing within my country. I'm terrified that I am not, have never been, and will never be enough of this part of me. I've never known my mother or my grandmother, and I've never been a part of their community. I may never know where I come from, and if I don't know where I come from, how can I claim this part of who I am?

"You're being stupid!" he yells. His face is flushed and spit is flying from his mouth. "You're being foolish. It's foolish! Some things you just can't know." He throws out his hands to hit his thighs. "Tough!"

I'm crying and I wish I wasn't. I can't think in a straight line when he's screaming this loud. Later, in bed, I'll tell myself I should have been stronger. I'm weak and he yells because I deserve it. Maybe, if I was capable of showing more strength, I wouldn't make myself such a target.

"You might never know where you come from!" He slaps the kitchen counter harder than Mom will say he meant to. It's always harder than he meant to.

"I know that. I just wish I knew something. Anything." I know it's always easier to hold this on my own, but tonight it's just too heavy. Tonight, my body is collapsing in on itself.

Dad yells and he screams and he reminds me, as he has many times before, that life is unfair and it's just too bad. He slams his hand on the kitchen counter once more before he marches out the front door to do his chores. It's silent between my mother and me—a silence I then break by apologizing to her. It's my way. It's our way.

"Let him cool off," she says. I can tell by the look in her eyes that she's upset with me. Sometimes, I think I'm angrier at her in these moments than I am with him. His anger cuts and it draws blood, but then it's done and I know how to tend to it. Her actions and inactions are subtle, the cuts small enough that I ignore them at first, until I look down and see that they're so numerous I have no clue how or where to start mending them.

Within seconds, Mom will act like nothing's happened. Within days, Dad will calm down and start speaking to me again. Within weeks, I'll convince myself that none of it was that bad and I was being overdramatic and, really, it was my fault because I should have known better.

I don't open my journal tonight, and I won't say another word out loud until I wake up tomorrow and whisper good morning to Jimmy, who will be lying next to me with one paw on my face. Instead, I turn on the thirteen-inch television on my dresser and pop an old home video into the VCR.

Chapter Twenty-Six

The bus sways and hurls itself along winding gravel roads as I drift in and out of consciousness, curled up on my torn-up leather seat. I'm worried I might see the porridge I had for breakfast this morning in reverse. The drive—which involves crossing the Manitoba-Ontario border—is three and a half hours, but these last thirty minutes have felt the longest.

When the bus halts abruptly, my stomach lurches. I grab the back of the seat in front of me and pull myself up, craning my neck to see why we've stopped. I watch, bleary-eyed, as a man exits a tiny shed the size of a fishing shack on the right side of the road and approaches the bus. Propped against the shed is a large plywood board, spray-painted to read "NO SOLVENTS" in big red lettering. This must be a checkpoint before we enter the reserve.

It's my first time here, on the land of the Wabaseemoong Independent Nations, and my first time ever on a reserve. I've been looking forward to this for months—since the moment

I said goodbye to the kids at camp, so many of whom live here. The kids reminded me of my foster siblings in so many small ways, from their sense of humour to the way they pronounced "yeah" as a short, deep "yuh." During my time at camp, it felt like a tiny hole in my heart sewed itself back up.

Once we're past the checkpoint, we park at a local high school. I step off the bus, the dry gravel crunching beneath my feet, and inhale the scents of balsam, spruce and tamarack—a tonic for my lurching stomach. "We're here to show the kids and the community that we care," one of the church leaders says, after we've all gathered inside the school. The leaders explain that today is just about spending time with any children that show up. It's less regimented than camp and with less of an agenda. I keep my head on a swivel as I listen half-heartedly, trying to take in as much of the school as I can. I wonder where my birth family is right now, whether any of them have ever lived on a reserve. I walk a few steps to look at photos of graduates on the wall. I note there are only a handful of faces on display from the last decade.

As the group begins to disperse, Shana catches me up on the plan for the rest of the afternoon.

"Do you think anyone will notice if we're not here?" I ask, another plan in mind.

She shrugs. "I guess not?"

As she and I walk down the main road to the east side of the reserve, I fill her in. We can still hear one of the church boys singing and playing his guitar from the school. I roll my eyes, and Shana shakes her head. We smirk at this boy who has brought his instrument and, instead of spending any time with any children, feels called to sing songs of praise through the halls of the school to offer protection to its walls and students. I wonder what he thinks his songs are protecting them from?

"Aw, man." Shana shakes her head again as we tandem-leap over a puddle. "I just can't." And the two of us laugh.

"God's probably gonna punish us and make us slip in that puddle on our way back," I mutter, and we laugh a bit harder.

Her house is a bungalow, like most of the homes on the reserve, and there are framed school photos everywhere. The walls are brown and have no mouldings, which Mom would hate, and there are dishes in the sink and boots lying on a pile in the entrance, thrown haphazardly by the many kids running in and out of here all day, which, of course, Baba would have something to say about. But it's warm and it's filled with the type of love that families should have for each other, and I feel this in my chest more strongly than I can smell the spruce trees outside.

Shana and I have just entered the kitchen at the house of one of the girls we met this summer, Kate, who is twelve years old and was in my cabin. Kate and I spent an afternoon on the dock down by the lake, watching as the other kids swam because her toe cramp—that godawful toe cramp I didn't stop hearing about for the rest of the week—kept her on dry land. We laughed and threw wet lake clay at the swimmers and then decided to see how the clay might work as a face mask. It didn't—and I had tiny red bumps around my nose for the rest of the week. It felt like Kate and I had known each other for years. I told myself that the connection was likely one-sided, and she would forget about me after the week was done. But she has written me letters since then and, in them, asked me to visit her. This was reason enough for me to spend seven hours on a rickety school bus with a bunch of Mennonite kids and no air circulation.

Before we had a chance to walk up the steps of Kate's front porch, I heard a voice call my name. I stepped back and looked around to the back of the house to see a group of young girls, maybe seven years old, playing by the bush. One of them came running to me and, although it was the first time we'd met, she wrapped her arms tightly around my waist. Kate's youngest sister, Isabelle. I hugged her back just as tightly. She offered me an uneven smile, and I noticed her two front teeth were coming in at different rates. Then, as fast as she'd come, she left, calling out a goodbye as she ran back to her friends.

We say hi to Kate and Isabelle's mother, Eleanor, who is in the kitchen, holding open the door to the fridge. She has long black hair that falls to her mid-back. A baby sits on her left hip, and I notice how much he looks like his mother.

"This is David," she tells us, and I feel the urge to snuggle him close, but I restrain myself. A year from now, when David is two, he'll run around the reserve, sticking up his index finger at everyone he sees, thinking he's giving them the middle finger. This will also be the summer when Kate will forget about him while she's babysitting, and he'll stay outdoors for an entire afternoon before the thought occurs to her and she runs outside to find him.

"Kate's in her room," her mom says, motioning to the room at the end of the hall. There is another bedroom across the hall with its door open and I can see one of Kate's sisters sleeping there. I will learn that it's her older sister—the oldest of all the girls at thirteen, Albertine—and that she shares the room with their mom and the baby. I will come to know her in the years that follow and I'll discover that she's different from her sisters, especially Kate. Whereas Kate loves makeup and boys and reality TV, Albertine never wears makeup and could not care less about celebrities. She loves her mother and she loves the reserve, and she never dreams of leaving it. She dreams of one day having children and raising them in a house near this one. Or, maybe, with her first child at least, she'll live here and raise her baby with her mother's guidance. She wants nothing more than what she can find here.

We step into the other bedroom and see Kate sitting on her bed with a compact mirror in one hand and eyeliner in the other. Her ten-year-old sister Olivia, whom I also met at camp, is sitting beside her, leaning against the wall and scrolling on her iPod, one headphone in her ear. Olivia's eyes widen at the sight of us and she tugs the bud out of her ear. "Hi," she says, leaning her body forward and tapping Kate on the shoulder like she doesn't already know we're here. There is no break in Kate's concentration—she moves the mirror closer to her face. I feel embarrassed. Does Kate really want us here? But then I remember her letters; she even used a different colour of highlighter for each paragraph.

"Hey," Kate says, moving from eyeliner to mascara.

Shana and I sit on the floor and begin chatting with Olivia when another of their sisters—younger than both Olivia and

Kate—leans into the doorway. I know from process of elimination that this must be Ashley.

"Not gonna help, Kate." Ashley smirks. "Still not gonna be able to hide those hickies, ayyy."

Olivia nudges Kate, then she and Ashley laugh at their older sister.

As we motion to leave, a smile suddenly spreads across Kate's face. "So, when are you guys coming back?" she asks.

"Uh . . ." I hesitate. "Do you want us to come back?"

She looks at me like I've just asked her the most idiotic question. "Yeah, obviously."

I know this family isn't technically my family and I know this home isn't my home, but I find myself feeling happier here than I have in quite some time. Happy with these girls and their mother and baby brother. It's not so much that I think I might come from here, from these same people—my government papers state I'm Métis, whereas they're Anishinaabe—but there's just something about being here. About being in a community that still holds its language—that regularly hosts ceremonies, culture camps and powwows for its members. No one is telling anyone that they *don't even look that Native* because being Native isn't something they have to hide here. This family helps me believe in a family and in a home and in a community that I do come from. They help me feel more connected to a culture I have never had the chance to know, even if my culture may be different from theirs.

I'll continue to sleep on the bumpy bus ride once a month to visit this family. I'll write to the girls, who I'll eventually call my sisters, and David will grow up asking his mom if I'm his biological sibling. The family will visit my parents' farm and I'll pour us some iced tea and ask Dad to show them his horses and they'll all squeal, having never been so close to animals so large. He'll take us all for a ride on one of the buggies he's built in his shop (a hobby he'll pick up in the coming years, fascinated by the ornate craftmanship of Amish carpenters).

I spend the drive home from my first visit to the reserve thinking about families, about my family, and how much less painful it would be if our histories were erased right as we entered the world. How few questions I'd have if my life truly had started when my parents first picked me up, first held me, first changed my name. I think it would feel a lot emptier, but I also wonder how much simpler it would all seem. It's hard not to yearn for "simple" sometimes.

When I return home in the early evening, I walk swiftly up to my parents' bedroom, where Mom is lying on her bed, the TV on in the background, and sit down next to her feet, tugging Jimmy onto my lap. I'm excited to tell Mom about my day.

"You're home," she whispers, having just woken up from a nap. I begin telling her about my day—about Kate and Isabelle and Albertine and Olivia and Ashley, about their mom and baby brother—but she starts flipping through the channels and turns the volume up. There's an *I Love Lucy* marathon on.

"Mom," I say. "Are you listening?"

She looks at me for a moment and huffs. My stomach does a flip. I can tell she's angry, but I can't piece together why.

"If you're going to act like this every time you go to the reserve, I'm not going to let you go again."

I hesitate for a second before getting up. "Fine," I say, grabbing Jimmy, and I leave the room.

PART THREE

Chapter Twenty-Seven

JUNE 28, 2007

TWO PHOTOGRAPHS

One. I'm in my cap—tassel hanging in front of my face—and long black gown in Baba's backyard. My hair is smooth and I'm wearing mascara, foundation and blush. Baba's arm is around me and she's smiling big and proud. We're only permitted two guests at my graduation, so she won't be there. But this day is just as much hers as it is mine.

Two. I stand between my parents outside the graduation reception hall. My hair is up now and there's a thin smudge of eyeliner across my lids. I rarely see Dad smile like this, never mind for a photo, but he's doing it here. I think this day means more to Baba and my parents than it does to me. Sure, I'm excited to graduate and itching to move on to university, but none of them graduated high school. Mom almost did, but she dropped out in the eleventh grade; Dad didn't even come close. He's been marvelling, in his way, at having a high school graduate in the house, which is to say he's mentioned it twice. But at one point,

I could have sworn tears welled up in his eyes before he turned away. Mom's proud too, I think, but she's only commented on how pretty I look with makeup on. Baba's been telling everyone, including the cashier at Shoppers, that I'm going to the University of Winnipeg—and, did they know, I graduated on the honour roll, and even went to Paris and Rome for a school trip on Spring Break, and she paid for most of it! "Yup, this Baba knows how to take care of her granddaughter," she says, without staying to listen to the cashier's response.

I step off the city bus and the frigid winter air blows harshly, almost sweeping me onto the street. I bury the lower part of my face in a yellow scarf Baba knit for me. Although the university is only a three-and-a-half-block walk from my stop, it's in the windiest part of the city, and the strands of hair sticking out from beneath my toque will have frozen stiff by the time I reach the school. I shuffle my feet along the sidewalk, careful not to slip on the ice.

I've been studying biochemistry at the University of Winnipeg, downtown, for six months now. I chose my undergrad major with medical school in mind—it's still my dream to apply as soon as I'm able to, in two years' time. I moved to the city from my parents' just over a month ago, and I'm finally starting to get the hang of the transit system. I count my steps to the first stoplight, hoping it'll turn green by the time I get there so I won't have to wait. It takes me twenty-eight shuffle-steps to arrive and the red light turns green and I cross Portage Avenue.

I pass the Aboriginal man I've come to expect to see each morning; his wheelchair is parked at the corner, shielded by the overhang, as always. His right leg is amputated just above the knee and he keeps a wool blanket draped over his lower body. He's wearing a waist-length parka with a broken zipper and a few puffs of insulation poking through holes near the elbows—it looks as thin as a windbreaker. Sometimes, when it's not minus fifty outside, I try to make eye contact with him. When it's warmer out in spring and I won't be in such a mad rush, I'll ask him his name and he'll tell me it's Albert. We'll say hi most days when we see each other moving forward.

I walk down Portage, my hands freezing despite my gloves, the wind biting at my eyelids. I try to shield myself behind a taller man, but he turns when we reach the next stoplight and I'm exposed at the coldest corner. I wonder if I'll see the Aboriginal man I'll eventually come to know as Joe. He has black, shoulder-length, dishevelled hair, and he's at least a foot and a half taller than I am. He's standing at the corner nearest the school today, holding his Tim's cup. His black sneakers are so beat up that the soles flap when he walks. I wonder if he's lost feeling in his feet from the exposure.

Mom and I often saw Aboriginal men on the street when we drove downtown during my childhood. We'd come into town for me to see the orthodontist, and Mom used those monthly appointments to collate any and every city-specific errand she could think up. Trips to Costco, if Mom brought along a friend who had a member card, and Walmart and Zellers and, if Baba was with us, the Liquor Mart so she could stock up her cabinet. Mom reflexively locked the doors as soon as we were stopped at a light if there was a Native person standing nearby. Sometimes,

Baba would roll down her window and I'd think she was about to give someone a toonie from her purse, or maybe even a Werther's, since neither were ever in short supply with her. Instead, as Mom drove away, Baba muttered, just loud enough for the person to hear, "Ah, get a real job." I eventually realized, though, that if I asked Baba for a toonie, she'd let me hand over the money myself. Sometimes I wondered if Mom and Baba forgot that I was Native too, or if they simply didn't care. Right now, it's too cold to reflect on the thought for very long.

I walk this path from the bus stop to the school every morning, waking up well before the sun has risen, so I can spend a couple hours in the library before my classes start. I walk this path in the early evenings, my eyelids heavy from the day and my heart missing home more than I expected I would. There are no pets allowed in the building where I live, so I couldn't take Jimmy with me. I miss knowing he'll be there to greet me when I get home, to lie on my textbooks when I study, on my pillow when I sleep. I walk this path every day in winter and into spring, as the days begin to grow a little longer and the wind softens against my skin and I am still no less lonely, no less convinced that, somehow, I'm screwing it all up despite my best efforts to get it right.

I don't know how many Native bodies I pass on the short walk from my bus stop to the school. Even in the worst weather, there are people on the streets. There are too many to count. No one seems to want to count them anyway. "I have a right not to want to see homeless people on my streets," I will hear someone from my hometown declare, and others with whom I grew up will comment in agreement. I encounter people who rationalize stances like this by volunteering that they "know some Natives" or that their "girlfriend is part-Native," as if that permits their racism. The proximity to Native bodies, I have realized, is enough for some people to justify their ambivalence or disgust. In a few years, *Maclean's* magazine will publish an explosive article titled "Welcome to Winnipeg: Where Canada's racism problem is at its worst." There will be shock and there will be denial—but not from Aboriginal people.

The high heels I saved up for this summer so I no longer have to borrow from Baba's closet clack loudly on the concrete. I'm running late. I'm always running late. I figure it must be something in my blood that I just can't erase. "Indian time," my adopted uncles joke, and I wonder if there are things that truly do run deep through the generations.

I've just returned from two weeks at camp with kids from the reserve—it was my third year volunteering there. I spent the first week looking after a group of campers that included Kate, Albertine and Olivia, and the second with one that included Ashley. Regardless of how much I feel like an outsider amongst the staff, I don't find it difficult anymore. I like the fact that I feel different from them. Plus, I'll take any opportunity to see the kids from this community and, specifically, to spend time with the girls who are starting to feel more and more like family. I'm home now for the next six weeks, working at an arts day camp in town, before I'll return to school again. I'm happy to be home for the most part. To wake up with Jimmy beside me, to feel the air, warm and fresh against my skin, in a way it never is in the city, to fall asleep to the sound of the crickets whistling in the grass. But right now, I'm late—and I can focus on little else.

The door is lighter than I anticipate and as it closes behind me it catches the back of my heel. I clench my teeth, not wanting to bring myself any more attention, and glance down at an angry red mark. I exhale. *Okay,* I tell myself, *the ceremony hasn't begun. Okay, okay. We're okay*. I slow my pace and smooth my top as I walk toward the sanctuary. I see the back of a familiar head in the corner of the foyer. My feet stop and I pause for a moment, looking at my cousin. George is in a white suit, standing next to a pastor. I don't remember the last time I saw him. I worked with his mom at Canadian Tire on the weekends and in the summers the last two years, and she would often fill me in on what was happening in his life, but I can't remember the last time he and I spoke, the last time we were in the same room. The thought hits me sharp like the back of that door. I shake my head, as if to dislodge the unexpected pang of sadness.

I find my parents sitting in an aisle near the front. I slink along the side of the room and down the pew to join them just as George and the pastor walk to the front. Mom peers at me with a smirk. "I know, I know," I mouth to her. Dad is sitting next to her and, as expected, fails to acknowledge my arrival. *At least my hair is dry,* I want to say, but I don't.

Music wafts up to the rafters and the entire congregation turns to look toward the back of the room. A blonde woman dressed in white stands in the doorway. The natural light from the foyer frames her, making her look like she's literally glowing. I look to my cousin at the front of the sanctuary, his arms at his side, his eyes deep and dark. *When did he grow up?* I wonder. *How has so much life passed between us?*

AUGUST 10, 2008
PHOTOGRAPH

George's arm is draped around my shoulders in a church foyer a few blocks from the one in which we were raised. My skin has browned from days at camp spent down by the dock, despite my tendency to stay in the shade, and it matches George's, which looks deeper than usual against his white suit. I'm reminded of when we were children and we spent our summers in the backyard, jumping on the trampoline with the sprinkler spraying up at our feet. When we came in for a break and iced tea, our moms wiped our faces with wet kitchen rags, only to realize what they thought was dirt was actually just our skin.

George and I smile at the camera. We don't have on matching red shirts, baseball caps or those thick black glasses from the dollar store today. We are cousins and we are strangers and we're both embarking upon paths we're carving out for ourselves. And, although we don't know each other like we once did, there is a look in our eyes that betrays the awkwardness we both seem to feel. It's a familiarity. Family.

I'm sitting next to my parents at a table in the church gym where the reception is being held. Once the scheduled speeches are done and the *faspa* has been eaten, there is an open invitation to us all.

"If anyone would like to share a story," the pastor says, "please do!" I make a mental note, if I ever get married, to definitely *not* include this. But then I surprise myself by looking over at one of my cousins, shrugging, and mouthing "Wanna?" He nods, and we push our chairs back and walk up to the microphone.

I peer at George and his wife, Rebecca, and I wonder how I could possibly offer up a childhood of memories in a moment like this. I think back to the time George convinced one of our younger cousins to eat a watermelon peel, and how we all laughed. I remember the hitchhiker seeds from the trees on our grandparents' farm always sticking to our clothes, and how we spent what felt like forever plucking them off. I think of the day I learned he'd been taken away and how I cried myself to sleep for days. How I would wake up in the morning and, for the tiniest sliver, I'd forget he was gone before it hit me all over again. I stare at the uncles and aunts staring back at me. My cousin has just finished his speech and is now looking at me too.

I glance at the back of my heel, which now has some crusted blood on it, then at George, and I smile.

"So, George," I say. "Remember that time you convinced me it was a good idea to climb under the electric fence in my backyard when it was raining?"

Chapter Twenty-Eight

The room is dark and crowded. I can feel the bass thumping through the floor and all the way into my chest as I weave my way in and around strangers' bodies. There was a six-month period this past winter when my friends and I went to clubs on the odd weekend when I wasn't studying or working, and I'd fall asleep at four in the morning for two hours before having to wake up for work. The hassle never seemed worth it to me—I certainly wasn't going to let anything get in the way of university. But tonight is special. It's my friend Shayli's nineteenth birthday and she's spent most of the last year travelling, and now she's home and we're out dancing in downtown Winnipeg.

I'm looking around the club, trying to find the bathroom, when I feel a tap on my shoulder. I turn around to see Shayli's older brother.

"Hi!" I shout over the noise, and we hug. A guy about his age walks up and puts his arm around Shayli's brother's shoulders.

"Hey," the guy says. I can barely hear him over the music. "Have we met before?" He looks at me with interest, but I'm not sure how to read it.

"I don't think so!" I shout back. But this is a lie. I recognize him from a few weeks ago, when he came through my checkout at Canadian Tire. He was buying fishing supplies with a few friends. I was scanning their hooks through when the phone at my till rang. I picked it up.

"Tell Andrew I say hi!" It was one of my female co-workers calling from an aisle several checkouts down.

I held the receiver against my shoulder. "Uh . . . Andrew? Beth says hi."

A guy standing in the middle of the group looked up. His light blue eyes were bright, and he looked full of energy. He reached his arm into the air, waved, and yelled a cheerful "Hey, Beth! How are you?" across the store. He was obviously an athlete, probably a hockey player—it's pretty easy to tell them apart from other athletes from their builds and the way they carry themselves—but I liked the friendly way he'd responded to my co-worker. I'd come to expect a different attitude from hockey players. I handed him his bag of tackle and hooks, and he thanked me before yelling goodbye to Beth and leaving the store.

And now he stands here, not even a foot separating us, and even though the room is full of so many women prettier than I am, whiter than I am, dressed in less clothing than I am, I feel like I'm the only one he's looking at.

"I'm Andrew."

"Brittany."

"We're going to go grab a drink. Want to come?"

"Yeah, sure," I answer. I'm surprised by the excitement that comes through my voice.

He smiles softly. The light blues in his eyes have darkened to almost navy in this low light. I've never much appreciated light eyes before. I've always seen them as a symbol of the difference between me and my parents, between so many of my friends and me, but immediately I find myself drawn to Andrew's. There's a look of freedom in them, a certain abandon, but I see care and sweetness there too. I immediately notice his politeness as he steps back from the bar to make space for me between him and my friend's brother.

"So where are you from?" he asks me, and I tell him.

"No way, I can't believe we've never met before!" he says.

"Well, we sort of have," I say with a smile, and I tell him the story.

Just as he's in the middle of apologizing for not recognizing me, a man standing behind him hears the mention of our small town and turns to us. "A bunch of Mennonites, eh? What are you guys doing here? Aren't you supposed to be at church?" He and his friend break out into loud laughter.

Without skipping a beat, Andrew and I start unleashing on these men.

"You know what? You fucking wish you could be a Mennonite," I say. I'm taken aback by my unexpected show of pride. It's admittedly a tad ill-fitted.

"Hey hey hey," Andrew adds. "A Mennonite can still kick your ass."

I will later learn that Andrew's mom is French-Canadian and he really didn't have a Mennonite upbringing in the way I did, and this will only make me appreciate his response even more.

The men look stunned. Andrew turns away from them and toward me. "Wanna dance?" he asks. I offer him my hand and leads me to the dance floor.

I'm at the beach with Shana and another of our friends. We're lying on our towels and resting after the night we had at the club. Two guys wearing sunglasses, baseball caps and swim shorts are walking down the boardwalk. *I recognize that walk*, I think, right as one of the men cocks his head at me and smiles. That's him, I realize, with Shayli's brother again.

"I didn't know if I'd ever see you again!" I say to Andrew.

"Uh, yeah . . ." he says, his face reddening. "Sorry about last night."

I'm surprised. I'm not sure what he means, but I wait for him to continue.

"We haven't really slept in forty-eight hours . . . I can't really remember a lot from yesterday."

"We went a little too hard this weekend," Shayli's brother explains with a half-hearted laugh.

"Ah," I say. "You really weren't bad at all."

Andrew raises his eyebrows in surprise. "Really? I feel like I was a gong show."

"No, no, I promise! Not at all!"

"Were you even drinking last night?" Shana asks me.

"Nope. Well, I had one."

"Oh." Now it's Andrew's turn to look surprised. "Well now I feel like even more of an ass!"

When I return home from the beach, I receive a message request on Facebook from Andrew. He apologizes again, and his earnestness makes me smile. I write that it's truly okay and offer that it was nice seeing him again.

He responds within minutes. "Well, from what I remember of the night, which I have to admit is not very much, I think it was a lot of fun. Thanks for being so nice."

Hours later I receive another message from him. "What are your plans for fall?" he asks. And, "What's B. J. all about?"

My shoulders reflexively tense up. I hate that my childhood nickname is sticking around, even though I've deliberately gone by Brittany for the last year, using the change in schools as an opportunity to start fresh. A lot of my friends still call me B. J., though, so I imagine he learned my nickname through Shayli's brother.

"Ugh. Ok, so the initials of my first and middle names are B. J. and there were a million Brittanys in my class growing up, plus Britney Spears, so my Baba shortened my name. She thought it was cute but . . . not so cute for a girl growing up around a bunch of hockey boys. So I decided now was the best time for me to switch back. You can probably imagine the comments I received growing up. So, that's that. Thanks for reading my personal essay. Goodnight and good luck."

I bite my upper lip. I have no idea why I typed that last part. I wait for his response, annoyed he would ask me about my name in the first place.

"Uh, yeah. I sorta meant, like, what are your interests? As in, who are you? What do you do for fun . . . that sorta thing? But we can talk about names if you'd like too!" I will learn later that he laughed for an entire minute and had to reread my reply before responding.

"Oh," I type. "My bad."

I think I might marry this guy.

I feel a pang of panic at the thought. He's white and he's a hockey player and I've never pictured myself with anyone like him. What would it mean if I were to be with someone white after everything I'd been through with the white boys in junior high? Someone with a Mennonite last name? I'd always seen myself with someone from outside the world I grew up in. *Relax, Brittany,* I tell myself. *You literally just met. Get over yourself.* Still, this feeling persists for days. When, as a teenager, my parents told me god had already chosen a man to be my husband, I adamantly disagreed with them and declared I would never get married. Instead, I would become a doctor and travel the world and work overseas. But despite this, and despite never envisioning myself with anyone like Andrew, I'm drawn to him in a way I've never been toward another person.

"I just don't know why she didn't want me." I'm next to Andrew on the pullout couch in my apartment, and I'm crying. "What was so wrong with me?"

"You don't know that she didn't," he says. He gently places his hand on my knee and rubs it with his thumb.

"Obviously she didn't," I say, the tears falling harder now. "If you want your child, you keep your child."

I've just finished the last of my exams and I'm exhausted. For the six months of our relationship, I've been terrified to let Andrew see beneath my exterior. I've felt strong with him. Funny. Brave, even. But with the lack of sleep these last few weeks and the stress of exams and moving my few belongings into this new apartment nearer the university, I feel exposed, like a crab without her shell. I feel tender and easily bruised, and this is when my insides start to spill out.

"Not everything is that simple," he offers.

I know he's trying, and I nod my head. Of course I know it's not that simple. Nothing ever is. I just wish my heart could know this in the way my head does. I lie down next to him on the pullout couch and rest my head against his arm. I inhale the scent of his neck and nestle in closer, before my eyes close.

"I know," I say. "I just wish it could be that simple."

Chapter Twenty-Nine

Jimmy and I are trying to nap on my bed at my parents' house. I've spent most of the summer here, working at the arts day camp in town. So far, I've managed to get through school on scholarships, but I don't know if that'll always be the case, so I'm trying to save up as much money as I can. Plus, I'm studying—I was up until four in the morning studying for my MCAT. I've heard that some people have to write it several times before they get a score they're satisfied with, and I don't want that to happen to me.

My body jumps at the sound of the cordless ringing on my nightstand. I reach for the phone and sit up, my hand reflexively landing on Jimmy's back. He watches me. My voice cracks as I say hello.

"Hello, can I speak with Brittany?" I don't recognize the man's voice, but the formality in his tone straightens my spine.

"This is her."

"Good afternoon, Brittany. My name is Steven, and I'm a social worker with Child and Family Services."

He pauses. I wait.

"I understand a few years ago you applied to unseal your adoption records? Is that correct?"

"Yes," I say. "Shortly after my eighteenth birthday." I remember that day, over two years ago now, clearly. Some kids go out for dinner and drinks to celebrate their coming of age and legal right to drink. I asked my parents to drive me to the Child and Family Services offices in Winnipeg so I could petition the government to unseal my records. The whole affair was anticlimactic. We entered the same rundown building where my parents had met with a social worker nearly two decades earlier. I asked a disinterested receptionist for the correct forms and filled them out in the waiting area. Mom sat by me with examining eyes. The forms were straightforward and I completed them within minutes.

"So, is that it?" I asked the receptionist, as I handed the forms back to her.

"Yup," she said. "You'll get a call if they find anything. Might be a few years, though."

My parents had felt it was only fitting they come with me for this moment. With how curious I'd always been about my birth mother and where I'd come from, they'd known it was coming for years.

"I've always said, we're grateful to her," Dad said when I discussed wanting to unseal my records. "I mean, sure, it'd be nice to know who she is."

"I'd like to see what she looks like too," Mom said. "Like Dad says, we're grateful to her. She coulda had an abortion or something. She coulda abused you or you coulda gone into foster care or, like Dad says, grown up on the street."

I appreciated their support, though Mom also liked to remind me about her cousin's husband, who was adopted too. "He's never looked for his birth parents. He's always said, 'Nope, my parents are enough for me.' So, everyone's different. But, no, hey, we'd like to see what she looks like and say, 'You know what, thank you.'" Sometimes, I'm not sure if she's trying to convince me or herself when she says this.

"Because your previous social worker has retired, I've taken on your case." David's voice on the other end reorients me to the present moment. "And I have some news for you . . ."

I don't respond, my breath catching at the back of my throat.

"Your birth mother had the option to veto future contact when you were born. She did not check that box off and stated that she would be open to you contacting her."

My stomach feels like it's in my chest. Jimmy has fallen back asleep next to me, his chest rumbling faintly.

"Is this something you would like to do?" David asks.

"You mean, contact my mother?"

"Yes, exactly."

What is this moment? Seconds ago, I was asleep, answers from the verbal reasoning sections of my practice tests replaying on a relentless loop in my mind, and now—what?

My chest feels like it has been whipped by the wiring on my grandparents' old electric fence.

"Yes," I manage to say.

"I don't have contact information, but I do have a name for you. Would you like to know her name?"

"Yes," I repeat—the only word I remember how to say.

"Your birth mother's name is Crystal."

I'm sitting at the kitchen counter at my parents' house, unable to study, listening to the high-pitched tone of the dial-up internet connecting. Mom and Dad have piggybacked off our neighbour's internet service since I was fourteen, paying him a small "rental fee" every month and, because of this, the signal is weak at best and non-existent at worst. Thankfully I've been studying from books and paper practice tests for my MCAT, but the task I'm about to undertake relies heavily on the internet.

Crystal. The name echoes. It's like a Ping-Pong ball bouncing in slow motion in my mind, never stopping, never settling. I don't know what to do with it. I don't know how to process it. It's been a few hours since that call. I've decided I'm not going to google her name until I feel ready. All I can seem to think about in the meantime is when I was eight years old and I begged my mother to change my name to Crystal. Did I know? Did I somehow know that was the name of my first mother? The name of the woman who carried me and then released me? How could I have known?

A few weeks ago, I noticed a birthmark at the nape of Andrew's neck. "Did you know this was here?" I asked. He did not. Children who grow up with their first parents—or at least know who their birth parents are—don't seem to notice those types of things. They don't spend their entire lives looking at their noses and their smiles and their various marks, asking themselves where they come from and whether there's another person who shares them. It's as though their bodies are not mysteries to them. Or, perhaps, it is just Andrew who doesn't notice—he's too excited about life and all the places to go and people to see. It's one of the things I've come to love about him, this intensity and exuberance. He runs before he stops to think; I've never run anywhere before assessing my surroundings. Sometimes, I wonder how he could possibly find me as interesting as he seems to.

Jimmy is asleep on my lap with his paws hanging off my crossed legs. I pull my laptop close to me, but I can't type out the words. I push it back on the counter and look down at Jimmy. He's unbothered and relaxed. I pull the laptop back to me. I push it away. I pull it and I push it, and I continue to do this until finally, I take a deep breath. "OK," I say to Jimmy with a gust of decisiveness.

This morning, I woke up next to Jimmy in a bed that was already worn down when Mom and Dad bought it second-hand a decade earlier. I woke up, in the house in which I was raised, to the sound of the old woodpecker who had woken me so many times before. This morning, my first mother was just a woman I'd dreamt of and I was just a daughter she had never known. Now, our worlds are about to collide. Slowly, I type out her full name. I press enter.

The faces of many women who share a name pop up on my screen. My body feels frozen, and I wonder, for only a second, how I'll ever be able to recognize her. Until I see it. There is no mistaking it. There is no second-guessing, no wondering if maybe, possibly, could this be . . . ? It's her. This is my mother.

—

I zoom in on her face, inspecting its contours for almost an hour. She has dark hair, shorter than I've ever dared to cut my own. Mom has always thought long hair is beautiful—I didn't even receive my first haircut until I was in the third grade, when my hair hung past my hips. Crystal's eyes are lighter than mine, more hazel than brown, but they're shaped like mine, angled like mine. Her cheeks are round, high up on her face, and they shape themselves in the same way mine do when I smile. But her hair is straight. My hand migrates to my curls. I expected her to have curly hair, like my adoption papers said. Maybe mine will straighten with time too? Or, maybe, hers was never curly to begin with.

The dogs start barking outside and I can hear Mom's car pull up on the driveway. I put my screen on the "rest" setting and wait for her to walk into the kitchen. When she does, I lift Jimmy and uncross my legs, folding them under my body so I'm perched up onto my knees.

"Mom," I say. I know to not leave anything dangling, lest she think someone died. "CFS called."

She stops mid-step and braces herself against the counter in front of her.

"They gave me my birth mom's name."

"Was it Ted?" she asks.

"No, it was a different guy. Some new social worker, David. He said Ted retired a few years ago."

"He retired? I didn't know that."

"Apparently."

Silence hangs in the air. She looks at the laptop and it dawns on her. I have already seen her face.

"Show me," she says.

Mom cries when she sees the photo of Crystal. I tell myself they're tears of happiness, but I know they're not. I can't deny the anxiety in her eyes. I can't blame her. I look her directly in her alligator-green eyes. "You okay?" I ask.

She nods and glances back at my birth mother's face. "She's gorgeous," she says. Crystal's not wearing any makeup, and she has an undeniable natural beauty.

"I want to send her a message on Facebook. Are you okay if I contact her?"

She takes a deep inhale. "Yes . . ." She slowly exhales. "Yep. Yes."

"Crystal," I type. "My name is Brittany. I think I am your daughter. I received a call from a social worker who gave me your name and I think you are my birth mother. If you are not my mother and you are another lady with the same name, I really apologize."

Mom and Jimmy are beside me when I hit send. We wait.

She responds within the hour. I'm still sitting in the kitchen when the notification pops up on my screen. I feel a chill, like ice water was just poured down my scalp and neck.

"She responded," I say, and Mom looks up from the sink. Her face drops and I can see the emotion in her eyes. I hold her gaze. "It's okay." Mom walks around to stand by my side, and I open the message.

"Yes, I am the right Crystal McMahon," I read. "I am so thankful you reached out. I am here to answer any questions you might have. I know this is probably a lot."

Mom is carefully reading the words and I can almost hear her heart firing in her chest. I look back at the screen—at my other mother.

"I have so many questions," I type. "I'm so thankful for the chance to speak with you. Thank you for being open to this. Maybe it would be easier to do this through email? Is that okay with you?"

She replies within seconds. "Of course, hun." She sends me her email address, and I tell her I'll be in touch.

"Talk soon, sweetie," she writes.

Before I even think to respond, I see the tears streaming down Mom's face. I close my laptop and nudge it away from us both. "Are you all right?" I ask, my voice soft.

"She called you 'hun.'"

I wait for her to continue.

"She doesn't really know you and she called you 'hun' and 'sweetie' and it's like . . . you just met. Why would she call you that?" The tears are falling harder now and her nose is running.

"You're my mom. You raised me. This doesn't change any of that. She's probably someone who uses words like 'hun' and 'sweetie' for everyone. I don't think it means anything."

She closes her eyes and tries to shake the emotions out with more force, but it doesn't work. It never works.

"You're not gonna leave me?"

"No," I say. "I'm not going to leave you." Silence hangs in the air between us. The chair protests slightly as I push it away from the counter. I take a step toward my mother and wrap my arms around her. "I'm not going to leave you."

—

Baba takes the news as I expected. She doesn't cry. She reminds me, as she does from time to time, that she thanks god every day for me and for my birth mother. She tells me that she thanks god every day for choosing my parents and her as my family. "Hey," she says, shrugging her shoulders. "She could've had an abortion."

A week later, Mom calls me. "Baba said she had a nightmare," she says. "We were in the backyard having a party for your birthday. Then your entire birth family came storming in from all sides. And apparently you told us, 'Sayonara! Thanks for nothing!'"

Chapter Thirty

It's August. The sun hangs around until at least 10 p.m. and the moisture has begun to migrate back into the earth. I can feel it in my lungs—the air feels slightly thinner on its way down. The canola fields are brighter than the highlighters mothers will pack in their children's backpacks in a few weeks, and the wheat is nearing harvest. There's an earthy, bready scent cloaking the province; I feel as though I'm back in my grandmother's kitchen as her buns are rising for *faspa*. There's an endlessness to this time of year—you can be lulled into believing it'll last forever.

I've borrowed Andrew's vehicle for the day. He lends it to me whenever I need it, and I enjoy driving it and sneaking the toonies and loonies he stashes in his console into my pockets—until one day he'll mention he can never find the change he could've sworn he'd left in the car. "I had to use my debit card for my coffee at Tim's. It was so embarrassing!" And I'll confess I've been the toonie thief all these months.

"It's been you this whole time?" he'll say, at once relieved, mock-outraged and amused.

"I thought we had a sort of unspoken agreement!" I'll laugh.

I step out of the vehicle and jump at the sound of the car door slamming. I've hated that sound since the accident, and today my nerves are especially raw. I can feel my heart bumping like it's a ball of thread being swatted by a kitten. I want to get back into the vehicle and drive until I'm somewhere I don't recognize. But, of course, I also want to be here. I've wanted this longer and with more intensity than I've ever wanted anything else. Right now, I'm in the "before," waiting for the "after," and the enormity of this moment lends a surrealness to my surroundings. Somehow, my legs manage to carry me toward the restaurant, where I know she's waiting for me.

I've chosen this restaurant because it's the nicest one in my hometown. It sits on a golf course. Mom is intimidated to dine here because the women who do are the type who shop at the Winnipeg malls—and not at Walmart or SAAN or, on very special occasions, Reitmans.

My birth mother and I have spent the last six weeks writing to each other, catching up on two lifetimes. I've learned that I was born on the day of her high school graduation. That she went on a bumpy drive down a gravel road the night before and woke up a few hours later with intense contractions. That her mother drove her from their town northeast of Winnipeg all the way to the Women's Hospital downtown to give birth, and her sister accepted her diploma on her behalf. It was that same sister who confronted her about her pregnancy after months of suspicion and brought her to her first prenatal appointment when she was well into her third trimester. I've learned that the man she is fairly certain is my father had been living out of the province for months by the time I was born. I've learned she has not spoken to him since and doesn't know where he might be. I've learned his name.

I've learned my name, Meagan McMahon, from her, and eventually, I received my official, unredacted birth certificate from CFS with Crystal's name on it and the father's information left blank. I've read it over and over until it has stopped feeling foreign. It is the puzzle piece that's finally found hiding under the couch. The name that never was.

She's told me about her childhood and her tenuous relationship with her parents, about her own mother's childhood, which was filled with more pain than she ever spoke of aloud, and of the suffering that has echoed through their family for decades. She's told me about her cats.

I want to tell her I'd had a good life, a happy life. That I am trying to make meaning out of the life I've been living. I want her to like me. I want her to feel proud.

"I was so scared, not knowing who you ended up with, not knowing if you went to an abusive home or what happened to you," she wrote to me in one email.

I want her fears to settle. I want to be the daughter who settled them.

I've still only ever seen one photo of her. *Will I recognize her?* I wonder, as I reach for the restaurant door handle. Will I stand awkwardly in the entrance as I search for her, not knowing what to do with my body? If I should cross my arms or put them in my pockets or hold them clasped in front of me? Will it turn out that we don't actually look anything alike—that objects are not actually closer than they appear? I've never been in close proximity to another person with whom I actually share DNA. What does it feel like, I wonder, for a person to know her own mother?

The steel handle is cold as I pull the door open. I glance at the clock in the entranceway and I'm pleased to see that I'm early. I wonder if my mother is also chronically late. Time seems to slow around me. I can feel my breath enter and leave my chest, and I feel both inside and outside my body. The room does not feel real. I do not feel real. The host greets me and asks if I'm meeting someone. I scan the room and see a now-familiar face by the window.

"Yes," I answer. "She's already here."

I walk across the room to the woman I recognize as my mother. She's sitting next to a big window that looks out at the golf course. Her shoulders are hunched forward and her hands are on her lap. As I reach her table, she stands up. We hug, and her embrace is kind and her body is soft, but a fleeting thought enters my mind: they belong to a homeland I've never visited.

We sit across from each other and stare, neither of us saying a word. Her hands are on her lap again, but quickly rise to her face as she smiles. "This is so weird!" Her palm grazes her cheek, as if it doesn't know where to land, and finally settles on her chin.

"So weird," I say.

She tells me more about her life now, about the man with whom she has lived for years and whom she will one day marry. I ask her about my aunts, about my grandparents and my cousins, and, although I already know she has no other children, I ask whether she ever considered having more.

"No," she answers. "I never wanted any more children." And a part of me withers inside. I always envisioned myself having siblings.

"I didn't feel I was ready to have a child when I had you," she says. She tells me that when she was pregnant, a classmate of hers who was adopted approached Crystal and said she shouldn't "be selfish" and keep her baby for herself just because she might want it. "I wanted you to have a better life than I thought I could give," Crystal reiterates to me.

Our meal is finished. The server is clearing dishes nearly as full as they were when she first set them down. I suppose we're similar in that we don't eat much when we're nervous. We walk out to the parking lot, where Crystal's partner meets us. I shake his hand, introduce myself and ask if they're comfortable following me in their vehicle. This is part two of the visit: they're coming over to the farm to meet my parents.

I climb back into Andrew's vehicle and don't allow myself a thought until I pull out of the parking lot. She looks like her photo. Her straight hair, her makeup-less face. She is beautiful and she is my mother. But I also expected something, someone, a little different, and I'm only realizing that now. I turn off the radio. It's already too loud, too crowded in here, even though I'm alone; I need silence. I'd thought she would be an older version of myself, the wise, old soul I pictured myself someday to be. A woman reluctant to show her emotions and calculated in her responses. An elegant and understated dresser. But she's different. There's a girl-like quality to her, a giddiness I don't recognize in myself. She dressed casually for today, in a dark beige T-shirt a few shades lighter than her skin, a pair of loose denim capris and well-worn sandals. This woman is beautiful and she is my mother and I have waited my entire life to know her, and she is different than I'd imagined.

As I drive down the highway, past the farmers' fields on the way to my parents' house, past the spot where Mom and I had our accident ten years ago and past the turnoff to my grandparents' farm, a heaviness settles within me. Until now, my mother was a faceless woman with no name. And today, I have seen her face and my body has held itself against hers, and I know her name. She is real enough to lose now. Again.

Dad and Mom are peering out the kitchen window when I pull into the driveway, my birth mother and her partner behind me in their truck. I think I would have liked to keep this day just for myself, but it didn't seem like an option. Mom made it clear she wanted to meet Crystal today and I know she needs this. I feel a responsibility to offer her this. I can almost feel her anxiety pulsing through the window and I feel guilty for being the one who's placed her in this position.

When I enter the house, Crystal and her partner behind me, Dad looks more cheerful than I've seen him in years. I can tell he's excited to meet Crystal, and he's rarely excited about much. Mom can't stop her tears from falling. My birth mother and my parents hug, and Mom ushers everyone to the kitchen table where she's laid out snacks, cans of pop and two photo albums. Jimmy rubs his body against my legs before trotting over to Crystal and pawing at her. She picks him up and scratches beneath his chin. Before we sit down, Mom pulls out her camera to take some photos. Afterwards, I sit at the table in between my parents and my first mother, and I watch as they exchange pleasantries. Dad's smile doesn't leave his face as Mom takes Crystal through the album, page by page, narrating the story of my early years. I watch and I witness these two worlds, these two stories of parenthood, mix and collide, and I try my best to ignore the confusion rising within me. *I've found what I was looking for. I should feel grateful.*

AUGUST 8, 2009
PHOTOGRAPH

I'm in my parents' kitchen, standing next to a woman who is not much taller than I am and whose smile is uncannily like my own. Dad is beside Mom on the other side of the lens. The look on his face reminds me of the one he wore the day I graduated high school.

Later, when we're alone and looking at this photo, Mom will quietly say, "Wow, she sure is pretty."

"You two look so much alike," others will tell me, and, "She could be your sister." Yes, Andrew will say, he can maybe see the similarities, but he's actually never been good at noticing that sort of thing, and, really, whenever he looks at me all he sees, still, is just me. I will look at the photo and see evidence of where I come from. Evidence that I did come from someone.

Chapter Thirty-One

It's a few weeks later, and Andrew and I are driving to my birth mother's hometown. My could-have-been hometown. He holds my hand in one of his as he steers, periodically glancing at me for longer than he should and hitting the strips on the side of the road. He's like this. Not even the fact that he's driving can pull him away from giving me his full attention. "I just want to look at you," he says, and I can never stay angry at him, even though I was in a serious car accident as a child and almost died and could he, maybe, at least try to stay on the road?

We're heading to a barbecue my birth mother is hosting for her friends and family to meet me. A homecoming, I suppose, although it doesn't feel the way I imagined a homecoming would. I feel nervous and untethered—and I'm thankful for Andrew. He has a way of making me feel safe.

As we near Crystal's, the lack of Bible verses on billboards coupled with the fact that I can spot only two small churches make it immediately obvious that this is not a Mennonite town. We pull up to her address to find an unassuming bungalow with a well-tended yard, and there are two cats roaming her driveway. I know I'm at the right place.

The evening is a blur of faces I don't recognize and names I've never heard before. I meet my aunt, who tells me about seeing me through the nursery window the day I was born. She laughs at the memory of Crystal's first prenatal appointment, where she had to pee into a cup to confirm she was pregnant when she was only two months away from giving birth. My aunt also reveals she gave her daughter the same name I was given at birth, and how she'd first asked Crystal if she was comfortable with it and how much it meant to them both.

I walk through the house that could have been my house and take photos with the family who could have been my family. Who . . . *are* my family. I can't hold back my smile when strangers come up to me and tell me how much I look like my mother, how much I look like my grandmother. I listen to Crystal's friends refer to her as my mom and I feel guilty. I don't know whether I'm happy or sad or angry, or if I'm just confused.

I remember a movie I watched when I was a kid. A boy who'd been kidnapped as a young child is removed from the only home he's ever known and returned to his true family. There's a scene where the family has pizza for dinner and the boy asks for milk. His older brother scoffs and his mother smiles, and it's painfully clear they don't really know him. They're strangers, connected only by blood. Sometimes family doesn't feel like family at all.

I want to cry as Andrew and I walk back to the car, but I don't. I want to cry on the ride home, but I can't.

"It just didn't feel like home," I say.

Andrew squeezes my hand in his and I can feel his eyes move from the road to me, the light blues in his eyes, I know, mixing with the darker shades of the night. I avert my gaze—I don't want him to see my pain.

"I thought it would feel more like home."

AUGUST 22, 2009
PHOTOGRAPH

A gentle man in his seventies has an arm around my shoulders. He has a head of hair thicker than I've ever seen on a man his age, and glasses delicately perched midway down the bridge of his nose. He's tiny, round in the middle, with a charming, crooked smile. I'm posed between him and an elderly woman with hair whiter than his. I barely know this woman—we have only just met today—but I know this much about her: she has permed her hair since she was a teenager. She picked this habit up from her mother. Her Métis, Anishinaabe and Cree blood mean her hair has always refused to do much other than lie straight. I learn that she also permed my mother's hair for years when she was a child. Later, I'll wonder in amusement—because I know the science doesn't actually work this way—if the generations of perming affected my genes. As if god said, finally, "Okay, okay, I get it. I'll give you the curly hair you've been asking for for generations!"

Chapter Thirty-Two

AUGUST 26, 2010
PHOTOGRAPH

Andrew's arm is draped over my shoulders. I lean into his side as he hugs me a little tighter. He looks down at me and I look up at him. "You did it," he says, smiling. I smile too.

He and my parents sat in the crowd as I walked up on stage and poked my arms through the sleeves of my white coat, in a ritual signalling that I and one hundred and nine of my new classmates are embarking on a journey that—the faculty tells us—will forever change our lives. The hours will be long and the nights even longer, but we will save some lives along the way, they say, and hopefully find some time to sleep in the middle of it.

Andrew's right, I've done it. He likes to remind me of all the ways I should feel proud. He will always like to remind me of this, but it's difficult for me. I've worked hard to get here, I know, and it's no small thing, but I hardly ever allow myself any moment of self-recognition.

For a moment, though, amidst all the smiles and the hugs, I feel hopeful—optimistic even—that maybe one day that might change.

I'm sitting at my desk, a lined notebook in front of me, as I try to plan out the next few weeks. It's 2010, and my first day of medical school is tomorrow. I moved into a new apartment this past week with two roommates, and most of my things are unpacked already, mainly thanks to Andrew. This place is closer to the University of Manitoba's downtown campus than my last apartment, but it's still an hour-long bus ride each way. Sometimes I wonder if it wouldn't be cheaper and not much more of a time loss to live with Andrew back home and drive to school every day instead. He'd spend his days working at the lumberyard while I was in my lectures, and then we'd come back together every night. In moments like this, with only textbooks to keep me company, even the thought of having Andrew in the next room makes me feel a little less lonely.

I take my glasses from my nose and place them on the upper shelf of the desk Dad built me from scrap wood in his shop. It fits so neatly in this corner of my new room. My fingers rise to meet my temples and I close my eyes. I rub along the sides of my jaw, in front of my ears, trying to ease the discomfort. I was grinding my teeth again last night. I can feel it in the way my masseters ache this morning.

My mind flashes to images from the past week. The party at my parents' house. Mom had taken extra time to poke through the clumps in her mascara with a needle before the party, while the lemon cheesecake sat and frozen *perishky* thawed downstairs. She invited her friends and cousins, some of my aunts and uncles, and my birth mother and her parents. Mom welcomed Crystal and my grandparents—it still feels a little alien for me to refer to them this way—and introduced them to everyone. Baba was a gracious host—perhaps even better than Mom. It was her second time meeting Crystal, and she hugged her as though she were also her daughter. She put her arm around my grandmother and ushered her inside, showing her which chair she should sit in and ensuring her plate was never empty. She grabbed Crystal for a smoke break at one point, and the two of them stood outside on the driveway, blunting their cigarettes in Dad's potted pink petunias.

I wanted to feel happy. My worlds were combining—and this should have felt more like the swirling of colours that had merged to form the sunrise that morning, like a mosaic of love. It was as though everyone else had received a memo I hadn't. I felt like a bystander to the celebration.

My birth mother and I both prefer to communicate through emails, and sometimes it still feels like we're sending little love letters to each other. Our notes are filled with lengthy paragraphs, although they're shorter now than they were a year ago, which makes sense. We don't have as much to catch up on now. But, somehow, it still feels like we have everything to catch up on. How do you condense an entire life spent apart? She's my mother, and yet I'm starting to think it's impossible for her to know me in the way a mother does. She doesn't know I preferred 7 Up to ginger ale when I was sick as a child. She doesn't know my first words were "Baba" and "Dada." She can't yet tell when I'm secretly sad in my emails and using distancing language to hide my emotions, and I don't think she'd guess what my greatest fear is. Now that I think of it, I'm not sure Mom knows any of this, either—but we have photos, we have home videos, we have memories.

I'm not sure what my mother-daughter relationship with Crystal is supposed to look like. I'm not her protector, so who am I? And I don't know her well enough to read into her emails and discern what emotions she's hiding, either.

I run my fingers back and forth against my eyelids. My eyes have been so dry lately, it might offer some relief if I could cry, but the tears aren't there.

In the bathroom, I stare at my reflection in the mirror and I can see my birth mother. But I can also see the ways in which I'm not her, the ways in which I am her daughter but I also am not. I don't nod with my whole body after I've made my point. I don't prefer to keep my hair short and despite rarely, if ever, wearing makeup, I enjoy the theory and application of it.

I paint a line of toothpaste on my brush and lift it to my mouth. My reflection reminds me that, still, it cannot offer me the whole picture. Still, I'm left with holes in my family portrait—in the map of my lines and curves and dimples. "I would have raised you if your mother wanted me to." The last words my birth father wrote to me after I reached out to him a few months ago. *I would have raised you.*

Our exchange was brief, a few carefully chosen words in a few deliberately short emails. I learned his name from my mother and she learned from a friend of a friend that he was living in Alberta. It seemed clear to me that any warm feelings she ever felt for the man—boy, I suppose, at the time of her pregnancy—had long dissipated.

I made sure to sound kind in my first email to him. So many sentences prefaced with "I am not offended if" and "no worries at all" and "I hope this doesn't overwhelm you." Such an odd way to speak to your father, I reflect now, but how is one supposed to speak to a father she has never known? I wasn't even sure I wanted to meet him—my government documents explained that he "denied being the father," and so the birth story I'd coloured in for myself had always revolved around my mother. She had carried me those nine months. She had handed me over to Child and Family Services. She had gone into labour, and she left the hospital without me. I was hers to have and hers to give away. My father had seemed irrelevant. A passer-by that made it all possible. But I wanted to know if I had siblings out there. A brother or a sister with whom I could connect. Something, someone, my father might have left for me.

I would have raised you. I made the mistake of repeating this claim to my birth mother. She rolled her eyes and scoffed, and I wished I hadn't mentioned it.

When it came time to respond to his note, I tentatively typed: "Absolutely no worries, but that's not the story I was told and it's not the story that was written in my papers." *Does that sound too aggressive?* I wondered. I deleted it. "I guess I've always just had a picture of you running away," I wrote instead. "Although I'm not saying that's what you did! I'm not accusing you of anything at all, but what you said confused me."

A few weeks later, I received his short reply: "I haven't forgot about you just had no chance to get into the office. I have to get to work, sorry."

It's been months and I haven't heard from him. It will be years and I will not hear from him. Apart from a spam email I receive from his account, to which I will not respond, I will never hear from him again.

I step off the bus a block from the school. I've traded in the scent of potato and barley fields, which are in harvest right now back home, for urine and trash and the faint smell of old blood. I cross the street, walking alongside several others from my bus and more who've parked their cars in the nearby parking garage. I'm wearing a white fitted T-shirt and a pair of looser-fitting jeans. I want to look casual but classic. A mustard-yellow cardigan is hanging over my bag, and I'll immediately wrap myself in it when I enter the chilly building. I walk with my shoulders back and my chest proud, hoping I at least appear a little more confident than I feel. I've been waiting for this day for so long.

The entire front of the school is a wall of glass, and the morning rays sparkle upon it like flecks of silver. Everything is shiny. Big and unfamiliar. The atrium is buzzing with new students and nurses and doctors and about fifteen people standing in line for their first cup of Tim's of the day. Years from now, I will remember this moment and laugh at myself for thinking it was only their first cup. The morning sun streams brightly on us through the endless windows. For the next four years, these windows will be our saving grace, a rescuing force on painfully early mornings and exhaustingly long nights.

I walk toward a desk with a sign on it that reads "Orientation," where a woman tells me to grab a manila envelope sitting atop a pile. I feel a little unfooted in this organized chaos. I can see that several of the students milling about already know each other. I hold my envelope against my chest and search for an empty seat at one of the tables spread out across the atrium. I find a chair and I sit next to a guy I don't know, reaching across him to grab one of the pencils at the centre of the table. I open the envelope and pull out an array of forms and a questionnaire. I quickly scan the questions.

What is your educational background? Easy. I just graduated with my degree in biochemistry a few months ago.

What community do you come from? This feels somewhat more complicated, especially since meeting my birth mother. I now know the community I originally came from. Crystal is Métis-Anishinaabe-Cree. She grew up in a mostly white town not too far from mine. I've been to her house, but it didn't feel like home in the way I thought it would—but it still was a home of sorts. My first home. But all of this is too complicated for a simple survey. I list the community I was raised in.

Which of the following income brackets describes your family? This one is also easy, I think, scribbling in the answer. *Whose family actually earns over two hundred and fifty thousand dollars a year?* I wonder. I do some quick math to determine that it would take at least nine years for my parents to earn that much. I'm about to move on to the next question when I glance over at my neighbour. I don't mean to snoop, but I can't avoid noticing where his checkmark has landed . . . Toto, I have a feeling we're not on the farm dodging rogue electric fencing wires anymore.

Which of the following describes your ethnic background? I close my eyes. I hate this question. I've never known how to answer this question. I've never checked the "Aboriginal" box on any form, anywhere. I've never felt I had the right to. What classifies me as Aboriginal? My name? Because that was changed. My upbringing? No. I thought meeting my birth mother would finally allow me to feel more Native. I thought seeing her and meeting her family and seeing the ways in which I looked like them and maybe even talked like them would grant me some understanding of this part of my identity. I always imagined her as some sort of bearer of worlds for me, a carrier of generations of women who were more connected to their culture than I ever had the chance to be. I thought meeting her would help me feel closer to these women I never had the chance to know, but whose stories were still carried by those they left behind, by those I had now finally found. But there were no stories.

Crystal told me early on that she has never really felt connected to her culture, and that she doesn't know much about that part of herself. She added that she wasn't interested in free handouts. Her words broke me. She never wanted *free handouts*? I thought back to when she'd shared with me that her non-Indigenous paternal grandparents used to refer to her mother as a "squaw." She'd never been denied access to who she was or to her culture, so I couldn't understand why she didn't feel connected to that part of herself.

I didn't know how to ask her for stories after that.

I'm walking from one lecture hall to another, my oversized, weighty laptop in my bag tugging at my shoulders and already causing me a headache. Everyone else has MacBooks I can't afford; I'm still existing off scholarship money, but luckily Andrew was able to find a laptop on sale through a company he works with. I push the heavy door to the lecture theatre open as another student pulls it from the other side, and I startle as my body skips forward.

"Sorry!" we both offer at the same time.

He seems to examine me. "Hey, you're Brittany, right?"

I nod.

"I heard you're Métis?"

I nod again, my neck reflexively stiffening.

"That's awesome," he says. "I'm Métis too."

I soften a little when he says this. I notice his eyes are similar in colour and shape to mine. There's a playfulness in them that belies his age. A picture flashes in my mind of my first brother, James, at my fourth birthday party, his arm slung across my shoulder. His eyes were bright and his smile stretched wide, like it always did. *His eyes,* I think. *James's eyes look just like this guy's.*

"Listen, there's a centre for students like us. There's a bunch of us neechis that hang out there. You should drop by. It'd be awesome to see you there."

I offer him my thanks before walking up the steps and finding a seat a few rows up. I exhale as I sit down, my chest feeling lighter than it has in weeks.

A tension headache is starting to scream behind my eyes. I want to go home and nap, but instead I turn right instead of left on my way out of the theatre and find myself walking to the Centre for Aboriginal Health Education at the front of the school. I open the door and see a man and two women I've never met sitting at a big table. This is the largest group of Native people I've encountered at school so far. The feeling of being an imposter comes over me. Although I'm not seven and dressed up as Pocahontas today, once again I feel like a Native kid pretending to be a white kid who's pretending to be a Native kid.

"Heya," the man says. He's a physician, I learn, and the woman sitting to his right, perhaps two decades his senior, is the Elder in residence. The other woman is an administrative assistant for the centre.

"So, what's your family name?" one of them asks. "Where are you from?"

"I'm adopted," I blurt out. I launch into the explanation of my upbringing and how I was raised Mennonite, but I'm not really Mennonite, although this doesn't feel completely truthful. "But I recently learned my name," I share. I wish a name was all it took for me to feel like I belonged here. I wish a name was all I needed to feel a sense of kinship with these people.

The man smiles and shares a story about his daughter who works as a teacher up north. I listen politely for a while before I excuse myself, feeling like I don't have much else to offer. I don't return for the rest of the year, unable to shake the feeling that I'm a fraud, even here.

When I do eventually find my way back, I mention to this same man how painful it's been for me trying to figure out who I am, how painful it still is, and he cries, along with me, as I speak.

Chapter Thirty-Three

JULY 2, 2011
PHOTOGRAPH

We do this thing called a "first look" on our wedding day, before the ceremony. Andrew and I stand back-to-back for the photographer. We haven't seen each other yet today. Andrew's wearing a dark-grey suit. My dress is satin and fitted, my hair half pinned up. I'd first wanted a simpler dress that I found when I went shopping by myself, one without ruching or stitched jewels along the waist, and I wanted to wear my hair down without any bobby pins poking at my scalp. Mom's always hated simple, though. When I did a practice run for my hair, she said, "Uh . . . really? That's how you want to do it? But you could look so pretty if you put it up." So I compromised and put half of my hair up and bought the dress she loved. No matter, anyway. I like this dress too, and I think she's right—it does look prettier.

It's been easy to feel overwhelmed by wedding planning, by the back and forth between the caterer and my mom and Andrew's mom and the stress over a guest list that's ten times bigger than I wish it was. I didn't want any of this to be stressful. Even though we're not married yet, I know if I could do it all over, I'd do it my way and invite maybe ten people. But I know this day is about more than just me and Andrew. And I'm thankful to have everyone under one roof: Andrew's parents and siblings, my parents, Baba, my birth mom and her sister and parents, and George and my aunts and uncles, many of whom I haven't seen since George's wedding. Kate and Olivia and Ashley have all come out for the day too. I asked Kate if she'd be a bridesmaid and she said yes. Later today, she'll walk down the aisle with fellow bridesmaid Shana beside her so she doesn't feel overwhelmed—she's never been in a wedding party before. In a parallel universe, one where we haven't been cut off from each other, all my siblings are here too—James, Marion, Julie, Sarah, Fred, Shanny, everyone.

This moment, this first look, feels just for Andrew and me, and I try to settle into it. He and I turn around at the same moment, and I have no more than a second to look at him before he envelops me in a hug so tight, it makes my dress feel loose by comparison. This is the photo. Me, hugging Andrew lightly, as his arms are wrapped around me more securely than anyone has ever held me.

I close the front door of our new house behind me. Andrew meets me in the entranceway and wraps his arms around me. His hug is tight and energetic and he holds on for a few seconds longer than I used to think hugs were supposed to last. My head rests against his chest and I think the thought that always pops into my mind during moments like this: *One day, I won't have this chest to lean against; one day, I won't have this heartbeat to listen to.*

He slides his hands from my back and onto my shoulders, gently pushing me away so he can look at me. He smiles in the way he does when he knows I'm exhausted or sad. His look is saying, *I'm here baby, I'm here,* but I still don't know how to accept this from him. "How was your day?" he asks.

I sigh and walk past him into the living room, where our new kitten is curled into a ball on the couch. We moved into this house a few months ago, the same week as our wedding, which I planned around my school schedule. Our house is six hundred square feet, over a hundred years old, and in a historic French part of Winnipeg. Our bedroom is barely big enough to fit our bed, and Andrew can't walk into the basement without ducking his head. He'll make the mistake, more times than either of us can count over the years, of rushing downstairs, nearly concussing himself and going to work with a cut on his forehead. This home is tiny and old and might not be very much, but it's ours—Andrew's and mine and our little buddy's too. We feel like a family, and I feel both desperately grateful for and terrified by this. I don't want to lose my husband or what we're creating here together, but I can't shake the thought that one day, without warning, I'll lose it all.

At first, we brought Jimmy here. I brushed him and fed him and he slept between Andrew and me, but I couldn't deny that, even after weeks, Jimmy seemed unsettled, unhappy even. He was used to running outside and climbing trees and catching mice out by the barn. Living in the city where he had to stay inside every day wasn't for him, clearly. Seeing him trapped in an environment that made him miserable made me think of when Child and Family Services took George to live in the city with a foster family. I knew the comparison wasn't really fair—Jimmy is just a cat—but still, the connection made me uneasy.

Finally, we brought Jimmy back to my parents' house, where I knew he'd be happier, even though it pained me. Later that week I drove to a farm a few miles north of our town where a farmer was giving away kittens. The moment I stepped out of the vehicle, a tiny tabby kitten approached me, pulling away from his mother, and I had eyes for no one else. His white paws, muddied from the wet earth, reminded me of Tabby's, and I knew he was the little soul meant for me and Andrew. For the first month, he snored loudly beside me each night, so sick he needed two rounds of antibiotics to clear his infection. It felt good to take care of him. We call him Rua or Roo or Roo-Boo or Ruby Tuesday.

I make my way over to Rua on the couch and I pull him into my lap where he starts kneading my sweater. Andrew sits next to me, his body facing mine. His hand migrates to my leg and starts rubbing it tenderly.

"Just when I think I'm starting to get the hang of med school, I feel like such a failure."

Earlier today, we were divided into groups of fifteen to practise our clinical interviewing skills with actors posing as patients. I volunteered to go first, figuring I'd be less anxious getting the exercise out of the way. A young female actor walked in and sat on a chair at the front of the class. I was instructed by our preceptor to leave the room and come back in as if I were meeting this patient for the first time. *This feels so weird*, I thought, as I made my way to the door. In the hallway, I took a deep breath before knocking and re-entering the room.

"Hi," I said, extending my hand to the woman. "My name is Brittany." I smiled with my teeth showing, trying to act like there wasn't a small audience watching me.

"I'm pregnant," she blurted out. "I don't know what to do."

I felt my insides deflating like a balloon popped by a toothpick. *Are you kidding me?* I thought. *This is my scenario?* My mind pounced from thought to thought, and I felt fragmented in a way that was so familiar and so unwanted.

I fumbled my way through the rest of the interaction, trying to figure out how to conclude our pretend-appointment gracefully. I talked the woman through the options available to her and arranged for her to come back for another visit. "Ensure follow-up," they tell us. At last, it was coming to an end. As I was trying to decide whether to shake the woman's hand, invite her to leave or walk out myself, the preceptor's voice interrupted my thoughts. "How do you feel that went, Brittany?"

My shoulders tensed and I pressed my lips together. "I'm not exactly sure," I said, trying to keep my voice steady.

"Your body language changed when she said she was pregnant," a classmate said.

"You . . . just got really small," offered another.

"Did you notice your body language change?" the preceptor asked.

I suddenly felt overwhelmed with emotion. And, as if the emotion had nowhere to go but through my mouth, I started speaking. "I'm adopted," I said. "My mother was young when she had me, and I never knew her or my family, but I just met them last year and . . ." My voice trailed off. I could feel my heartbeat in my ears as so many white faces stared back at me.

I tell Andrew about my day and about how the preceptor pulled me aside once everyone had left and told me to do something nice for myself. "So, I bought myself a Starbucks," I say. It was my first one and I had no idea what I was ordering or if this was what the preceptor meant, but I asked for a vanilla latte and it made the bus ride home a little nicer.

The snow fell dense and early this year; by October, it already felt like we were in the middle of a shaken snow globe. After the first storm of every year, the traffic in Winnipeg is always awful. It's as though we're in a slumber every spring and summer and forget what it's like to drive with snow on the ground. Then we remember, and spend the next five months battling through it until it's spring and we forget all over again.

It's the holidays now, and Andrew's brother and sister and their families are visiting from Alberta. Andrew uses a few of his vacation days to spend time with them and his parents, and I'm genuinely confused by this. Although they've helped me feel like a part of their family since I first met them three years ago, their closeness still feels strange to me.

Theirs is the type of family that texts and calls each other every few days. It's clear to me that Andrew has never spent a night crying himself to sleep, wondering why his parents don't seem to want him. He has this unbridled sort of faith that they will forever be in each other's lives, and although I know some of this blind trust comes from the nature of his personality, I also know that some of it comes from the fact that it has simply always been this way for them. They have never left each other. They have fought and they have gone without speaking and they have been angry, but they have never left. And, sometimes, I pity them. I pity them for being so naive, for not knowing that our lives and the people in them can change, can be gone, in an instant. Except I know, on some level, that what I feel is not pity at all. I think it's jealousy. I think it might be breaking my heart.

We're sitting in the family room at Andrew's parents' house—a house that, decades ago, his grandfather built. Andrew's father is sitting in a brown leather recliner that once belonged to his own father. Everyone laughs at it because it's dated and worn out, and Andrew tells us how often he sat on his grandpa's lap in that chair; his grandpa always squeezed him tight before letting him go.

My dad actually worked at Andrew's grandfather's logging and building company for years. It was his first job. I knew he'd worked there when I was younger—I'd even gone to the building centre with Dad to pick up two-by-fours a few times—but I didn't connect it to Andrew's family until after I was married, when Dad mentioned it to me. "He treated everyone like they mattered," Dad said to me of Andrew's grandfather. "Didn't matter if you worked in the back or were some big shot, he'd sit down and have a cup of coffee with you, no matter where ya came from." If I close my eyes, I can still remember the smell of the warehouse at the back and when I mention this to Andrew, he says he remembers that smell too. A small thing shared between us that doesn't feel so small.

"Oh!" Andrew's dad jumps from the recliner. "I almost forgot." He walks out of the room and we can hear his tread up the stairs. They are a family of loud walkers, I learned quickly. Loud walkers who like to wake shortly after sunrise.

A minute later he's back in the room, and he hands little boxes to me, his wife and his daughter. For a moment, he looks shy, and his six-foot-two frame cowers a little. I wait for Andrew's mom to begin opening hers before I unwrap mine. Inside the box sits a chain-link bracelet. I pick it up and I lay it in my hand. There are words on each link, words like *trust* and *hope* and *faith* and *family* and *love*.

"When did you get this?" my mother-in-law asks. She sounds surprised. It's not like her husband to do something like this. Not because he isn't caring; he's the type to sooner give someone a cheque so he can be sure they'll be happy with their gift.

"When you were buying groceries a few weeks ago."

I feel the bracelet in my hand and lightly rub my fingers against the word *family*.

Chapter Thirty-Four

I'm on my way to a family reunion. Mom and my aunties on Dad's side have rented out a nearby park and arranged a potluck barbecue. The last time I saw George and my aunts and uncles was at my wedding two years ago. The last time I saw my entire family together, cousins included, was over ten years ago. I pick at the skin around my thumbnail as I drive down the highway, nervous but excited to see everyone.

I've been coming back to my hometown less and less these days. Life has been busy, but I'm not sure if that's the full reason. Lately, coming home is like returning to an amusement park that was so colourful, wild and exciting as a child, but feels dingy and rickety as an adult. And those spinning green apples that looked magical and left your stomach in limbo for an hour afterwards? They're just metal tanks covered in chipped paint.

I drive to the gathering by myself—and I guess I really have been gone from this town for a while because I'm caught speeding and get a ticket. When I pull up to the park, I see all of my aunts and uncles there, arranged on lawn chairs, no longer divided with the men on one side and the women on the other. Well, I guess that's not totally true. I realize after I get out of my vehicle and approach my relatives that they're in one big circle, yes, but all the men are in one half and the women in the other. Old habits die hard, I suppose.

Mom's face is cheerful as she waves me over. I walk toward her to offer her a hug, waving at my aunties and cousins along the way. I don't even recognize some of the people here—some must be my oldest cousins, others the children of cousins, others still the children of children of cousins. I make my way over to George and his wife, Rebecca, and sit down at a picnic table near them.

We haven't seen each other since my wedding. I'm not sure we spoke much that day, and I'm not sure what to say now. But before I can feel awkward about it, I notice their one-year-old sitting on Rebecca's lap. Those brown eyes deep as the prairie night sky, those cheeks like honey-glazed donuts, the way he looks like he's about to start giggling at any second—I feel like I'm looking at George when he was a baby.

"Can I?" I ask Rebecca, holding out my arms.

"Of course," she says, handing her son over to me.

The baby settles into my arms. I rest his head against my chest and close my eyes, breathing in the scent of him—the baby powder, milk and innocence—and of the potato salad and the fresh *roll kuchen* plated nearby. I hold my cousin's son on my lap for the remainder of the gathering. When Andrew arrives late because of work, I walk over to meet him with the baby on my hip. This is the first time Andrew is meeting many members of my family, but I don't even try to introduce him. Instead, I walk around the circle, showing the baby to different relatives. "He looks so much like George, doesn't he?" No one seems as amazed by this as I am.

I sit down next to George's mom. "He looks so much like George," I say.

"Oh, yeah, he does. Little Georgie Porgie."

I grin. I feel like I want to cry. I hold the baby a little closer as he plays with the beads hanging from my ears.

It feels nice to be around my family. I'm happy to have the chance to show Andrew a sliver of what it was like when I was a child. He grew up in a very different Mennonite family, with only two uncles and one aunt and four cousins. He had no clue what *meddachschlop* or *faspa* were, and no matter how often I remind him, he will never be able to differentiate between *roll kuchen* and *schnetke*, which feels as much like a sin to me as anything possibly can.

I thought I would feel a little sad being here, reminded of what we once had as children, of the ways we gathered every Sunday with my grandparents, but sadness is not what I'm feeling. It's not nostalgia, either. All I can think about is George's baby. How remarkable it is that he'll never have to know what it feels like to be taken away.

Crystal didn't want her to come to the wedding—that much was clear. My birth mother was getting married in a week when a friend I'd made from Wabaseemoong arrived to stay with Andrew and me. She'd just been discharged from a detox program and I didn't feel good about leaving her alone, so I asked Crystal if I could bring her to the wedding. I also thought it might help me feel more grounded to have her there with me—even though Andrew, Baba and my parents were attending too. The wedding reception was taking place at a local restaurant and I'd been told there would be no strict seating arrangement, but Crystal didn't take the request easily.

We had a fight over the phone. One of those arguments where one person thinks it's about one thing and the other thinks it's about another. Crystal was overwhelmed with the planning of her wedding, with the health of her parents, with the health of her in-laws. I was overwhelmed at the thought of leaving my friend alone and of being surrounded by a bunch of biological family members I hadn't yet met or didn't know well while Crystal, my connection to them, was understandably occupied for the day. I had been anxious for weeks leading up to the wedding, but how could I tell her that? Of course I never did. She'd seemed so happy at the prospect of her only child attending her wedding. I worried that telling her I felt anything other than excitement would break her heart.

SEPTEMBER 13, 2013
PHOTOGRAPH

My birth mother's cheeks glow, flushed to a deep berry shade. Her wedding dress is simple, with a V-neck cut and beading on the bodice. Her hair is short and tousled, her makeup minimal and sheer. She and her new husband, along with her parents, sisters and I, are gathered on a small bridge. I smile in a way Baba hates, with my lips pressed together. She's always told me I have the most beautiful smile she's ever seen—that I need to show it off in photos. But I feel awkward in my own skin today. I feel like the child peeking through the neighbours' window on Christmas, watching them celebrate in the warmth.

I feel ashamed of not feeling like I belong with my first family. And I feel ashamed at the number of people who've come up to me today in front of Mom and mentioned how much my birth mother and I look alike. Mom begins to cry at the reception, and Andrew and I both try to comfort her, reminding her that she's still my mom as much as she ever was. I feel ashamed for feeling ashamed when so many around me are celebrating.

What happened between us was nothing gargantuan. There was no shouting, no insults to sever what connected us. What followed in the months after the wedding was more of a fading away, which felt, in its own way, gargantuan enough. Crystal and I have since spoken only a handful of times, and our once-lengthy emails have shortened to only a few sentences. Soon, they will shrink to even less than that. Eventually, we will wish each other happy birthdays and merry Christmases, and that will be all. I prefer not to talk about it much with Andrew; when he asks me how I feel about the status of my relationship with my birth mother, I tell him I'm fine. "I lived most of my life without knowing her," I say. "Really, I'm okay."

It's January 2014 and I'm about to return to med school to complete my third year. About a year ago, I emailed the associate dean to request a meeting, not knowing what I could or should do, but knowing I needed to do something. My sleeps had been worsening. I'd just finished a surgical rotation and all I could think about were fractured tibias and femurs, bones shattered after crush injuries. My body refused to relax, whether I was on call or not, whether I was in my quiet home or on a stiff bed in some dingy hospital basement, where the cacophony of pinging pagers and howling pipes mixed with the whistling of my own breath that wouldn't settle. I didn't understand why this was happening. Why did I feel so alert and on guard when there was nothing obviously alarming occurring?

Andrew had just recently switched jobs and was working almost as many hours as I was some weeks. There were days when I returned home from the hospital only to catch him walking out to his car on his way to work.

The conversation with the dean was short. He's a kind man who's spent years working with remote Indigenous communities—I feel comfortable around him. "I think this is a good idea," he said. "Just a short while away from school to take care of yourself." He genuinely seemed to think a break was not a big deal; to me, it felt like a catastrophe, the end to my career-that-never-was. But the thought of working in such a busy career while also not being able to sleep seemed unfathomable to me.

"Brittany," the dean said as I stood by his doorway, my bag hanging off my shoulder. "It'll be okay. It really will be."

Despite my disbelief, his words proved to be true. I spent the first few months sleeping—late into the morning or in the middle of the afternoon, whenever my body would allow. I met with a pastor in my hometown who invited a female staff member into his office then turned to me and said, "I think you need a real dad hug." (I'd liked him, and I sensed that his gesture was kind, but I felt terribly uncomfortable. Besides, what was so wrong with the stiff sort of hug Dad offered me the day I moved out of the house?) I reconnected with friends. I helped Andrew in his job to open up a new business. I slept some more. Olivia—who by now was fully a sister to me—came to live with us for a bit. I spent time with Rua and our new orange kitten, Abby. I slept a bit more.

When I return to school, it feels like jumping into a deep pool of cold water as someone yells "Now *swim*!" My third year of medical school is a succession of six-week rotations and my first introduction to what it's like to be on call and in the hospital full-time. In a few years, the university will institute restrictions on how many hours students and residents are permitted to be awake and working, but for now, there are no rules. I'll be thankful when I'm finished my training that I learned in this environment, if for nothing else but the appreciation it gives me when I'm finally able to dictate my own schedule. Yet there are still Mennonite tendencies I can't shake, and when I come home from work or school exhausted and sore, I trust I'm doing something right. A part of me thinks my father would be proud of how hard a worker I am, though I'll never ask him.

I'm surprised by how much I enjoy my obstetrics rotation, although maybe I should have guessed that I would. Human births, I realize, are not that dissimilar to animal births. The steps it takes for the cervix to dilate, the stages of labour, the contractions, the afterbirth, the smells, all make me think of being home on the farm. I've often watched my dad, dressed in his overalls and rubber boots, tying a struggling, labouring cow or horse to a tree, then pulling on a glove that extends all the way up to his shoulder. He reaches inside the animal and grabs a foot, and a few seconds later a calf or foal is on the ground. Mom is inside, of course—peering through the blinds occasionally, though she can never watch for long.

The scent of blood and placenta sticks to my hair and I carry it home with me at the end of each shift. Andrew is kind and doesn't comment on it, but I know he can smell it when he hugs me, resting his chin on my head briefly before rubbing his nose. Rua sniffs at my hair and bites a few strands before sneezing, and Abby doesn't seem to want me holding her—and I know it's time for me to shower.

After drying off and putting on my pyjamas one evening, I perch myself on our bed to tell Andrew about one of the births I attended earlier in the day.

"Her delivery went faster than we thought and I was the only one in the room," I say, my hands gesturing wide like they do when I'm excited. "I called for the attending, but the baby came fast. So, I delivered a baby all by myself today!"

"Good job, baby!"

Rua and Abby are sleeping next to each other on my pillow. Abby is still just a kitten and she tries to feed from Rua sometimes, which he allows without protest. I can see her kneading against his belly, her purrs almost alarmingly loud for such a petite kitten.

"Wait," I say, "there's more. Her placenta wouldn't come out, so the attending had to reach inside of her and pull it out."

Andrew looks horrified.

"I felt just like I was back home!" I laugh and tell him how many times I saw my dad do the same thing on the farm.

After we say goodnight and turn out the lights, I rest my head against Rua's back, feeling the light vibration of his purrs against my ear, thinking of my dad and his animals, of Grandpa raising sheep and of Grandma birthing ten children. I think of my mom laughingly saying it was probably a good thing she couldn't have biological children because she never could have handled the pain. I think of my birth mother and I picture her entering the hospital with me still in her belly and leaving the next day with nothing at all. I think of how we're barely speaking anymore.

Chapter Thirty-Five

I'm on call at my rotation at the Women's Hospital in Winnipeg when I'm paged to attend a delivery in the case room, a space designated for medically high-risk deliveries. It's across the hall from the operating room, where the team can prepare for a caesarean within minutes, if necessary. When I arrive, the resident I'm working with is already there and unpacking what looks like a suction cup for the baby's head. The room is set up like an operating theatre and the bed is not really a bed—it's more like a makeshift operating table.

The air feels heavy, like there's a blanket of thick sap cloaking the room. The mother, an Indigenous woman, is lying on the table, her feet propped up in stirrups. Her hair is straight and black and beautiful, the way I've always wished mine was, and her eyes look like there's an entire world locked behind them. The father is standing by the head of the bed, and neither parent is saying a word. They're not speaking to each other and no one is speaking to them. I know birth is not necessarily a comfortable experience, but everything about this moment feels overly cold and sterile.

I hear a nurse whisper to another that, yes, Child and Family Services has been notified and, no, it is not this woman's first child and, no, this will not be her first to go into foster care.

This is a birth-alert delivery. Child and Family Services places "birth alerts" on the files of pregnant people they believe to be "high risk." Hospitals, in turn, are required to notify CFS when these "high risk" individuals come in to deliver their babies so that CFS can step in and apprehend the baby before the parents take their child home. Birth alerts are issued to mothers for a variety of reasons: exposure to the foster care system with their older children or when they were children themselves; a history of drug use or incarceration; poverty—or any reason, really, that the agency can find to indicate the baby might be in potential danger of harm. The definition of "harm" varies. In reality, this policy disproportionately impacts Indigenous and other racialized women. It always has. It will take several years before Manitoba officially ends the practice on my birthday in 2020. Ontario will follow suit three months later, and in 2023, Quebec will too, becoming the last province to do so.

The doctors, nurses and I are all here to help usher in new life. But that's not what this moment feels like. It doesn't feel magical or beautiful, but rather like it's draped, already, with mourning. We are not the midwives. We are the pallbearers. I wish I could stand by the mother's side, have my eyes meet hers, and let her know she's safe and that everything will be all right. But I'm not sure either of these things is true.

My mind flashes to the daydream of my first mother that I used to have when I was a child—a faceless woman who has just given birth, alone in the corner of a room—and I wonder how similar Crystal's experience felt to this woman's. There are still so many questions I haven't asked Crystal, questions I've never thought of asking. And now that we're not really speaking, I'm not sure we'll ever be back in a place where I'll feel comfortable asking her more.

Does she remember the first moment I kicked inside her? Did a doctor or nurse tell her the colour of my eyes? Did she see that they look just like her mother's? What was our goodbye like across that nursery window? How long did she spend staring through the glass? How long did it take before she could wake up in the morning and not think of that day? Did she truly leave the hospital emptier or did she leave with something still inside her, not a child but perhaps something just as profound?

The tightness that creeps from my chest into my neck doesn't come from the pain of not having the answers. It comes from having to mourn her all over again, when I'm not sure I ever properly mourned her the first time.

It's clear from the mother's body language that this is not her first child. She's seasoned. If you were to study only her face, you would think she's in very little pain. She makes no noise with each contraction that mounts, and she holds on to nothing but herself. The rhythmic waves do not sweep her under. This moment does not overtake her.

I watch as the resident attaches a tiny monitor onto the baby's scalp, which is taking its sweet time to crown, so we can better hear the heartbeat. She then takes a vacuum and suctions it over the baby's occiput. There is a beep-beep-beeping with the baby's heart rate. The attending obstetrician stands at the resident's side, her arms crossed. I'm trying to read body language. I'm trying to read the faces in the room. The moment is solemn.

The baby's father grabs the headphones cradling his neck and whispers something to the mother. She nods, and he places the headphones gently on her ears. I wonder what he's playing for her. Music he chose specifically for her in this moment? Her favourite song? Their favourite song? This moment should have left little room for tenderness, but this man, he has managed it for her.

Then, without warning, a nurse rips the headphones from the mother's head. "No!" The nurse's voice is harsh and her index finger is inches away from the couple's faces. "No!"

I'm embarrassed and ashamed, and I don't know why. *No.*

The resident is pulling with the help of the vacuum now. "You don't want or need to use much force at all," the attending obstetrician explains to me. We're standing off to the side and she is watching closely. The woman is pushing as the nurses tell her to push and the resident is pulling in a straight, slightly angled direction. The father is still standing next to the mother, watching everything unfold like a bystander at a crash who doesn't want to get in the way of the professionals doing their work.

I recall the delivery I attended a few days ago, and the contrast between then and now feels painful. This other mother was a teenage girl, a white girl, still in high school and pregnant by her out-of-high-school boyfriend. She'd spent the last seven months planning for that day. She'd met with several families and chose adoptive parents who reminded her of her own. There was no social worker. There was no birth alert. Child and Family Services was not involved. Both of her parents were in the delivery room with her. And both of her baby's new parents were there too. Her mother and the baby's new mother cried and hugged each other when they heard the baby cry, and the new parents cried even harder when they held their child in their arms. The nurses smiled, and even I couldn't deny the sweetness of the moment. I couldn't deny that I felt lucky to be in the presence of a baby so loved, so wanted, so cherished.

The room is getting louder and bodies are whirring and my attention is jolted back to the present moment. And then the umbilical cord is cut, and the baby is hurried to the incubator, and the mother is told to push again. She rests her head against her pillow in relief as the placenta slinks out of her. Bodies begin filtering out of the room until it is just the father, a nurse and me at the mother's side.

The baby is placed on the mother's chest and I hear the woman whisper her child's name. She has chosen a name for the daughter she will be prevented from bringing home with her. The daughter she will not raise. One thing has changed since I was born: whether this child stays in foster care or is adopted, her given name, although still subject to change, will not be hidden, and her information will not be sealed. I suppose it is something, but I can't say it feels like even close to enough.

Two weeks later, I'm downstairs in the emergency department, on call with the gynecology service. It's the middle of the night and I'm carrying a small carton of chocolate milk; one of the residents taught me chocolate milk works just as well as coffee and won't give you the jitters. I throw the carton into the trash before I knock and peek around a curtain to introduce myself to my next patient. I'm here to gather her history before the resident arrives.

"I knew something was wrong," the Indigenous woman says. She's seventeen weeks pregnant and has been cramping and bleeding for hours now. Although she's only a few years older than I am, she has several children, and I feel shy in the face of her knowledge, which comes from experience and not a textbook. "I knew something was wrong and he didn't listen. No one listened to me."

She's referring to her obstetrician. After her symptoms began this morning, she told him she was concerned she was about to lose her pregnancy. He told her there was nothing wrong. It's clear to me that she's right, and I pass along everything she's shared with me to the resident.

An hour later, the resident and I are sitting at a desk across from the patient's room when we hear her cry out. The resident jumps up and I follow her, and when we pull the curtain back, the woman is in a labouring position with her legs on either side of the bed. Her eyes lock with mine. "It's coming out," she says.

The resident gloves her hands and lifts the blanket, reaching into the shelter to cup the fetus still housed in its amniotic sac. She asks the woman if she wants to see it. The patient shakes her head. "I just want to go home," she says, and the resident nods.

I find a pad in a nearby cupboard and bring it to the woman. "Take care," I offer quietly, placing my hand on her shoulder. It's all I can think of saying.

Once the woman leaves, after the resident assures her that she will personally be looking into what happened earlier that day with the obstetrician, the resident looks at me. "Come," she says, and she takes me to an empty side room. She places a sterile cloth on the counter and lays the fetus in front of us both. "Look," she says, and I bring my head in closer to see. I stare at the fingers and the toes and the tiny head with the tiny eye sockets, and I think about the woman who has just been emptied. It's a wonder that I can feel such awe in the face of such heartache.

This is not the first time I've been on this side of things, where an Indigenous woman tells me about her concerns being dismissed, her fears ignored. And it won't be the last. A few years from now, when I'm in my first year of residency, I'll meet an Indigenous woman, a day after giving birth, who cries and asks for pain medication as her uterus throbs, only to be scolded and told all she's permitted is extra strength Tylenol. She'll be ignored when she tells the nurse that it's not enough and, hours later, I'll see the back of her stretcher being pushed into the operating room, her bed pooling with blood. I'll meet her in the elevator days later, and she'll tell me they had to take it all out. They had to remove her hemorrhaging uterus. I'll apologize to her for not doing enough for her, but she'll thank me and tell me that she doesn't feel that way. I will know that I could have done more.

Six years from now, Joyce Echaquan, an Atikamekw woman from the community of Manawan, will die from pulmonary edema in a hospital in Quebec after receiving inadequate care because medical staff incorrectly assumed her symptoms were the result of drug withdrawal. Before her death, she live-streamed a video of nurses throwing racist slurs at her. "Had it not been for the video footage, it is likely that this event would never have come to public attention," the coroner's report will read. There will be national outrage for a minute, as though this has not been happening to Indigenous Peoples for generations. The coroner will ask the province to acknowledge the systemic racism living in its hospital walls. In response, Quebec premier François Legault will say: "Is there systemic racism in Quebec? [...] Is there something from on high that is communicated everywhere in the health system that says: 'Be discriminatory in your treatment of Indigenous people'? It's evident for me, the answer is no."

Now that it's morning and my shift is over, I toss my scrubs into the hamper in the change room, grab my bag and make my way home. I sleep next to our two cats until Andrew comes home at the end of his work day and wakes us up.

"How was your shift?" he asks.

"It was okay."

I carry the stories of these women within me with no place to lay them down. I can feel them seeping into a crack between Andrew and me, and I don't know how to repair it. I want to say more. I want to tell him that I need him and ask that he hug me so I can forget my day. But I say nothing. Andrew is white and he isn't adopted and he's never been in foster care and he's never asked his mother when CFS is coming for him. I don't know how to make him understand the way these women's stories affect me. I don't even know if their stories *should* affect me in this way. I'm only part-Indigenous, a "half-breed," and I've been told over and over and over how blessed I am to have been raised by a family who wanted me. I also know Andrew well enough to know how he deflates at the mention of any difficult experience or emotion. I can almost see the anxiety rising within him when he's confronted by sadness or fear, his brain working in overdrive to try to find an exit.

"It was a long night, but," I repeat, "it was okay."

Chapter Thirty-Six

I've just begun my next rotation in the emergency department of a hospital in downtown Winnipeg, where everything is so fast-paced I don't know where to look. This world is fascinating and terrifying, and I alternate between feeling exhilarated by the rush of it all and paralyzed by my proximity to the fragility of life. I know that at some point the novelty will wear off, and I'm not sure whether that's something I should hope for or try to stave off as much as I can.

A man several years younger than I am was just wheeled into the resuscitation room, or "resus" room, as we call it. I don't fully understand my colleagues' language yet, but I manage to pick up "hypotensive" and "bradycardic" and "hemorrhaging." I gather enough information from the sidelines to understand that he was stabbed a few blocks north of the hospital. It's unclear how long he was unconscious before the paramedics arrived.

The resuscitation attempt feels like it lasts seconds, but probably takes ten minutes. The young man was dead when he arrived and he's dead when the doctors and nurses leave. Slowly, the room loses its numbers, and then it's just me and this man's body. He can't be more than twenty years old. His cheeks are dimpled with acne scars and his skin is fair, like mine. He looks like he could be one of my cousins. That's how it is here. I have yet to meet a physician, paramedic or nurse who reminds me of any of my Indigenous relatives, on Crystal's side or Dad's. The only faces and bodies I recognize are the ones who are hurting or sick or dead on arrival.

I walk around the stretcher and look at his back. There is a three-inch wound with raw flesh protruding from it where his bottom rib meets his spine. It reminds me of a cut of beef Dad has laid out from a cow he's just butchered. It's so odd to me, that something so small could be so lethal; the knife that stabbed him punctured his kidney and an artery.

I wonder who will be searching for him tomorrow.

Two dayshifts and a day off later, and it's the Friday of Easter weekend. Andrew and I meet my parents at the apartment we helped Baba move into a few months ago. It's smaller than her house was and there's only one floor—and she won't have to go down any stairs to do laundry, a key detail about which she's thoroughly pleased. As an added bonus, it's across the street from her old home, so she can watch the new occupants through the blinds and complain to us about how they're letting her garden go to shit.

Baba has never understood how medical school could be busier than her life as a retiree. She keeps herself busy checking in on all her neighbours. Recently, she can't stop talking about the couple next door and how the wife—oh, how Baba hates her!—has been hiding the remote control from her husband ever since he had his stroke. "She only lets him watch cartoons, and she takes that damn remote and hides it up on the top counter!" She shoves her hands up in the air in disgust. One afternoon, when the wife is running errands and a nurse is looking after the husband, Baba will walk over to their apartment, grab the remote, and give it to the man. "Let him watch what he wants to watch!" she'll say to the nurse as she leaves. Baba likes to tell all her neighbours about her granddaughter the future doctor, and her new grandson whose grandmother used to sit right in front of her at Sunday mass. "He's a Penner," she says, "but he comes from a good Catholic family on his mother's side." Really, I don't think it matters all that much to her. Andrew's tall and handsome with blue eyes, and he made her laugh the first time they met so many years ago, and that is enough for her.

Andrew is sitting on the couch next to Mom, and Dad is asleep on the loveseat across from them. Baba is sitting in her pink chair, which she definitely does *not* sit in to smoke. She insists that she gave up cigarettes over a year ago, but whenever Andrew and I visit, we smell cigarettes mixing with her lavender air freshener; and Dad's asthma still acts up when he's here. I'm sitting on the floor, watching the six o'clock news, when the anchor tells the story of a murder in downtown Winnipeg. I recognize the face that flashes on the screen, though I make no mention to my family of the fact that I was there when they pronounced him dead. "Shame," Baba says, before switching the channel to curling.

—

Every time I walk through the door of my parents' house, I'm affronted by so many memories, so many ghosts whose stories I don't know how to hear. On Easter Sunday, Jimmy greets me in the entrance and I pick him up, gently throwing him over my shoulder. He hangs halfway down my back, pawing at Andrew so he'll scratch his head.

"I'm just going to head upstairs for a second," I tell Andrew.

The second floor has felt like a deserted town since my parents stopped using it. Mom's knees have been bad and the staircase has become too difficult for her, so Dad converted the living room into their bedroom and the upstairs now sits unused. I walk down the hallway, past the bathroom and their old bedroom, which now sits empty but for a chest of drawers, too heavy to carry downstairs. I round the corner where I used to see Tabby sitting in the weeks after she died and pass the spare bedroom, stopping when I reach mine. I stand in the doorway and look up at the stars still stuck to the ceiling, the Little Dipper in its place, Jupiter near the edge of where the fan blades spin, as it always has been. I know that in a few hours, when the sun has faded, those tiny stars will look like fireflies dancing on my ceiling, even after all these years.

I take stock of my old bedroom, which Mom clad in sandy-beige paint after I moved out. "Toasted wheat," she'd called it. It's easier on the eyes than the creamsicle orange that took me hours to roller onto the walls in high school. A thick layer of dust sits atop the old white dressing cabinet that used to hold my clothes. I remember waking up in the third grade and sitting in front of this cabinet, after George had been taken away and my siblings had all left, wrapping my arms around my legs and holding them close to my body. My sleeps had become so restless that I woke up in tears some nights, but I couldn't really understand why. It seems funny now to think about how I couldn't connect the dots back then. But how does a child make sense of loss when it has become such a normal and expected part of life?

I scan the rest of the room, my thinning cat still resting on my shoulder, unbothered and content. *There used to be so much life in here,* I think, and an ache develops in my chest.

"Brit, where are you?" Mom's voice calls from the bottom of the stairs. "Lunch is ready!"

I shake the feeling away and turn to leave the room, making a mental note to ask Mom if we can take Jimmy to the vet next weekend. When I reach the dining room, I see my family sitting at the table. I sit next to Andrew as Dad bows his head, signalling for us to do the same.

"Our gracious, heavenly Father," Dad begins.

Although I've landed at a complicated relationship with Dad's god, my body reflexively settles into this moment. It's familiar, and I'll take that.

It's Easter Monday and I'm back in the emergency department. A Métis girl, who seems both younger and older than her fifteen years, is brought in after one of the cuts she's carved into her thighs won't stop bleeding. This happens every so often, the nurses tell me, and her legs and abdomen are already marked with scars thick and pale, too many to count.

Her auntie arrives to pick her up a few hours later, and my attending and resident pull her into the family room to ask her a few questions. "Do you know why your niece might have done this tonight?" the attending says.

There are deep lines splaying from the corners of the auntie's eyes. She looks tired. "No, things have been going pretty good lately," she says.

"Has there been any stress recently?"

"No." She opens her mouth, then falters. "Well, she hasn't been sleeping the best lately. Her cousin who abused her when she was young is going to court tomorrow and she has to speak." The attending nods like he understands, and a few hours later, I watch the girl leave with her aunt. A part of me feels nervous for her. Nervous for court tomorrow and scared that she might be back here again in a few days. But I can't listen to that part of me right now. If I do, I'm not sure it will ever stop talking.

I'm a week away from finishing this rotation when, one night, I see a look of panic wash over the faces of the nurses and my attending. A woman is seizing, but it's not the seizures themselves that are alarming them. This woman is in her third trimester, and if I've learned anything while I've been here, it's that emergency room doctors don't feel comfortable treating pregnant patients. I think it's the stress of having to care for two lives at once. Their anxiety makes me miss my obstetrics rotation. It's difficult knowing what area of medicine I want to pursue when I seem to enjoy every area I explore, but I realize I would be sad if I never had the chance to be a part of a patient's pregnancy again.

The patient is wheeled into the resus room on a stretcher, and I watch as the paramedics and health-care aides transfer her to the bed. She's unconscious and still seizing. A young woman is in the corner of the room talking with a nurse. Yes, her sister has had routine prenatal care, she says, and, yes, it's a healthy pregnancy. No, she has not been taking any drugs. I hear her tell the nurse again that *no*, her sister has never used any drugs. The patient is in her twenties and she's Indigenous, and I'm starting to notice a pattern in the way the emergency department treats these women.

There are surgeons in the room now, as well as anesthesiologists and another emergency room physician. Eventually someone thinks to call obstetrics. One of the doctors yells that all non-essential staff need to leave because the room is getting too crowded. I motion to leave but my attending looks over at me and shakes his head. "No," he mouths. "Stay." And I'm grateful. I want to be here.

"Have you given her mag sulf?" I hear the obstetrics resident ask the anesthesiologist, and this is the first I've heard anyone mention treating this woman for what she has come in for. Everyone has been hyper-focused on determining whether she's taken drugs. The anesthesiologist tells her no, and the obstetrics resident looks unimpressed. "It's eclampsia," she says, shaking her head. She insists that the patient be transferred to the labour and delivery floor where she can be cared for properly, but the surgeons refuse; they'd already told the operating team upstairs to prepare a room.

If this woman had not been young and Indigenous, would different assumptions have been made about her? I know the answer already, but I can't suppress Dad's voice in the back of my mind, telling me that I'm making a mountain out of a molehill. Maybe some molehills really are mountains. Maybe it depends on the eyes that are looking at them.

A few hours later and I'm standing beside another dead body. Another dead Indigenous body. I'm learning to see the health-care system as a revolving door, and I'm unprepared for the ways in which it's breaking my heart. It's late and I'm tired, but I can't look away. My eyes don't want to stop looking at this woman's body—a woman who, hours earlier, was alive. A woman who hung herself with a wire hanger because, I can only imagine, being alive was more painful than that.

The grooves in her neck are deep. I couldn't see them until I stood a foot away from her and now her neck is all I can look at. There is no life here. There are only scars. Scars on her neck and scars on her arms and, I'm sure, many more that I can't see. Her body was cold by the time the paramedics found her. I didn't catch who found her, but I wonder. I wonder if it was a friend or a sibling or her mother. I wonder what that person is doing right now. I know that they're not okay.

Even though I don't know this woman and even though she's no longer alive, it's as though I can feel her pain just by standing near her. As though her pain is travelling through meridians in the air, making its way to me, hitting me in the chest. I'm struggling to understand why others seem so unaffected by this. Why am I the only one standing in this room next to the dead body of a woman I don't know?

Chapter Thirty-Seven

In my fourth and final year of medical school, I choose to spend a few weeks working in the child and adolescent psychiatric unit. Since I'm planning to apply for a residency in family medicine, I figure the experience of treating mental illnesses in teenagers will serve me well.

During my time there, four teenagers are admitted to the unit. One has a new diagnosis of schizophrenia and is not allowed near anything sharp. Another has just finished detoxing and walks around in a lethargic haze, as if his body is in the midst of a reboot. The third is a white boy who's been admitted in the middle of his first manic episode. He's been transferred from a community a few hours northeast, so we spend days trying to piece together his medical history while he raps about bumblebees and honey trees and how he's exactly where he wants to be. The fourth is a girl—in fact not even yet a teenager, at age twelve—from a reserve up north.

The nurses and health-care aides on this unit are kind. They have a way of speaking with their patients that conveys respect.

Sometimes I wonder if it's easier to offer respect to teenagers because we still believe there's hope for them.

Most health-care workers feel disillusioned at some point in their careers. You pursue medicine because you want to help people, but it's easy to fall victim to the harsh realities of an overburdened system. Medicine is a vocation, a calling, but it doesn't always feel like one. Not when it bleeds into every facet of your life: when you haven't seen your family in weeks, and distance is growing between you and your husband, and you can't remember the last time you slept more than a few hours without your pager blaring obnoxiously. It becomes so easy to lose faith in your patients and in your own abilities to help them. Still, I notice the differences between the doctors I want to model my career on and those I unequivocally do not. Sometimes my patients tell me about the way in which one of my colleagues has spoken to them, and I'll think, *Yes, I understand, because they speak to other doctors that way too.*

I arrive at the psychiatric unit one morning and check in on the twelve-year-old girl who was admitted overnight. Immediately, I notice how she clutches the cuffs of her sleeves in her palms, how she doesn't look anyone in the eyes. When she speaks to me, she holds one of her cuff-clutched hands in front of her mouth—a mannerism that reminds me of my sister Ashley.

When Ashley visited Winnipeg a few weeks ago, Andrew and I brought her to a bakery to celebrate her sixteenth birthday. After carefully examining the eighteen types of cake on display, Ashley looked at the server, her hand raised in front of her mouth, and said she'd have a slice of carrot cake. Andrew and I both chuckled.

"That's what you choose?" I asked. "Out of everything?"

She shrugged, lowering her hand to her lap. "It's my favourite."

Later that night, after we dropped her off at her grandmother's, she sent me a text message: "I haven't done anything for my birthday in so long. No one has ever really made me feel special like that before." When I texted her back, I told her I loved her and that I would never be able to eat carrot cake again without thinking of her.

The girl who reminds me of Ashley has a note in her chart that says she has social anxiety, but I'm not so sure that's true. I think she has simply learned that her voice holds little weight in most of the rooms she enters. She has been taught to equate silence with security. She has learned what so many of us learn—that sometimes it's safest to say nothing at all.

Her room is filled with a group of us: an attending psychiatrist, a resident, another student and me. I wouldn't think the crowd makes this moment any easier for her, but I don't get the feeling that she cares too much. We admit her quickly. We ask her questions about her history, her family, and the incident that prompted her admission, and she answers in as few words as possible. She tells us she has eight siblings. That, yes, she has spent time in and out of foster care. She explains that two months ago, a guy attacked her. No, nothing like that had happened before, she says. Or, well, yes, something sort of like that had happened before, but that was when she was younger, and it didn't leave her with nightmares like the ones she has now. The nightmares, they're the worst part. No, she's never attempted suicide prior to last night. Yes, when she was younger, she would cut herself—but, no, she hadn't wanted to end her life then. She had just wanted to end the pain. She doesn't volunteer any other information. She doesn't trust us or this place. She has no reason to trust us or this place.

In the coming days, we'll witness the intensity of her nightmares, how they jar her awake in a cold sweat two or three times per night. How sometimes she'll cry out for her grandmother, and other times, just moan until she wakes. We'll discover that Ativan calms her down in the short term and that Prazosin works like magic once we find the right dose. I'll be thankful to have learned this lesson. In a few years, my nightmares will overwhelm my Mennonite grin-and-bear-it ethos, and I'll walk into my own doctor's office and tell him the dose I think he should start me on.

I don't know what happened to the young girl who reminds me of Ashley. She was still an in-patient when my rotation ended. But I do know that her nightmares decreased in both frequency and intensity during my time there. That is the goal, I suppose. There is no perfect remedy when it comes to coping or healing, but there can be nudges in the right direction—tangible ways that we as doctors can make it easier for others to move through life.

I'm sitting behind a one-way mirror with six of my classmates, watching as a psychiatrist interviews a nineteen-year-old woman in an otherwise empty room. This is an intake interview for a community outpatient program for teenage patients with anxiety disorders. The young woman tells the psychiatrist she's having trouble leaving the house. When she tries to, her hands and feet get sweaty.

Her heart beats so loudly she worries others can hear it. Sometimes she gets confused and can't think straight. She says it's impacting her job, her relationships. She doesn't understand why she can't just feel better. I watch her intently as the psychiatrist asks her about her childhood and her relationship with her family. Two of my classmates are whispering and another is picking at a broken thread on his jeans.

She knows that we're there, watching and listening on the other side of the mirror. She's consented, agreeing to share the painful details of her childhood with anonymous students for the sake of our learning, but this doesn't sit right with me. It feels unfair to her—to offer us such an intimate window into her life when she doesn't know who's watching behind the glass. Shouldn't she get to decide who sees her tears? Shouldn't she have a say over who listens to her story, who analyzes it, who judges it?

·

It's a Saturday afternoon in late November and I'm driving to my parents'. I promised Mom I'd visit now that my rotation has ended, before I fly out on Monday for a four-week elective at the Norway House Cree Nation reserve.

I turn off the highway and onto the gravel road to their home and try to shrug off the twin sensations of comfort and dread that creep over me. Over the past few years, as I've spent more time in the hospital, listening to stories similar to my own, I've begun to see my home, my family, my childhood in a different light. I'm starting to wonder if we're not able to fully recognize our own pain until we see it mirrored back to us.

Dad is outside by the woodstove when I pull onto the driveway. One of the Labs runs up to the vehicle to greet me, while the other two stay at Dad's side, trailing him as he shovels pieces of wood into the stove. Inside, I find Jimmy lying on the couch, and once again I toss him over my shoulder. I notice he hasn't lost any more weight, but his fur is matted near his tail. I lightly pick at one of the tufts until he squirms. "I'll be right there," Mom yells to me from her bedroom on the main floor. I can hear that she's on the phone.

I feel an undeniable sense of guilt over how this house has begun to disintegrate. As though my absence has somehow caused the walls of my childhood home to cave in. Clusters of dust and cat hair dance in the corners of rooms and the cracks under the kitchens windows are leaking. When did it get this bad? The water dripping from the ceiling isn't new. I know this because Mom's complained about it for years. If I press on a certain part of the living room wall, it's so soft I can mold it, and that doesn't happen overnight. But then why are these not parts of how I remember my childhood? What else did I not see—or not allow myself to see?

By questioning the narrative of my childhood, by pulling at loose threads, it's as if I'm ripping my childhood home apart at the seams. I feel responsible for unravelling my family's narrative, for not knowing how to fix it. For not being sure that I should.

Two weeks later, I'm in my apartment near the hospital in Norway House, trying and failing to fall asleep. Andrew called me earlier today to tell me Rua snuck outside, and Andrew panicked until, twenty minutes later, he spotted him under the stairs at the back of the house. This made me miss home even more. My body feels numb, my vision hazy, from twenty-two hours—twenty-eight hours?—on call. A young boy was attacked by one of the rez dogs, needing fifty-four stitches in his inner thigh. My attending remarked on how well-approximated my suture edges were, and I relished the compliment—until a man came in after a machete fight, requiring almost as many staples on his scalp. Later, a woman arrived almost fully dilated and I excitedly delivered her baby by myself, while my attendings stood to the side.

The nurses at the hospital are mostly local, and don't seem to like me very much, although I deeply crave their approval. Early in my rotation, one of the nurses warns me not to expect them to clean up after me. I don't know what to say.

"I . . . I'd never think you would clean up after me."

They never warm up to me. But by the time I finish my four-week rotation, I manage to make one of them laugh. It feels like something, at least.

Chapter Thirty-Eight

I'm one week into a two-week consulting psychiatry elective, and it's approaching midnight. I sigh as I sit on the old spring mattress in the call room and begin untying my shoelaces. My body is ready to crawl under that blanket, so ready I don't even care that it's one of those thin, staticky hospital blankets that, although technically clean, feels like it's coated with the residue of interrupted sleeps from residents and students past.

There are only four months left in my final year of med school and I'm in the middle of preparing for interviews with residency programs across the country. I'm almost certain I want to go into rural family medicine, which would offer me greater independence, a broader clinical scope, and, given rural medicine's limited resources, added complexities. I feel like it would provide a chance to merge the parts of myself I haven't always known how to reconcile. And it would give me the opportunity to be a part of my patients' pregnancies—an experience I know I would love. That said, I also enjoy psychiatry. I find meaning in the hearing and holding of people's stories. I suppose there will be a lot of that in family medicine as well. I suppose there's a lot of that in medicine in general, if you're willing to listen.

I grab the edge of the hospital blanket just as my phone whistles from the nightstand. The text is from the resident who's on with me tonight. It says there's a patient in the emergency room who needs an assessment.

I meet the resident in the foyer of the psychiatry building and we walk to the emergency department together while she tells me what she knows about the patient. "She's a thirty-nine-year-old female with multiple comorbidities—diabetes, CKD and recurrent bouts of sepsis from an intra-abdominal abscess that won't heal." This patient is much too young to have kidney disease, and I wonder if it's the result of a congenital anomaly—or maybe she only has one kidney? Or perhaps she's had infections that were incompletely treated over the years, which has led to scarring and worsening functioning of her body's filtration system.

I suddenly realize that a year ago I would've understood little of what the resident was saying. Medicine makes so much more sense to me now that it has been translated into stories.

"She has a history of depression and anxiety," the resident continues. "And she's Indigenous. They're asking us to assess her capacity in making her own medical decisions."

There's a certain hum to the emergency department, as though it operates on a different frequency to the rest of the hospital. Bodies are being stretchered down the hallway. One nurse is running in one direction while another is running in the opposite. A family huddles outside one of the trauma rooms. Their arms are wrapped around each other and they're crying onto each other's shoulders. A failed resuscitation, I think to myself, and I remember the young Indigenous guy I saw in that same room, the one who had been murdered and who looked like he could have been my cousin. The hall outside that room was empty the night he died.

I follow the resident to our patient's room and see a woman who's just over a decade older than I am, although the gap between us feels wider. The resident and I introduce ourselves and the patient nods. I can tell this isn't her first or second time in this hospital. There's an ease to her, an absence of the fear that so many patients carry in their eyes. She's not startled when a nurse comes to check her blood pressure, nor is she alarmed when someone begins to shout in the hallway and security is called to escort him outside. She's seasoned, a veteran of sorts. Esteemed. Or perhaps I'm the only one who sees her this way.

I overheard one of the nurses complaining about this woman before we entered her room—a "frequent flyer," she called her. There can be resentment toward patients like this. Another patient—another Indigenous patient—who doesn't have the respect for the system she ought to. Who seemingly ignores the advice of doctors and nurses alike. Who "misuses" the system some days and refuses the system other days. I recognize another type of resentment within myself, pointing in the other direction: toward the system that doesn't serve these patients. Where does this come from? I wonder. Is the Indigenous girl in me pained to hear the same type of prejudiced speech and sentiment I was subjected to so often throughout my childhood? Or is the white girl in me ashamed to hear white nurses and doctors speak to and about Indigenous patients in a way that reflects something ugly back at me about my own whiteness? I'm a "half-breed," after all, and I don't know which part of me is entitled to feel angry.

She has been feeling unwell for a few days, the patient tells us. "It's just like last time," she says. She was here, in the same department, only a few weeks ago. She received IV antibiotics then, and when she started feeling better she didn't want to stay in the hospital for the rest of her treatment.

"This is what usually happens," we were warned by the nurses ahead of time. "Tell us if she understands the risks if she leaves." The staff wants to be relieved of any responsibility if the patient refuses further treatment and leaves against medical advice again.

"I know I do this," the patient says. She knows every time she leaves she'll likely get sick again, whether in a few days or a few weeks. But the point is she knows. She knows and, still, she chooses not to stay. Still, she chooses to be out there rather than in here. She has been here too often, she says. She can't stand it anymore. It doesn't feel any safer to her in here.

She tells us she was placed for adoption as a child and was raised by a Mennonite family south of the city. She mentions the abuse she endured from an uncle and how, as a teenager, she moved to the city and began doing drugs and drinking to escape from her pain. She describes the time she was almost killed by a boyfriend who pushed her out of a window, and how a woman she thought was a friend left her outside and unconscious in the dead of winter. She speaks of her grown children and how she wishes she could see them more often, and how she tries to see her adoptive parents but has a hard time finding a ride. She counts on many fingers the number of times she's been admitted to the intensive care unit and describes how her body hasn't felt right in years.

"I'd say she definitely has capacity," the resident tells our attending and the ER doc looking after the patient. "She might not make decisions we agree with, but she's aware of the risks if she leaves."

"Thank god," I hear one of the nurses say to another, and they both roll their eyes.

The doctors are still talking when I sneak back to the woman's room. I lean my head to the side of her partially open curtain. "Can I come in?" She nods and shifts her body over in her stretcher. I don't know if she intends for me to sit down in the space she's created, but I do and she doesn't seem to mind. Since I was a child, I've had these senses, call them intuition or guidance or even naivety—I'm not entirely sure—but they feel like a sort of deeper knowing, a recognition that my body and whatever exists within it is telling me to do something that my mind can't fully articulate. All I know is that right now, in this moment, I feel this is where I need to be. Here, with her.

"My mom didn't want me, you know?" the patient says.

I look her in the eyes and I exhale. Words just aren't enough here. When are they ever enough, I wonder. With the silent snap of invisible fingers, it's as though a dam breaks.

"Why didn't she want me?" The woman cries into her palms and I can see an at-home tattoo with initials on her hand. Her children, I think. She mentioned their names earlier. The tattoo makes me think of the times I sat with one of my friends on her bedroom floor as she traced tiny designs onto the skin of her calf or her thigh, wherever she could comfortably reach, with a needle and a Bic pen. "Why?"

I know she's not asking me this question. This is a cry she's putting forth to god or the creator or the universe. It's a plea I've made myself, many times since I was a child. If I were to count on my fingers the number of times I've wondered this, I don't think I would ever stop. She asks me and herself and our god why her mother didn't want her. What, god, *what* was so wrong with her that her own mother didn't want her?

I have no answers for her. The room has no answers. Our god has no answers. So, I sit in silence. With her. And I exhale. It's the most I can offer her and myself.

In the morning, I return home, and because it's a weekend, Andrew is home too. As usual, he jumps up from where he's sitting on the couch with Rua and Abby to greet me at the door, arms wide. I drop my bag on the floor in the entrance and let my jacket fall off my shoulders.

"Hi, love," he says. He looks at my deflated frame and concern washes over his face. "What's wrong, baby?"

"I can't," I say, and I lean into his chest. His arms wrap around me tightly, in the way I let only him hug me, and my tears start falling.

"It's okay," he offers.

The tears come harder now, and I don't know if or when they'll ever stop.

Chapter Thirty-Nine

A month after graduating and days before starting my residency, I learn that I've failed a major exam. I was given only the briefest moment to celebrate that I've graduated—that I've finally become a physician after years and years of work. Now, I feel like I'm being met with the judgment that this path is just not meant for me. Failing this exam means I'll have to repeat it in a few months, but it doesn't interfere with my graduation or entering residency. It does, however, make me question myself and my capacity to succeed in this field.

After a few brief emails back and forth, I meet with the dean of students. "Some people just aren't exam-takers," she says. "This is just how it is for some people." She pauses for a moment before she speaks the words that will end up being more life-changing than either of us realizes. "I think you should see someone. There's a psychologist at the school who I think you'd connect with. Let me put you in contact with him?"

I'm weary. The "therapy" I experienced with pastors in my hometown always left me feeling worse. But I'm desperate for anything that might help me with my exam anxiety, and I'm willing to give it a shot.

I sit cross-legged on a sturdy, cushioned chair across from a man with a clipboard on his lap. My mind briefly flashes to those lunch hours I spent with my school guidance counsellor in junior high—I used to sit cross-legged on her old brown couch too. The psychologist's eyes are soft, and he has an unassuming presence I'm not accustomed to feeling in a man my father's age.

"This is so foolish," I keep repeating. "I don't know why I'm here." My cheeks grow hotter by the second, my tears refusing to be contained. He will spend the next few years telling me, session after session, "It's okay to cry, you know. You're safe to feel what's happening inside."

"Well," he answers me, "why don't we start with what you're feeling right now? Here, in this moment?"

"No." I shake my head quickly, tears splashing down my face. "No, I don't know if I can."

He pauses and we sit in what feels like the longest silence of my life, his eyes never losing their kindness.

"Why don't you try?"

I pass my exam on the second try, but I continue to see the psychologist every few weeks, even on the days when I'm post-call and haven't slept all night. It feels important. So much of what I've started to share with him I've never said out loud. Although the psychologist works at the university when I begin seeing him, he eventually enters private practice and I follow him. I wonder how quickly it became clear to him that my exam anxiety was merely an entrance complaint. Like a black, gangrenous toe that a patient thinks simply needs to be warmed or treated with topical antibiotics, but that actually signals a severe, systemic reaction, potentially threatening the entire limb. "But, my toe," the patient will say, hoping, believing, it's truly as simple as that.

"I don't want to feel sorry for myself," I tell him on more than one occasion.

"You're not," he replies.

"I don't want to feel this way."

"But you do."

"I don't think I can call it assault," I confess, eventually.

"What would you say to a patient who went through that?" he asks.

It's like a part of me that's severely dehydrated is finally being offered water. All these years, I'd been telling myself the water wasn't safe.

I never thought I would return to live in my hometown. Yet, here we are. When I match to one of the two family residency positions offered here this year, Andrew and I decide to move back. I'm reluctant. He's excited. He grew up in a small town just north of mine and always loved it. He's never had the complicated relationship with his childhood or his cultural identity that I have. But the medicine is rich and the schedule is satisfyingly busy, and I'm quickly reminded why I wanted to match to this program in the first place. I get to do things like pop a shoulder back into place and treat a woman with eclampsia seizing in labour and diagnose all sorts of conditions that only seem to brew in farmers who delay coming to the doctor for as long as possible. Mennonites are nothing if not stoic and reluctant to complain. Whenever I spend time away from this community, I'm reminded of how unique their approach to life is.

I'm sitting next to Andrew in our local evangelical church one Sunday morning. I've hated coming to church, especially recently. I've become increasingly disheartened by the pastor's sermons and by the homogeneity in the faces that surround me. I've continued attending because Andrew's attached to church and I don't want to break his heart. Every drive home, for years now, he and I have had frustratingly tense conversations, and we never seem to find common ground. He's afraid of having a community stripped away from him that offered him comfort during a time when he desperately needed something to believe in. I'm afraid I'll spend the rest of my life not only unseen, but unseen in the face of a god I'm told can only look one way. And in that version of the creator, there's little room for someone like me.

Even if it were not for my husband, I think I would still struggle with deciding to leave the church. Although I learned early to hate church basements and although I have a layered and tenuous relationship with my father's god, I'm afraid to leave it behind altogether. As a child, our religion was our culture and our culture was our family. There was no severing them. And, I cannot bear to lose any more family than I already have.

Midway through the service, a face pops up on the overhead screen at the front of the sanctuary, and my stomach flinches in the same way it did fourteen years ago. I would recognize those eyes anywhere. Those eyes that were once reflected back to me in a rear-view mirror when I was thirteen years old. I haven't seen his face in over a decade. He's sharing his testimony, how his struggles have made life difficult for him, and how he would never want his children to have the life he's had. How he's dedicating his life to the Lord. How he's filled with the joy that that brings.

My mouth becomes dry and my body feels a sense of urgency that forces it out of its seat. I push through the doors at the back of the room and walk to the bathroom. In the stall, I sit on the closed toilet lid and rest my elbows on my knees and my face in my palms. I breathe. "I don't want to be here," I whisper. I stay in the bathroom for another few minutes and in the foyer for the rest of the service.

Andrew is one of the first to come out. He looks confused. "Where'd you go?"

"The bathroom," I say. "Can we go?"

"Of course, baby. Are you feeling okay?"

I shake my head.

Later that night, before we're about to fall asleep, I tell him what happened. I tell him about the time in the car and I tell him about the time on the ground outside the arena. He looks tired. Tired of me? I don't know if I'll ever tell him what happened when I was even younger. I'm not sure he can handle it.

"I don't want you to pity me," I say.

"I'm not pitying you." He's quiet for a few seconds. "I just wish this didn't happen to you."

"I should've known better," I say. "I mean, what did I expect?"

"Baby." His voice is so soft I almost can't hear it. "It's not your fault. You didn't deserve that."

But his words sound like one of those white lies people say to make someone feel better. Like when Mom told me CFS doesn't take adopted kids away. Like when people say my first mother's love for me was so great she *had* to give me to another family. Like when people say it was all in god's plan.

"I love you," I say. "But I think you're wrong."

I can feel the distance between us right now. It has been subtly growing since we moved back home, and I don't know how to fix it. It feels like a shade has been cast upon us and we're struggling to reach each other through the forced night. I don't know where to find the light that can help me find his hand. I think I've begun to lose sight of my own.

It doesn't happen immediately, but over the next several months, we stop attending church. One day, I run into the pastor at that church on the sidewalk by the clinic. We exchange niceties before he says, "Are you and Andrew going to a new church?"

I don't feel like talking to him about this, so I lie. "Yes, we are."

"Well, that's good," he says. "I always say, as long as you're going somewhere."

Damn, I think, *you were one of the ones that I liked. I didn't expect this from you.*

"Why'd you leave—can I ask?"

Surprising myself, I blurt out, "Well, I find it difficult to sit in church and look at someone in another row who abused you as a child."

"Oh . . ." He's silent. He doesn't seem to know what to do with what I just said. "Oh. I'm sorry to hear that. Is he still abusing children? Because I have a duty to do something, then."

"No," I say. "Obviously, if I had knowledge of him doing anything remotely close to hurting a child, I would report it."

"Okay, because you know, we have a duty and—"

"Yes, I know. And I have a duty within myself to report anything like that too. Trust me. Well, I've got to get back to work," I tell him, and I wave goodbye.

Chapter Forty

I do a rotation in one of the obstetrics units in Winnipeg as part of my first year of residency, but I'm able to live at home with Andrew and make the one-hour drive to work and back each day. I'm just about to begin my morning rounds when Ashley and Kate's mother's name, Eleanor, name pops up on my phone screen. She rarely calls me, preferring to text instead, and something inside me knows this isn't good.

"She's gone" are the first words out of her mouth.

"Who?" I ask. "Who's gone?"

"Albertine . . . Last night." She sounds numb—dazed.

My heart leaps into my throat. "What happened?" But I know without having to hear her speak the words. I don't want to hear her speak the words. "Did . . . did she kill herself?"

"She . . . she hung herself. She's gone."

Everything feels hazy after that. Like Eleanor, I feel empty. I tell her I'll come as soon as I can. I hang up and walk over to the labour floor where my senior resident is working. She's the senior resident who intimidates me the most. A no-nonsense, shoot-from-the-hip, we-focus-on-the-job-here type. I wait as she speaks with one nurse and then another, fighting back tears that feels like they're about to explode forth. Finally, the resident looks at me. "What?" she barks.

"Can I talk to you somewhere privately?"

She sighs. "Yeah. Come."

I follow her down the hall and down another until we reach an empty family room. She sits on the sofa and I in a chair next to it. I can feel frustration emanating from her.

"What's wrong?"

I don't know where to start. "I just got a call, and my sister . . . well, she's not technically my sister, but I call her my sister because she basically is, and, well, she . . . sort of killed herself today."

The resident's expression immediately softens. "Take the day. Take the day and the rest of the week. You're done your rotation next week and you'll be on to another one, so you can apply to take time off for bereavement. I'm so sorry," she says. I can tell she means it.

I offer my thanks as I stand up and head toward the door.

"Hey," she says, and I turn around. "It was really great having you on our service. You're going to do well."

A day later, I'm on the reserve with the entire family, looking at Albertine's body in a coffin in their living room, remembering the last suicide that happened here. It was her boyfriend a few months earlier. The cycle is relentless.

—

I'm walking through the Winnipeg hospital mezzanine for the first time since I received that call about my sister almost a year ago. I've been on rotation at other hospitals in the city and in our town since then. I'm doing a rotation in the ICU here because my local hospital isn't big enough to house one. Thankfully, enough time has passed that I don't want to cry at the sight of these hallways. The elevator's slow, so I take the stairs up to the second floor to meet my patient, a young Indigenous woman who's just been rushed in. She's pregnant and her membranes ruptured a few weeks ago. She presented to the hospital septic, which is to say, in her case, nearly dead, and with no fetal heartbeat. They will have to evacuate all that is inside of her uterus, but she can't go to the operating room like this. She's too sick.

She had been septic at home for days, as best we can gather. She managed to self-medicate but we're not sure what exactly she's taken—the tox screen isn't back yet—which only further delayed her presenting to hospital. By the time she arrives to us, her blood pressure is so low that the machine struggles to pick anything up.

"I killed my baby!" Her cries can be heard throughout the entire unit, even with the door slid shut. It's not a cry, actually. It's a wail. She's wailing for the child she has lost.

She is bleeding and oozing and she cannot contain herself. Although I've only just met this woman, I suspect this is a rare moment of vulnerability for her. Her skin has been hardened by the elements. Her spirit too. I can feel it. But right now, she is raw. I lean on her bed and rub her hair as she holds my other hand.

"You didn't kill her," I tell her. "You didn't."

She turns her head into my shoulder and I feel my scrubs becoming wet from her tears.

"I did kill her. I killed my baby!"

I tell her this now and I will tell her this again and again, however many times she needs to hear it. I say it because it's true. Perhaps her baby could have, likely would have, lived had the patient had access to medical resources and stable housing. But she did not kill her child. This much will always be true.

In a few weeks, when I am at a residents' retreat, I'll overhear some first-year residents speak of this patient in a way that makes me seriously consider punching them in the kidneys. I'll learn the doctors had to remove her uterus when they took her to the operating room. This woman, mourning her child, and with no chance at ever becoming pregnant again. Some might call it justice—some did call it justice, I suppose—but I cannot.

It's a few weeks from Christmas and I'm working an overnight shift in our local emergency department. Between both of our work schedules, Andrew and I have felt like roommates lately. We don't fight—we've never been ones to fight—but we're saying less. And every time we hug, it's like the two of us never want to let go, both wishing we didn't have lives that seemed to pull us apart so often. I listen to his heartbeat in his chest and I think, *I hope I never lose this.* I'm terrified of losing it.

It's just before midnight when a Mennonite woman is brought in. "She's sobering up right now," my attending tells me. "You can see her in a half hour or so." Despite being only a few months shy of her thirty-fourth birthday, her chart is thick, full of psychiatric reports and ER visits and admissions to the crisis stabilization unit. It's also filled with labour and delivery notes—she has five children. There's no mention of any reporting to CFS or of a potential hysterectomy, even though she's clearly struggling to take care of both herself and her children; when she can't find alcohol, she drinks hand sanitizer directly from the bottle. I've seen charts like hers, with the only difference being the other mothers were Indigenous, and I know that in most of their cases, CFS was involved and plenty of discussions were had about options to limit the women's fertility.

This patient doesn't want to speak to me initially. I can't blame her. This isn't her first admission. It's not even her first admission in the past month. I ask her if she remembers why she's here and if she can clarify a few details of her medical history. We sit in silence for the next few minutes. I note that she had actually been doing quite well from a sobriety standpoint this year. That, until a few weeks ago, she'd had no ER visits for roughly ten months. She nods. I ask if she can identify why this last month has been so difficult for her. She tells me she can't, but I sense there's a window within her, a piece of a story that needs to be heard. Sometimes, if we sit in silence long enough, a patient's story will slowly reveal itself, I'm learning.

"Christmas is coming up. Have you had any family gatherings?" I ask.

"Last Sunday," she says. Two days ago.

"Sometimes, the people who are closest to us are the ones who hurt us," I say. "We don't know how to say something, or if we should say something. Sometimes, I think it's too painful, and it's really scary to even say any of it out loud." I scan her face and see her eyes focusing on the bedside table in front of her. "Has anything like that ever happened to you?"

"Yes," she says. Tears spill from the body that has kept them in for so very long. I hold her outstretched hand and we sit in silence again. It's a different kind of silence now.

When I finally leave and return to the back room, my attending asks how I managed to get the patient to speak to me. "She's seen countless doctors and none of us have figured her out. How did you know?"

I tighten my lips and let out a quiet exhale. "Sometimes, you just know what someone isn't saying."

His eyes offer me a sort of understanding I wish I didn't see in them. He turns back to his paperwork and I to mine.

Chapter Forty-One

I'm standing on the road, a few feet from Eleanor's house on the reserve. Ashley hasn't lived here in months, but today, she's here. On record, it's a warm October morning, but when the air blows against my exposed skin it feels sharp. I remember the first time I came here and how the air felt so much lighter than it does now. How at home I'd felt, seeing children running and chasing after each other outside the school and the kookums standing in a group by the parked vans nearby. How at home Eleanor and the rest of their family made me feel without me asking for it.

A few months after Albertine died, Eleanor asked if Ashley could come live with Andrew and me. "I wish it could work, I really, really do," I told her. I had just begun another two-month rotation in Winnipeg, waking up at five in the morning and getting home fourteen hours later most days. On top of working more than full-time hours, I was also on call "one-in-four," which meant I was providing in-hospital call coverage seven nights in a twenty-eight day period. And Andrew had just started a new job.

Neither of us was ever home, and we wouldn't have felt good about leaving Ashley alone in an empty house with no one else she knew nearby. "Can we talk again in a few months?" I asked. By the time I was finished my rotation and working in town again, Ashley had moved in with her boyfriend and was no longer interested in living with us. I wish—oh, how I wish—I would have pushed harder.

The wind is picking up now and I'm growing colder. Andrew's hand is on my back. "Ready?" he asks, and I nod. I don't feel ready, but I walk.

It's been thirty minutes now. I've been sitting in one of the bedrooms with two of the girls I've called my sisters and who have called me theirs for almost the last decade. We're sitting in silence. There are no words to speak. This should not be survivable. But somehow, for us, what is considered survivable is constantly rewriting itself.

Kate—she's twenty-two now, and I can't believe I've known her since before she had her period—motions to get off the bed. "I'm ready," she says.

I take her hand and walk toward the living room with her. It's mildly easier if I tell myself I'm doing this for her—if I believe I'm offering her some strength. I'm not sure she actually needs it, but it helps me move my legs forward.

The casket is big and shiny, and it sits in the living room with chairs facing it. In a few days it will be hoisted into a plywood box so it won't get dirty, then lowered into the ground. I've never quite understood that part—a box held within another box—but I guess it doesn't really matter.

Her body has been here since last night, and people from the community have been coming and going ever since it arrived. As different as my Mennonite upbringing was from the Anishinaabe culture of Eleanor and her kids, as well as from what I'm coming to learn about being Métis, I'm noticing the overlap in the way we hold our losses and the way we surround each other in the midst of the pain. I almost feel like I can hear Dad's family singing in the distance somewhere, like the hymns are drifting in through the open windows in the kitchen.

I walk closer to the casket and all I can see is her face. Kate and I stand a foot away from our sister's body. I hold my spine stiff and place a hand on her back.

Andrew and I had just returned from a trip to Kenya to celebrate my graduation from residency, and I'd woken up alone in bed when the text message arrived. "It's Ashley," Eleanor's message read, and I knew what it meant. I sat on my bed in my empty, silent room, and somehow it felt like the loudest place on earth.

The phone call was short. "It happened last night," Eleanor said. The wake would be the following week. It felt like we were just there yesterday, in the school gym for the service, at the graveside, throwing dirt onto a coffin. But this time, I'm not sure any of us saw it coming.

Ashley's skin has darkened to a purplish, leathery hue and her hands are stiff, cold as snow. Her neck is positioned awkwardly and I know it's because of the way she died. I recognize it from the times I've seen it in the ER and from the way Albertine's body was positioned in the casket. A fracture in the C2 vertebra. A "hangman's fracture," it's called. I will never want to call it that again.

Kate has left, so I stand next to Ashley's body by myself. I will stay here for another ten, twenty, thirty minutes. I will try to move, but my legs will not listen. *Stay here,* my body whispers, *stay here, with her.* I stand next to her body until I can no longer feel my own. I've seen death before—in the emergency room and in hospital beds. I've seen the deaths of animals and grandparents and cousins. Shouldn't I be immune to this feeling? But I can't get past the way her body looks to me right now. She was only nineteen. Four days ago, there was blood pumping through the chambers of her heart. There was blood flowing to her brain and to her feet and she could speak and she could laugh and she could make sarcastic comments all the same. Ninety-six hours ago, she was alive. There was still life in her. Now, there is no life. Ashley is not Ashley anymore. Where has her spirit gone? Tell me, please, where her spirit has gone, so I can find her.

The lowering of the casket is the part I hate the most. Someone grabs two sets of ropes from the back of their truck, but no one ever remembers gloves or a pair of solid shoes. Every time I'm here, I stand to the side, watching, waiting to jump in case the box crashes to the ground because someone has slipped and let go of the rope. I always envision one of the men falling beneath the box and the box falling on top of him. I tell myself next time I'll stop by Canadian Tire on the way over and pick up a few pairs of gloves for this moment, but I always forget. But no one slips and the box doesn't fall.

I already know too many children and teens whose bodies have been lowered into this ground. Suicide rates among Indigenous youth are six times higher than the national average. And in my sisters' community, the rate is three times higher than the average in other First Nations. I used to track how many kids I knew who'd died of suicide, but once I could no longer count them on two hands, I stopped.

Ashley's boyfriend stands by the grave, shovelling. Even when it becomes clear his body is tired and sweat is beading his neck, he doesn't stop. "Please help?" I ask Andrew. He walks to Ashley's boyfriend and places a hand on his shoulder, but the young man shakes his head. Andrew begins to turn back, then stops himself. He leans in close to the man once again and whispers something I can't hear. The man slowly drops his shovel in the dirt and nods, stepping away.

An hour later, we're at the feast and one of Ashley's aunts sits with me and Andrew and Eleanor. She makes a comment about how attractive this white man is. "I think I might have to go home with you later," she says to Andrew, and she and Eleanor and I laugh. I can tell Andrew isn't sure whether or not he should laugh, which only makes me laugh harder. When we're met with such unspeakable devastation, what are we to do other than laugh? What else could possibly help make a moment such as this bearable?

I open my practice the week of Ashley's death—I'd planned my schedule months in advance. My days are filled with new patients and reviewing charts and medical histories and delivering new life into this world. Everything is new, but despite this, it offers no distraction from my grief over Ashley's death and guilt over not having had her come stay with us. I can't wake up without remembering how her body looked before she was buried. I can't fall asleep without thinking about carrot cake.

My therapist reminds me this is normal, reminds me that guilt is a common reaction after a loved one's suicide. I know this too, so I'm confused about why I still feel it. I know the stages of grief, I understand the psychology of it, so why must I experience it? I tend to think that if I can wrap my mind around something difficult, it should spare me from having to feel it. My brain has protected me so often in this way, but it can't manage it right now. It feels like it's operating on an endless loop, trying to calculate an unsolvable equation.

"You've faced a lot of loss in your life—there's been significant grief," my psychologist says, and this surprises me. This version of my life is all I've ever known. It's hard for me to assess what "significant grief" really means.

I know, with time, the intensity will ease. Loss, in some ways, prepares you for future losses. But knowing that doesn't make it easier now. In some ways, I find these recent losses harder, which makes it that much more confusing for me. It's as though there's a compounding effect; each loss adds on top of the last and the weight only grows. Andrew is hurting, too, I can tell, but he doesn't know how to talk about it. I know he doesn't share his pain with me because he thinks it'll only make me hurt more. I know this because I know him. I can feel him withdrawing from me to protect us both. I can feel myself doing the same. I've always known how to comfort those around me, how to set my emotions aside to help them realize theirs. But even I can't help him through this.

Months later, I'm called in to a delivery at night. Andrew is still at the gym kickboxing, which he's been doing quite a bit lately. I understand why. I think it offers him a place to step outside himself and feel the pain he cannot say aloud. I drive to the hospital and walk into the delivery room to see one of my patients, a woman with whom I attended high school. I always assumed it would be awkward to care for people I had some sort of history with, but I'm finding that's not the case. I am finding, surprisingly, it offers both me and them a sense of trust.

I check her cervix and it's not dilated any more than it was a few hours earlier. Her labour is stalling. "She's starting to have decels," the nurse says, with the fetal heart tracing in her hands. I can see my patient's mother pacing in the hallway just outside the room, and I nod to the nurse.

We have time, I think. *We have time, but I know there are special circumstances.* Years ago, when we were teenagers, this patient's younger sibling died suddenly of cancer. I remember it so clearly—my parents talking about it at the kitchen table. How, overnight, this family had grown smaller. I don't want this night to prove any more stressful for her or her family than it needs to.

"Listen," I say to her. She's lying on her left side, holding her abdomen, as her husband rubs her back. "We have the time to watch things here, but I want to explain what your options are now while you might feel a bit more able to process them."

Because the operating room is closed at our hospital this weekend, if she needs a caesarean section, we'll have to drive fifteen minutes to the nearest hospital, and this will take a few phone calls and some coordination to get everything in place.

"Whatever you think is best," she says. "I trust your opinion."

An hour later, I place her daughter, crying, on her chest, then I step out of the operating room to find her parents. "She's healthy," I say. "Your granddaughter is healthy. It all went perfect." Her mother hugs me and her father cries, and it's just about my favourite moment I've had in this career.

In the change room, I sit down and remove my amniotic-fluid-and-blood-stained shoes. I set my bare feet against the cold floor and my hands on lap. I feel the roughness of the scrubs against my fingertips as I rub them lightly against my legs. "I miss you," I whisper. I'm not sure if I'm saying it to Ashley or if I'm saying it to Andrew. I think I'm saying it to both.

Chapter Forty-Two

"There's someone in the house." My voice is quiet and my breath is fast and I'm clutching Andrew's wrist so tightly that, in a few hours, there will be marks on it in the morning light. He lightly places his hand on mine and unclasps my fingers.

"Brit," he says, "there's no one here—"

"Go check! Please go check."

Andrew is a good person, a dutiful and kind person, and he makes no complaint about having to get up at two in the morning to double-check that the doors are still locked and there's no one in the house.

After he's done so, he climbs back into bed and rubs my shoulder. "Nightmare?"

"Yes." Another nightmare.

It's the second tonight and the fourth this week. Always, I see the tall silhouette of a faceless man at the foot of my bed. He never moves. He never speaks.

For the rest of the night, my body jolts awake as soon it falls into any sort of deep sleep. In the morning, I drive to the hospital and then to the clinic, and even though I'm exhausted, the moment I step into those corridors, my body switches into another mode and I become efficient and organized. It's easier to focus on what's right in front of me, on numbers and lab values and vitals. Easier to allow myself to be engulfed by the pandemic that's just begun spreading like wildfire in our town. Easier to focus on a known entity during the day, however evolving it is, than on the dreams terrorizing me at night.

Night after night, I plead with my body for even a few moments of reprieve. But it will answer me tomorrow as it answered me today. *No and no and no*, it says.

I'm sitting on the floor in my home office, photo albums strewn all around me. I recently stopped by Mom and Dad's and picked up my childhood albums and VHS tapes. I found a VCR online and the proper adaptor for my TV, and I've been rewatching the old tapes I saw so many times as a child. I pull back the cellophane from the page of an album marked "1992" and gently tear an old photo from its sticky binding. There we are. James and George and Marion and me, sitting in the clawfoot tub in my parents' old bathroom. The sun and the dirt from the barn have darkened our faces, offering a stark contrast to the white of the tub. I smile, unsure if I remember this exact day or if I'm remembering the hundreds of others just like it. I know that after this photo was taken, Mom almost surely grabbed the empty margarine container with its label long worn away, dunked it in the rusty water, and released lukewarm streams over our heads, washing the day away. If I close my eyes, I can picture it, I can feel it. My toes pushing against Marion's, the sound of James laughing when George splashes him with water. Mom would then have instructed us to step out of the tub as she kneeled on the floor holding out a big mauve towel. I can hear the Trisha Yearwood playing in the background. I can smell summer wafting in through the bathroom window.

I want to keep this one close, so I place the photo to the side. I reach for my phone and begin scrolling through my images until I land on one of my biological mother as a child. Her cheeks are chubby, her brown eyes wide, and the edges of her two front teeth reveal themselves just below her upper lip. If the photo didn't look dated, I would think this was a picture of me as a kid. I don't think I ever resembled her more.

Until a few months ago, it had been years since Crystal and I had last spoken, apart from our birthday and Christmas greetings. But something made me reach out to her. Dad's favourite dog recently developed bladder cancer, which progressed quickly. There was no humane treatment, so Andrew and I accompanied him to the animal hospital, where the vet slowly pushed a syringe of that clear, lethal concoction and I felt the dog fade in my arms. I stroked her head and Andrew rubbed her back, but her eyes never deviated from my father, who sat across from her. I think she was maybe the best friend he had ever had. Right after, I felt a sudden strong desire to send Crystal a message—to tell her what had happened. Our love for animals is one of the similarities we share.

"I'm so, so sorry for your loss," she wrote back to me within the hour and, somehow, that was all it took. The door was open again. Slowly, we started reconnecting, sending messages back and forth every few weeks. Short at first, then lengthier with time. Perhaps the pandemic had this effect on many mothers and daughters.

Eventually, a thought dawned on me. "Are there any pictures you can send me?" I asked. "I never realized before that I've never seen a photo of you as a child. I also don't think I've ever even seen a photo of your grandmother." I gave myself a little time to digest each photo before I asked for another. *Pace yourself*, I thought. But I was greedy with these photos. I already knew I would never have enough. My hunger would exist forever.

I stare at the photo of my great-grandmother on my phone. Her cheeks are mine. The shape of her face. I feel like I know her without ever having met her. I swipe until I reach a photo of her with my grandmother. I see myself in these women. I don't look exactly like them, but I can see the thread that links us through time. I'd always thought I looked so much like Crystal—and I think I still do—but I hadn't realized how much I resemble these women that came before her. I feel connected to them and, by extension, to my mother, in ways I never have. Yes, these are the first photos of them I've ever seen, but I think it's more than that. I wonder if, maybe, I'm simply ready to see myself in them now—if I've finally found the space to let them in.

My grandmother currently lives in a personal care home. Her mind is forgetting most of what it has known—perhaps a welcome reprieve from a childhood of pain about which she rarely spoke, and with few details. She comes from a large Métis family and many of her sisters are still living. Lately, I've been reaching out to them. I've asked if I may call them Auntie, to which they've all emphatically replied *yes.*

One of my aunties, in particular, has a lot to share with me. I learn she's been heavily involved in the Manitoba Métis Federation for most of her life, and she tells me how involved her parents, my great-grandparents, were within the community too. How proud of our culture they were, and how they passed that on to her and my grandmother and the rest of their siblings. She tells me how my grandmother, the oldest of them all, was raised by their grandmother, a first cousin to the Métis leader Louis Riel.

She also tells me about my grandmother's birth. "Our mother hid in the bush with her," she writes to me one day. "She never spoke about it much. But the 'welfare agents'—that's what she called them—they came to try to take your grandmother away."

"Why?" I ask, although I suspect I know the answer. My grandmother was born in the 1930s, back when the Canadian government made it a practice to apprehend Indigenous children.

"Our mother gave birth in a maternity home a few days before. She didn't tell anyone who the father was and the agents found out she'd had a child. All she ever said was how terrified she was that your grandmother would cry and the agents would find them in the bush."

My grandmother never spoke to anyone about how long her mother hid her in the bush or whether the agents ever came back. But we know they didn't find them.

The "welfare agents" would have been trying to apprehend my grandmother to place her in a residential school. The Canadian residential school system was the government-sanctioned practice of forcibly removing Indigenous children from their homes and placing them in Church-operated boarding schools. The ultimate goal was to indoctrinate and assimilate Indigenous children into Euro-Canadian ways of living. As stated by Duncan Campbell Scott, the deputy superintendent of the Department of Indian Affairs, the system was designed to operate until there was "not a single Indian in Canada that has not been absorbed into the body politic."

While the Catholic Church had been operating residential schools as early as the 1600s, the Canadian government began actively funding residential schools and investing in the infrastructure to support the entire school system in the mid-1800s. Some people think of residential schools as a relic of the past, but the last federally funded school, the Gordon's Reserve Indian Residential School in Saskatchewan, only closed in 1996.

Within the residential school system, children were separated from their parents and other family members at incredibly young ages and forbidden from contacting their families, wearing traditional clothing or speaking their languages. Often, children were assigned numbers or given Euro-Canadian names, tactics that disconnected them from their histories and identities. What followed, naturally, was a widespread fracturing of families, communities and cultures.

The painful legacies of the residential school system include the widespread neglect and abuse of Indigenous children. Physical, emotional and sexual abuse was horrifyingly common, as was deliberate and sustained malnourishment—the result of the government's insufficient funding for food, and, in some cases, intentional nutrition experimentation on children. Today, many survivors and their families are still trying to heal from the trauma wrought by this system.

My auntie also tells me that, years after the government tried to apprehend my grandmother, one of their other sisters fell ill and, during her hospitalization, a white couple tried to adopt her because she had fair skin. My great-grandmother overheard this couple speaking to a nurse about the adoption and, again, she managed to save one of her daughters from being taken away. But she couldn't save her from everything. In that hospital, the staff ran experiments on her child. My auntie says they tortured her.

My auntie also tells me that one of Crystal's sisters went into care immediately after she was born, although it's unclear if she was apprehended or if my grandmother relinquished her. Regardless, in the end, my great-grandmother managed to help bring her home.

I lie in bed, thinking about my great-grandmother. I wish I'd had the chance to know her, to have at least met her. To have heard her voice, to have felt her arms wrapped around me. I wish, rather than including inaccurate details about my mother's appearance in my papers, Child and Family Services had offered me my great-grandmother's story. Something deeper, more meaningful for me to have held on to. Something to help me feel connected to the women who came before me.

As I fall asleep, I'm not sure if it's a dream or a vision or my own imagination, but my great-grandmother comes to me. We're standing by the Red River as she grabs my hand and walks me toward a circle of people who look just like me. She introduces her grandmother and grandfather to me. They put their arms around me. *We are with you,* they say. *We always have been with you.*

The next morning, I wake up and walk over to my laptop. My grandmother entered this world and immediately they tried to take her. They tried to steal her. From her mother. From her people. I try to put words to a story that has never been written down, a story that has never been told in its entirety. I know that I will never know the details of that day, how my great-grandmother felt or what lived on within her moving forward. But I want to try. So I write.

MAY 1938
ST. LAURENT, MANITOBA

I imagine motherhood suited her. Even without her child's father by her side, even alone, as she was, in this house. Madeline was almost two months past her twentieth birthday, a few days past giving birth at a maternity home for single, mostly Indigenous, women. I picture her—her head draped with thick, black hair, her baby nestled in the crevice of her bent arm. I imagine her swaying her hips slowly, side to side, as she sang in Michif, crooning in the melodic language her child would eventually learn to speak. After all of the pain, the contractions like rhythmic waves, the fire so intense she had felt shorn apart, she was now with her daughter. A daughter who had made her a mother. Did she feel, in this moment, like she had everything she needed? I picture the deep, black eyes of the baby meeting the blacks of Madeline's.

Was it the sound of the vehicles driving down the road that had alerted her? The sound of the nearby car doors slamming? Or had she been waiting? Had someone warned her that they would be coming for her daughter? This is a part of the story about which she never spoke.

I imagine her breath quickening, her eyes darting from the window to the door and back to the window once more. Did she have time to put on her shoes? Or did she run barefoot, ignoring the pain of the rocks and branches prodding at her feet, the ground soft and wet after the thaw of spring?

The welfare agents had come. "Welfare agents." That's what she called them, officials from the government who had come to take her daughter. Who had tipped them off? Was it a nurse at the maternity home where Madeline had stayed only days earlier? A neighbour down the road, someone who had heard that there was an Indian woman with a child, but without a husband? This was just how it was then, and how it would remain for decades for Indigenous women and their children. Never safe. Never free from intrusion.

I wonder how far she ran into the bush. One hundred feet? Five hundred? How far was far enough? I can feel the thud of my heart against my chest as I close my eyes, imagining what it felt like for her. I picture her crouched low to the ground, blood trickling down her bent legs as she hid behind some bush only starting to bud. Did she place her hand over her daughter's mouth, terrified she might make a sound? This was the moment she would come back to when asked about it years later—how terrified she was that her daughter would cry and the agents would find them in that bush.

Did she whisper some words into the sky, praying to her creator to protect the two of them? The smell of new earth would have filled her nostrils, mixing with the scent of fresh Seneca root in the distance, which she picked each spring and sold as traditional medicine in the city. Did it offer her any sort of protection? Or was there something else that shielded her and her child that day? Had she run deep enough to obscure their silhouettes? Or did her mother, my great-great-grandmother, who was presumably inside the house, distract the agents? Did she feed them, tell them a story? Or did those men simply grow tired of searching?

I imagine my great-grandmother clutching my grandmother against her body as she watched the white men through the branches. I can see those agents circling her house, pounding on the doors and peering through the windows. Did she wait for the sun to set? For the blending of those deep orange and fuchsia hues in the evening sky for which late prairie springs are known? Or did she count quietly, deliberately, to herself until she reached a certain number? Was it safe to come out then? How long was long enough? I wonder if she ever felt safe again.

In the fall of 2021, I begin an online Master of Liberal Arts program in Creative Writing and Literature at Harvard University. Since graduating residency a few years ago, I've thought about doing this. I've felt a need to map out my story in my own words, filling in whatever blanks I can on the page laid out in front of me.

A little over a year ago, I wrote a personal essay that was published in *The Globe and Mail.* In it, I shared about my Mennonite upbringing, about meeting Crystal and connecting with my first family. "Sometimes it still feels like I understand myself so little," I wrote. "The shame still awakens from its slumber every so often. [...] I suspect it will be a lifelong journey, but I'm thankful I'm further along and finding greater comfort in my own skin than I had at the start."

When Dad heard about my essay, he was furious and refused to read it. I'm still trying to forget everything he said to me during that conversation. I will never forget that he told me I should be grateful for all that his family has done for me. I don't think I will ever forget some of the other words, too. A few online strangers said much of the same thing, although I tried to ignore their words. Mom told me people were coming up to her at work and apologizing to her on my behalf. I didn't hear from either of them afterward for almost five months, until Mom needed my help navigating the medical system.

This was the first time I'd publicly put into words something I'd felt my whole life, and despite my parents' anger, I was surprised by how valuable it felt to share these parts of who I am. It felt like I was inviting the younger version of myself to speak, like I was hearing the sounds of her whisper for the first time. It felt like I'd lit a matchstick to gain a bit more light in the dark.

Since then, the desire to write has grown so persistent I spent a year trying to ignore it, debating whether or not it was right of me to shift my practice to allow space for it. If I wanted to study writing for real, I would need to stop providing on-call labour and delivery care to my prenatal patients, though I'd maintain the other parts of my practice. I also knew that writing anything about my experience that wasn't steeped in gratitude might cost me my family. But I came to realize I've paid a tax for my silence, and I wasn't so sure I wanted to keep paying it. Eventually, it became too difficult to deny that longing to share.

I feel shy when I start my classes, embarrassed that I don't know the terminology that other students seem to know, self-conscious that I haven't read the books so many of them have read. I don't make mention of the fact that I'm a physician until I'm midway through the semester, fearful of making them think I'm smarter than I actually am. During a meeting with one of my professors, I confess to him that I think I'm one of the dumbest people in the course. He laughs and thinks I'm joking, but I'm not.

After I publish a piece about holding a place in my heart for both of my mothers, Crystal tells me how much the piece meant to her. Mom calls me to tell me how many people have approached her to offer her condolences for having a daughter who would betray her like this, and to reassure her about what a good mother she is. Someone online "encourages" me to show my gratitude. "You would have been raised molested by uncles and brothers. Be thankful your family saved you from that. You were raised in a good, generous family that loved you. You should feel grateful." Another person calls me a "savage."

I'm sitting at my desk, having just finished my classes for the day, when I receive an email saying my DNA results have come in.

Andrew gifted me the test last Christmas after I'd connected with my grandmother's sister. What she'd shared with me left me wanting to know more, igniting a fire inside of me that hasn't gone out. There's still so much about my family I don't know. I wondered if a DNA test could help colour some of it in. I'd taken a swab to the inside of my cheeks and mailed it off the next day.

Months later, I learned the company lost my test. They had to send me another in the mail. It was as though the gods of recreational DNA testing were saying to me, "Are you sure about this?"

I thought I was.

Chapter Forty-Three

We've been tentative, treading lightly, neither of us wanting to get hurt as we slowly reveal parts of ourselves. Parts others wouldn't really understand. Over emails and texts, he's told me that building a relationship with the land has been invaluable in reconnecting with his Cree culture. I can't say I've found a single entity to bridge that gap for me. I was finally able to apply for my Métis card—and although a simple laminated card shouldn't be a factor in confirming a piece of my identity, it did help a little. I also found a video of local Métis elders making traditional bannock while speaking Michif and followed along, adding the ingredients to a large mixing bowl. I think it tastes a little like *schnetke.* Recently, I've welcomed an Elder into my practice who has taken to calling me "my girl" every time she sees me. She and her husband bring me pickerel they've caught and bannock she's baked. She told me in Cree the other day that I was a woman "of great beauty and strength," and I wish I could tattoo those words on my heart. She still perms her hair, and she reminds me of my grandmother and the photos I've seen of my great-grandmother. Her kindness has helped me feel a greater sense of belonging than anything I've tried on my own.

George sent me an email last year after my essay was published in *The Globe and Mail*. We hadn't spoken in years. The last time I'd seen him was before his fourth child was born. I'd held his youngest son at the time, marvelling at how much his eyes reminded me of George's, of the child I once knew.

In his note, he told me how much he related to the words I shared in my essay. How he has struggled with feeling like he doesn't belong anywhere. How he has grown his hair, thinking it might help him feel more connected to where he comes from. And how, when he was taken away as a child, he wasn't surprised.

"A lot of people don't know this," he writes now, over Facebook Messenger, "but we were actually part of the Sixties Scoop. It lasted until after we were adopted."

I stare at my screen. I'm not sure what to reply.

The Sixties Scoop was a period, beginning in the mid-1950s and ramping up in the 1960s, when it was common practice for the Canadian government to remove First Nations, Inuit and Métis children from their homes and communities and place them, largely, with non-Indigenous families, often in other provinces or even other countries. The term "Sixties Scoop" was first introduced by Patrick Johnston, the author of the 1983 report "Native Children and the Child Welfare System." He coined it after a social worker in British Columbia told him how common it was for the government to "scoop [newborns] from their mothers on reserves."

Often, children were apprehended outright, without their parents' consent and sometimes without their knowledge. Parents were rarely told where their children were being sent, and often never heard from them again. An estimated twenty thousand Indigenous children were removed from their families during the Scoop. Many of my aunts, uncles and older cousins were adopted during this time.

By the 1970s, roughly one third of all children in care in Canada were Indigenous, while the vast majority of foster families were not. The legacy of the Sixties Scoop has continued into the twenty-first century, with some dubbing the continued overrepresentation of Indigenous children in foster care and their subsequent placement in non-Indigenous families "the Millennium Scoop." As a result, the Sixties Scoop and the Millennium Scoop are largely understood as extensions of Canada's genocide against Indigenous Peoples.

"Just like the residential school system, the Scoop didn't fully stop until the nineties," George adds.

"Do you think it matters that we weren't apprehended? I mean, we were given up," I write.

"I don't think so. It's all part of the same thing. Even though neither of us were actually apprehended by the government, a lot of women were still coerced into placing their children into care. Or there was so much intergenerational trauma they believed they weren't equipped to parent—that their kids were better off without them."

It's like a stubborn gear stick suddenly shifts for me. Going back to the earliest days of colonization, through to the residential school system—which tore kids from their families and forced them into white-run institutions designed to strip them of their Indigenous cultures and languages—and on to the Sixties Scoop and beyond, the system was always designed to tear us away from our cultures and our peoples. Deep fracture lines were drawn through families for generations, and people were stripped of their rights to the point where relinquishment might have, for some, felt like the best available option. When George and I were placed into the care of a government that had only ever tried to suppress and erase our peoples, this was a fulfillment of that same colonial legacy.

"So," I say to Crystal over the phone. I hesitate, trying to determine how to ask her this question. Our relationship still feels fragile, and I worry about dismantling the building blocks we've only just begun to carefully stack. "I took a DNA test."

"Oh?" she asks. She sounds intrigued.

"My results are a little confusing. They don't really make sense," I manage. The surnames that showed up on my paternal family tree weren't at all the ones I was expecting. "So, I was wondering—"

"I know where you might be going with this," she interrupts me. *Thank you, god,* I think. "And, yes . . . there *is* another man who could be your father. But there's no way I ever thought it was him. The timing just didn't make sense."

As it turns out, some seventeen-year-old girls aren't aware that pregnancies can last for forty-two weeks.

I sit on the floor of my office to draft my second "I Think You Are My Father" letter. Although this is more of a "I Thought Someone Else Was My Father and Now I'm Not So Sure" letter.

I must not expect a confirmation email, I promise myself. After spending one day in limbo, wondering if he's hiding my note from his partner or if he has deleted it, pretending I don't exist, I ask my biological mother to ask him if he has received it. It's useful that the two of them, unlike she and the previous man, are still on speaking terms.

"Yes," she responds later that day. "He has received it. I've asked him not to leave you hanging."

Another day passes with no response from him. Then a week. Then two, then three. But the sting feels only mild this time. Like the bite of a sandfly, compared to an infected cat scratch or a broken ankle. The first letter to my first potential father prepared me for this.

"I won't leave her hanging. We'll talk soon," he messages Crystal.

Finally, we share a brief exchange where he tells me he's interested in figuring out if I'm his daughter or not.

I don't hear from him again.

In late 2021, I write an essay for *Salon* about taking the DNA test and searching for my birth father. In it, I call myself a "child of the Sixties Scoop" for the first time. After so many years of hiding my feelings, I'm finding it freeing to share my experiences in writing—though it's slightly terrifying to do it so publicly. I receive a few messages online from people who say I put words to their experiences. A female physician reaches out to me and tells me about her childhood, and we share how lonely medicine has felt for us both, how uncommon it is to hear stories like ours from other doctors. I hear from a few older women in town who tell me how brave it is of me to share. Their words are different in tone from the apologies Mom's told me she's received. At night, the faceless male figure waits for me. I've stopped clutching at Andrew's arm when I gasp awake and he manages to stay sleeping.

Crystal reaches out to me shortly thereafter to tell me that I wasn't part of the Sixties Scoop and shouldn't claim to have been. "I didn't give you up because I'm Aboriginal," she says. "I gave you up because it was my choice."

That same day, one of my biological aunties contacts me too. "I'm afraid you're misleading people," she writes. My chest feels like it's going to collapse in on itself.

I email George and he tells me he understands, that he's sorry I have to deal with this. I call a friend from medical school who's also Métis, and he reminds me that none of this changes my experience. Their words offer me a penny of comfort, but I can't stop myself from spiralling. I google and I read and I try to find the stories of other Indigenous adoptees. I find very little. I'm looking for an answer that will tell me whether I'm allowed to feel the way I feel. Are the ways in which my life unfolded really, when taking the wider perspective, not that big of a deal? I email George again.

"One could argue," he writes, "that after colonization and the intergenerational trauma that our families faced, when a social worker presents adoption as the only option to a woman in this circumstance, it is coercion."

I find the work of Dr. Raven Sinclair online. She's an internationally recognized scholar on the Sixties Scoop and a child of the Scoop herself. I decide I have nothing to lose by reaching out to her, and surprisingly, she responds to me within hours, offering to meet me over Zoom.

A few days later, I sit at my desk, Rua purring on my lap, as I speak to a woman I instantly come to revere. She possesses both a strength and a sense of humour that come through immediately.

"The scoop lasted until 1991," she tells me. "The fact of the matter remains, whether a kid was apprehended or placed into care, there were systemic policies in place with no regard for cultural continuity and preservation. These mothers and their communities had no say in the matter. The decision as to where the child ended up was left to the government. That's the point."

"But . . . my birth mom says I wasn't part of the Scoop," I say. "Her sister too."

"Yeah . . ." She pauses. "What your mother says—that's on her. That's for her to deal with. And she has to make peace with that."

It sounds so straightforward coming from her. *I don't have to fight to be seen here,* I think. Dr. Sinclair was adopted too, and I imagine she's wrestled with some of the same things I have.

I suddenly remember something Crystal said to me years ago: "I felt like I had no other option than to give you up."

Perhaps it's too painful for a mother to realize she held less agency than she thought she did. Perhaps, as soon as you start pulling at that thread, there's a chance for so much more to come unravelling with it. Or perhaps both things can be true: my birth mother made a choice that was her own, that was true to what she wanted at the time—*and* that choice was shaped, at least in part, by forces and systems outside herself.

The café is busy for a Tuesday morning, filled with retired Mennonite women. It's March 2022, and social-distancing restrictions have lifted enough to allow us to be here. I glance around, but don't spot him at any of the tables. We haven't spoken in a few days. We sometimes go days between emails, occasionally weeks, and, more rarely, a month or two.

"Are you looking for someone?" the server asks.

"I don't think he's here yet." I take off my coat and pick a table by the windows. It feels a little more private here, away from the talk of grandchildren and scrapbooking and prayer requests.

The server sets down my latte and I glance up to see him. George's hair is almost as long as mine and falls with a wave down his back. I think of the child I remember with short black hair and glasses. I think of the children we used to be, playing out in the backyard, shooting at each other with potato guns from the dollar store, raking leaves into a big pile so we could do cannonballs into them. It feels like a lifetime has passed between us, a lifetime since we were those two children playing out by the electric fence.

We both sip at our coffees, the calming hum of the coffee shop surrounding us.

"You know, I used to do this thing," George says. "I used to look at my papers, and there was this paragraph at the end that I clung to. It said, 'The birth mother wants the child to know that she thought of the adoption a great deal and thought it was best. She wants him to know how much she loves him.' I held onto those words so hard. I was like, 'She thinks of me. She loves me!' Then I was talking to a friend who was also adopted around the same time, and we realized we had that same paragraph at the end of our papers, almost word for word."

"George . . ." I say, my mouth gaping. "I had those exact same words in mine. I'm not kidding. I used to sneak into my mom's drawer and pull my papers out all the time, and at the end of my documents, it said, 'The birth mother wants the child to know she thought of the adoption a great deal and that she loves her.'" I shake my head. "Those words helped me survive."

We can't help but laugh. What else is there to do? It's our way. At some point, I imagine, the tears might come, but we will both save that for later. That's also our way.

"Did they let you take anything with you? You know, the day you were taken?"

"Yeah. I took a stuffed animal—a dog." He shakes his head and laughs. "I still have that thing. It's so old and torn, and I've tried to get my kids to care about this stupid dog, but they just don't get it. Last year, my youngest drew on it with marker and I was so upset. Over this stupid stuffed animal."

I see the child I used to know sitting in front of me. The quiet one who becomes so chatty as soon as he feels comfortable.

The calculated one who, when he doesn't think anyone is watching, lets his guard down. My cousin.

"I've never told anyone this, but there's a memory from that time that I've never forgotten. It was after I was taken away and I was visiting home. My parents were sitting with the social worker at the kitchen table and they were talking about where I was going to live. Your dad was there. He was furious—so angry. And he was telling the social worker that I had to come home. That I needed to be with my family. That a child should be with his family. I've never felt like anyone fought for me like your dad did. I'll always remember that."

"Huh." I look down at the last of my latte. I bring it up to my lips, but it's long grown cold. I don't know exactly what I'm feeling right now, but it's something like the feeling I have when I return home after a call shift and Rua climbs onto my lap, or when I'd hug Tabby as a child and she'd nestle in under my chin. "How about that."

Chapter Forty-Four

There are moments in my life I wish I remembered but can't piece together. Memories of siblings and family upon which I wish I had a firmer grasp. Then, there are moments I wish to forget, to cast into the wind on a blustery night never to see them again.

Andrew is sitting on the couch when I walk into the living room of the house where we have lived for the last six and a half years. His elbows are resting on his knees and his palms are clasped together. He looks broken. He has looked this way for quite some time, but I haven't wanted to admit it.

"What's up, love?" I say, walking toward him. His eyes move from his palms to me. He looks like he's about to throw up.

I know. I knew last night, and I know in this moment.

An hour later, he's packing an overnight bag, and I'm letting him go. I grab two pillows off the bed—the thin ones, the ones that don't bother his neck—and place them next to his bag. When he walks back into our bedroom to grab a few more pairs of pants,

I tuck two Coke Zeros and a bottle of extra strength ibuprofen next to his sweater. I know he'll want them later.

He stands by the front door, about to walk through it and out of the life we have shared for the last decade.

"I love you," he says. "I'm so sorry."

"I know. I'm sorry too. I love you too."

We wrap our arms around each other the way we always do, like neither of us wants to let go but, of course, we know that we must. That is how this works. I wish I could take care of him through this but, of course, I know that I can't. That is not how this works. Later I'll realize the thought of taking care of myself never occurred to me.

As I watch his taillights fade down our street, I think, *I won't be hearing his heartbeat tonight.*

I can't sleep tonight. I can't sleep and it's not because of the faceless man at the foot of my bed, but because my mind feels more haunted than my house. Nowhere feels safe right now. I pull Rua in close to my chest and tug the blanket to cover us both. Abby is curled in a ball near my feet. Andrew and I rescued two more cats in the last year and a half, and now, in the quiet of the night, they're both offering me solace too. I'm lying in the bed in the spare room, the bed that we bought a few years ago when Eleanor and her son, David, stayed with us for a few nights. I will sleep here for the coming weeks and then months. It's smaller than the other bed, but there's no imprint left in it from Andrew's body.

Dad stops by to fix a few broken panels in my floor, to install new light fixtures, to inspect the sump pump that's leaking again. Mom stops by and cries until I tell her, in a tone that's harsher than I intended it to be, that if she needs to cry, she needs to do it before she comes or after she leaves. Eventually, I mention to Crystal what's happened with Andrew, and she tells me how sad she is to hear the news. Despite the different ways in which we see my adoption, we haven't stopped speaking, and our messages flow back and forth.

How does one explain something that seemed to happen both overnight and over the span of years? Is it my job to explain it to anyone, anyway? People ask me what happened—my mom, Baba, friends of friends who feel entitled to information, friends of friends who ask those same friends who then ask me—but it's all too painful. And, quite frankly, for maybe the first time in my life, I do not give a shit. My story is my own to share, and I do not wish to share this.

Ten days after Andrew leaves, I'm on an airplane. First to Calgary, then to Paris and Rome and Naples, and finally to Positano for a writers' retreat to which I was invited several months ago. Andrew was supposed to come with me, and we'd planned to extend our trip by touring around Italy for a few weeks. I've managed to shorten it since, and will only be on my own for a few days outside the retreat.

While I'm waiting for a train in Rome later that week, I read about the First Nations, Inuit and Métis leaders from Canada who've just arrived here to ask the Pope for a formal apology for the role the Catholic Church played in the cultural destruction and forced assimilation of Indigenous Peoples across Canada. Soon, my auntie will join them as a Métis leader. I will be in Positano then, wearing the ribbon skirt I packed, sewn for me by an Indigenous patient who'd also been adopted.

I'm standing on the beach in front of our hotel, having spent the morning workshopping a piece of mine with a group of women who, days earlier, were complete strangers. I feel the breeze from the Mediterranean Sea blow my strands softly against my neck and I close my eyes. One of my new friends told me this morning about the many bits of ceramic tile scattered across the beach here—how she and her husband had walked along picking up pieces of all colours and sizes, admiring their unexpected beauty.

I gaze at the shattered ceramic beneath and around my feet. These fragments feel like a reflection of my spirit right now. I've been broken into so many pieces I can't count them.

I spot a blue-and-white ceramic shard by my toes and I bend to pick it up. I hold it between my thumb and index finger, rubbing its sides, feeling the ridges of the blue paint, noticing how much smoother it feels than it looks. Maybe, I think, the beauty of where I find myself right now is that I have the opportunity to decide what pieces I take home with me and what I let wash back into the sea. I take the tiny, smooth shard and stick it in my pocket.

Chapter Forty-Five

The coffee is still hot and it burns my mouth just a little. I hold the paper cup against my lips as I sit across from my once-mother and once-father at their kitchen table. I haven't seen my in-laws in months. When I lost Andrew, I lost an entire family—a mother and a father and a sister and a brother and a niece and nephews. So many names to add to the long list of people I've loved and lost.

"What are your plans for the holidays?" Andrew's mother asks me.

We're about a month away from Christmas. I tell her I'll spend it with my parents and also with my best friend. I'm at Shana's house most nights of the week, her husband washing up after cooking us dinner, while she and I take care of bathtime for her daughter and son. Sometimes, I climb into bed with her five-year-old and we read a bedtime story and play a game where she makes me guess which Barbie she is on each page of her fashion book. It's no great secret: she's always the pink one. The one with sparkles.

As I stand up from the table, ready to leave, Andrew's parents both tell me they would love to see me more often. They both remind me I can come over. "Any time," Andrew's mother says, and I can see in her eyes that she means it. She hugs me, and then his father steps forward to hug me too. I was thrown off by being surrounded by so many huggers when I first met this family years ago. Now, there's a throbbing in my chest at the thought of not being one of them any longer. His father's arms wrap around me and, for the first time, I don't stiffen. I let myself feel the warmth of his hug too.

"Oo, hold on a second," his mother says, quickly running to the kitchen counter. She hands me an envelope and hugs me again. "See you soon," she says.

I get into my heated vehicle, which has been running for the last ten minutes, and pull out of their driveway. I drive down snow-packed streets, drifts already forming on the edges of the roads, and turn in the direction of home. I considered moving to the city after Andrew and I ended, to move away from the pain and the memories, but lately I've been thinking I want to stay put.

I turn the volume dial down and grab the envelope Andrew's mother handed me. There's a thoughtful gift inside, but it is not what I notice first. "For our daughter," the front of the card reads. And inside, in his mother's handwriting: "You will always be our daughter."

The snow doesn't stop falling for days. Next week, it will stop abruptly and won't start again until after Christmas. My vehicle climbs up and plunges downs the tiny hills in the parking lot to the personal care home where I round a few times a month. I pull the zipper of my ankle-length parka all the way up to my chin before stepping out of my vehicle for the twenty-foot walk. The wind, even with distances this short, will still make your cheeks sting on days like this.

I meet the charge nurse at her desk and we start reviewing. "Mr. Peters had a fall this week," she says, sighing. It is not Mr. Peters's first fall this month. "He knows he's not strong enough to get up on his own, and we put the call bell right beside him, but he still insists on doing it himself." I smile, understanding all too well the Mennonite insistence on self-sufficiency, born not of pride but of an assured belief that if one has legs, one must at least try to use them.

I follow her into Mr. Peters's room. He's sitting in his wheelchair, head leaning back and to the right, eyes closed and a slight snore coming from the back of his mouth. His bible lies on his lap—I can see that it's open to Job. There are photos displayed all around his room. Photos of his children and grandchildren, of his wife, who has already passed on. In these pictures, he and his wife remind me of my grandparents, and I find this comforting. There's a laminated quotation on his nightstand; in big, bold letters, it reads: "Consider it pure joy, my brothers and sisters, whenever you face trials of many kinds, because you know that the testing of your faith produces perseverance. Let perseverance finish its work so that you may be mature and complete, not lacking anything. James 1:2–4."

The nurse taps him on the shoulder and talks loudly into his good ear. "Mr. Peters, the doctor is here to see you!" His eyes slowly blink and he smacks his lips as he reorients himself to his surroundings.

I squat beside his chair, so that he's looking down at me. "How are you feeling today?" I'm used to speaking a few decibels louder whenever I'm here.

"Great. In the middle of *meddachschlop*," he says. His accent is thick like my dad's. He looks confused but not annoyed about why we've interrupted his nap.

"I heard you had a fall," I say.

"Oh, no. Just a little one." He bats his hand in the air. "I'm fine."

"This time," the nurse says. "This time you're fine, but next time you might hurt yourself. We need to make sure you're safe and don't hit your head. That could be really bad."

"No, no," he says, smirking. "I'm fine. If I fall, I just get back up."

"Well, not exactly," she says. "You need two health-care aides to help you up when you fall because your legs aren't strong enough right now. And something worse could happen."

He is still smiling. "Well, if it's my time to meet my maker, it will be my time." He shrugs. "And I don't think that's too bad."

Mennonites have an honest acceptance of death I have found nowhere else.

"I'm wondering something," I offer, treading lightly. "I know that you feel strong enough to move on your own and sometimes, I know, it works. But what if you at least pressed that button to call someone before you tried getting up?" I point to the call button pinned to his pillowcase. "That way, we can avoid falling altogether. And the last thing any of us want, including you, is a broken hip, which would make moving a whole lot harder."

"*Yo, yo,*" he says. *Yes, yes.* "I'll try."

I push myself off my knees and pat him on the shoulder. "I'll let you get back to your *meddachschlop,* then." I know he won't be using that damn call button the next time.

As I walk back to my vehicle, in the frigid cold, I chuckle at the Mennonite reluctance to complain and the steadfast belief in self-reliance. And I feel really thankful to have inherited these qualities myself.

I turn down my street to see that my dad's dirty old truck is parked in front of my house. He's dressed in his beat-up winter coat and his worn-out jeans, shovelling my driveway. I know without asking that he's wearing two pairs of thick woollen socks underneath his weathered boots, too stubborn and too Mennonite to throw away a pair of boots that are still technically functional.

I pull onto the path my father has already cleared on the left side of the driveway and weave around him into the garage. I turn off the engine and walk to where the garage meets the icy pavement. I stand with my hands in my pockets as my dad heaves a heap of heavy snow onto the side of the yard.

"You want something?" I call out to him. His wheeze cuts through the wind and I know his asthma is giving him trouble. "A coffee? Pop? Tea?"

He looks my way for a second before answering with a "no," and the intonation in his voice makes me think of Grandma.

"You sure? It's pretty cold out." I'm already shivering. In my new jacket and insulated boots.

He turns, swats his hand in the air and keeps shovelling. I smile, giving my head a little shake as I walk to the house and close the garage door behind me. Fifteen minutes later, I check my front window to see where he is. His truck is gone and my driveway is clear. For now. I'm sure in the morning there will be a new layer, a few inches high, but that's not the point.

"Thanks," I text my dad.

"Yup."

He is nothing if not consistent.

"I'm not here to tell you what to do." My voice is soft, my words gentle. I'm sitting cross-legged on the floor, next to her. "I'll stay here as long as you need. I'm not going anywhere. I promise."

She looks at her hands in her lap, her legs crossed just like mine. "I'm scared," she says.

"I know. But I'm not. And we don't have to go anywhere—not until you're ready, and only if you feel safe, okay?"

She nods.

This is a ritual we have done every night for weeks. I tell her that she's safe and she nods, staring at her hands and sometimes looking back at me. "I'm scared," she says again and again. And I remind her, again and again, that it's okay to be scared, and that I'm here to protect her in the ways others couldn't, until eventually she starts to believe me. I can feel it.

One night, she scoots her bum across the bare basement floor and settles her chest against mine. "I think I'm ready," she whispers. "I think I'm ready to leave."

I hold her tight, rubbing her back and brushing her hair with my fingers. I look down at my six-year-old self, and I kiss the top of her head.

"Do you think we can bring her?" She looks to the even younger version of us, whom she has kept safe for so long, hidden for all these years. My four-year-old self is sitting behind her with a kitten—a kitten with little white paws and a tiny grey moustache. Tabby.

"I know you're scared," I say to them both. "It's not your job to protect her anymore," I tell my six-year-old self.

I stretch out my hands. My six-year-old self reaches out first. Next, my four-year-old self. I wrap my arms around them both and I kiss kitten Tabby on the forehead before I whisper, "Okay, loves, let's go."

I spend every night with the younger versions of myself. Four and six years old. Eight years old. Eleven years old. Thirteen and fourteen and twenty years old. I spend as much time with each of them as they tell me they need, and each one needs something different from me.

I begin going for walks every night. Sometimes I start just as the sun is setting and I return home in the pitch black. The pain of losing my husband is still so visceral. It's an ache in my chest and in the pit of my stomach that refuses to relent. There is no answer to it. I still can't eat very much most days, even though months have passed. But, somehow, I manage to walk. One foot finds itself in front of another as I make my way down the bike path by my house. As winter nears, I watch the colours around me pixelate from yellows and oranges to greys and whites.

The loss of Andrew has thrown me into the loss of every sibling I have ever known. It takes me back to the day George was taken away and to the moment I heard those two words echo over the phone when Ashley died: "She's gone." Although Crystal and I have reconnected, it throws me into the loss of her I carried with me as a child and then the loss of her again as an adult. Andrew is gone, and the loss of him is a reminder of all the ways in which I, myself, have been lost too. Night after night, I spend time with a younger version of myself, and step by step, I move myself forward. At times it feels as though I will not survive it. Like a once-severed nerve beginning the torturous process of regenerating itself, I am feeling everything. But I keep walking. I keep walking. Step by step, I begin walking myself home.

Chapter Forty-Six

It's a few weeks before Christmas, and I'm on my way to my biological grandmother's funeral.

"I can come with you," Mom offered over the phone a few days ago. This was a gesture so generous it nearly overwhelmed me.

"No," I said. "I need to do this alone."

It'll take me a few hours to drive from my house to the small church where my grandmother's service is being held. The bright sun through my windshield is burning my eyes on this unusually warm autumn morning. I feel nervous about seeing my family. Although we're speaking again, I haven't seen my first mother in years. And there will be cousins, aunts and uncles at the funeral I've never met before. As I drive, I think about how my grandmother went by the name Bea, similar to my nickname "B," which Baba loves to call me. I think about how this was something we shared. This was just one of the ways in which I was similar to the woman my great-aunts tell me I looked so much like. *Your eyes,* they tell me. *And your cheeks. Your smile.*

I sit next to my younger cousin at the church, the son of my aunt who took my mother to her first prenatal appointment. My mother and two of her sisters stand at the front of the room, reading their tributes to a complicated woman who held a complicated motherhood. I watch my family mourn. I'm surrounded by people I resemble and whose blood I share, relatives of a grandmother I hardly know, and I feel grounded in a way I never quite have before. I grasp my hands tightly as tears sting at my eyes. This time, I don't stop them from falling. I don't wish to push away the unexpected sense of oneness I feel being here with my family.

One of my aunts has created a slideshow for the service, a collection of photos and memories that are not mine, but that I lap up nonetheless. Photos of a woman—I have to agree with my aunts—I can't deny I strongly resemble. I feel connected to a history, to my history, in this moment. It's a river so vast and deep, I can't see where it begins or ends. For all I know, it does neither.

I don't know that my identity will ever have tidy boundaries. I'm not confident I will ever fully understand it, and I think I'm learning I have to be okay with that. For so long, I've felt that I wasn't enough of anything. Never Indigenous enough. Never white enough. Never Mennonite enough. Where could I fit? But what does it even mean to consider yourself "part" something and "fully" another? As I've come to know my Indigenous friends and family better, I've noticed that they view parts and wholes in a different way than I've seen in the non-Indigenous people in my life. They don't often separate degrees of relations. There are no first cousins and second cousins—only cousins. There are no half-siblings—only siblings. Why must I separate the parts of myself, when they combine to create the sweeping landscape of who I am? I'm Métis with Anishinaabe and Cree ancestors and I have European settler ancestors too. I can't deny my settler lineage, but it would feel dishonest to not acknowledge that being Indigenous has shaped my life from the day I was born.

Even though I was raised in a time and place where being adopted and Indigenous meant I was often viewed a *certain way*, no one was ever able to take my culture and my history away from me. Even when I was unaware of exactly who and where I came from, the truth still existed within me.

My life, like so many others', is full of strands and stories that sometimes feel difficult to hold together. I've stopped going to church, but I'm not certain that will always be true, and I'm still a prayerful person. I lived away from my hometown for a decade, convinced I would never return; now, I'm back, and I feel tiny bursts of joy whenever I see an elderly woman wearing a headkerchief like those worn by Grandma. I'm the daughter of a woman who always wanted to be a mother, but for whom motherhood was kind of tricky, and who still craves reassurance that I'll never leave her—and of course I never will. I'm also the daughter of a woman who feared becoming a mother, who believed my life would be better without her and who, now, I can see is proud to know me. I'm the daughter of a farmer who had a plot of land and an inherited set of tools, rickety and rusted and not much suited for the seed he was given to grow. But he tried. I'm also the daughter of a man I may never know. I'm the granddaughter of a woman who offered me more mothering than grand-mothering, whose body is growing smaller with each passing year, but whose spirit continues to bite back at it all. I'm the granddaughter of a woman who, for whatever reason, chose to spend her life raising more children than anyone else I've ever known. And I'm the granddaughter of a woman whose mother hid in the bush with her to protect her from those who wished to steal her and their culture away. In my hands and my bones and my heart, I carry it all.

I drive home later in the afternoon, passing a familiar piece of land that sits forty-five minutes north of my hometown and forty-five minutes south of what could have been my hometown. My hands turn the steering wheel and moments later, I'm standing on the cool, wooded earth, surrounded by trees and feeling the autumn sun across my cheeks. I walk down a path that's been worn into the ground, not knowing how long I'll be here but with the knowledge that, at some point, I will find my way back.

A handful of days have passed when Andrew's truck pulls into the driveway. I steady myself with my breath. *It's okay,* I remind myself. *I'm going to be okay.* He's come to pick up the last of what he left behind when he moved out, a few boxes I've packed and brought to the entrance.

He doesn't look like he's been taking care of himself. There's a new hollowness in his cheeks and a sadness in his eyes that his attempt at cheeriness can't hide. Before he leaves, I feel the urge to say something. "I'm feeling really overwhelmed lately. Do you think you could take Caesar?" Prior to our separation, we spent months feeding a fluffy orange stray cat with two missing teeth and calloused paws until we eventually trapped him in the garage. We had full intentions of finding him a home after we brought him to the vet, but after spending six weeks with him in our garage, shielding him from the onset of one of our coldest winters in years, there was no way either Andrew or I were saying goodbye to him. Caesar is surprisingly affectionate, and he and Andrew developed a bond the moment he came inside for good.

"I don't want to take him from his home . . ." he says. "I'll only take him if it'll help you."

"It really, really would," I say. Secretly, I think it'll be helpful for Andrew to have someone to return home to. Someone to sleep next to at night.

I'm not sure if I'm imagining this, but I see a faint look of relief wash over his face.

Andrew and I hug after I've kissed Caesar on the nose and helped him into the carrier.

"We'll talk in the new year," I say.

"We'll talk in the new year," he says.

Just as I did eight months earlier, I watch as Andrew walks out that front door and the lights of his truck fade down the street. I'm crying before I see them disappear altogether. I am standing, looking out the front window, unsure of when I will see either of them again. Emotion sweeping through me, a thought hits me as hard as the one I had the night I met Andrew so many years ago, the one that told me we would fall in love.

You will be together again, it says. *You just need to find your way home to yourselves, to each other.*

—

It's a crisp evening one week before Christmas—the sky growing dark before 5 p.m. and the stars beginning to pepper the sky—as I push through the glass door of the funeral home to see Mom and Dad and the rest of Dad's family. The last time I stood in this building was a year ago, after my aunt, George's mother, suddenly died. Her illness had been short and unexpected, and all I'd wanted to eat for weeks afterwards was takeout from McDonald's. I couldn't understand why the pull was so strong. A few weeks later, Mom had randomly asked me if I remembered how often she and my aunt used to take George and me and our foster siblings to McDonald's. I hadn't remembered, but suddenly the memories broke through like water through a dam. How I would finish my Coke before the rest of my meal and ask Mom if I could have a sip of hers. How I'd diligently put my shoes into one of the cubby holes beside the play structure before launching myself through the tunnel and into the pit with its blue and yellow and red and green plastic balls. How those balls would leave my hands sticky for hours afterwards and how the pit always smelled like a mix of stale fries, chicken nuggets, ketchup and dirty hands. How my hair would catch on the screws on the sides of the slide and the strands would lift into the air, held there by static, when I emerged. And how none of it—not the stickiness or the dirt or the static—bothered me when I was there with my siblings and George.

Mom holds me tight inside the funeral home and I shudder at the sound of her sniffling back her tears so close to my ear. Dad nods at me, his hands remaining in his pockets. I hug one of my aunts and wave hello to a few others before I tell Mom that I'm going into the sanctuary. "I want to go alone," I say.

I see the body of my young cousin in his casket straight ahead, and I see his father, George's older brother, sitting in a pew at the front. *His first-born,* I think to myself. *How does he begin to make sense of this?* I tuck my chin slightly as I walk down the aisle.

I approach my cousin's body. His nineteen-year-old body. His hair is thick and black, and his features demure. He was a beautiful boy. He has a rose tattooed on his right hand in shades of black and grey. I recognize the familiar position of his neck. It reminds me of Ashley's and Albertine's and the many others I've known who have died too soon and in this way.

I touch his hand and kiss his forehead, a practice I've adopted since Albertine died. The cold flesh against my lips somehow helps my brain connect with my body in a moment where everything feels incomputable. "He's with his grandmother," I hear someone in the distance say, and I think of my aunt, of George's mom, and I wonder how we're expected to bear this. Our family that has not felt like much of a family for so long now. A family that stopped singing those beautifully haunting hymns in hospital corridors and at family gatherings and funerals years ago. But tomorrow, one of my Indigenous uncles will place an eagle feather atop the casket as it's being lowered into the ground, and not one of my aunts or uncles will be absent.

I walk over to George's brother and we wrap our arms around each other. His daughter, his youngest child, will not leave his side for the remainder of the evening. She'll sit on his lap and rub his back and they'll mourn the life of a boy they should not yet have to mourn. A line has formed behind me now, a queue of relatives wanting to offer condolences and prayers. I release my grip and tell my cousin I love him.

I find George on the far-left side of the room and make my way over to him. We don't say a word to each other, but he hugs me like he has never hugged me. I feel myself holding up some of his weight as his sobs flow heavier now, and I don't know if I'll ever let go. Words do not have much to offer us here, like fireflies in the morning light. As our parents and aunts and uncles and cousins file into the pews, I feel his arms around me and I close my eyes.

DATE UNKNOWN

PHOTOGRAPH

My grandparents sit together on the wooden glider swing in their yard. They look to be in their sixties. Grandpa built this swing years earlier, sanded its edges until no sliver could be produced. Like most things he crafted, it was built to withstand the weather and it always glided without a hiccup. He painted it a cherry red that I imagine, in its early days, shone bright amidst the trees on their acreage. By the time George and I were old enough to race each other to the swing, the paint had mostly chipped away, but there were still some red flecks to be found that I couldn't resist picking. It always stood unadorned, with no cushions on its seats. In the summer, the fireflies danced around it, flickering like a broken halo. I think to myself that my grandfather was right: the swing never needed anything more.

I picture George and me sitting on this swing, as we did throughout our childhood, faspa *after* faspa, *more times than I could ever recall. The wind rustles through the trees and the sun weaves its way through the canopy of leaves, touching our faces. George leans back as I lean forward and the swing glides up into the air, its top edges skimming the lower branches of the trees. We push and we pull, laughing so hard we get a cramp in our sides, and the swing glides higher and higher until it feels like it might tip over, but of course it never does. We sway back and forth, never tiring, and we tell our stories as the stars begin to mix with the fireflies, with the hope that we will be back next week to do this again.*

Epilogue

I'm back, walking this path that I've returned to again and again since the day of my grandmother's funeral. The snow is starting to thaw and the first signs of spring have begun to declare themselves. What's fallen asleep is in the midst of reawakening. Tiny leaflets are beginning to bud from the bushes and the trees are dressing themselves once again. Like all that surrounds me, I can feel a sense of renewed life within me too.

When Andrew and I separated, I stopped wearing the fox necklace he'd bought me for Christmas years earlier. It felt too painful—it had always felt more valuable to me than my wedding ring. I've recently started wearing it again, and I reach to touch it, running the pendant along the chain, feeling its coolness against my skin.

Chickadees send a flitting melody above me and I watch as they fly away. A squirrel dashes up a tree and around its branches. There is so much life here. So much to feel, so much to be found.

I walk down the path my feet have carried me across so many times before and I think back to when I visited this place just after my grandmother died. So much had been lost. So much had died. But my feet, they carried me onward, and the trees, they lost their leaves, and eventually the air grew harsh and the snow fell so thick upon this path there was no traversing it. The land, it rested, and it asked me to do the same.

As I'm walking, I notice a creek I haven't before. Perhaps, when I first started coming here, it was dried up. I wind through the roots and the rocks and the wet earth to kneel at the creek's edge. The water flows softly downstream and I can hear the birds overhead skirting through branches, the sun shining on us all. I trace my fingers along the water, cold against my fingertips, and I bring my face in closer. In the ripples left behind from my fingers, I see the faces of my mother, my grandmother, my great-grandmother and the ones who came before them.

Nicâpân, the trees whisper. *Wahkômâķana. Ancestors.*

I look over my right shoulder, and then my left. I see the younger versions of myself standing along the stream's edge beside me. My eleven-year-old self has her arms wrapped around my four- and six-year-old selves, pointing at something beneath the surface of the water. I see my thirteen-year-old self and my fourteen-year-old self and my twenty-year-old self. I see us all. We're all here together.

I look across to the other side of the creek and see my parents. Mom and her family. Dad and his. Crystal is here too, with hers. Baba is leaning against a tree with her arms crossed, and I smirk at how funny it would be if, in this moment, she was smoking a cigarette. My aunts and uncles and cousins and Grandpa are all standing amongst the trees. Grandma sits on one of those chairs they'd always pull up from the basement, her hands on her lap, at the centre of them all. She's wearing a blue-and-white dress with beige stockings underneath. That dress has always been one of my favourites.

On the earth in front of Grandma sit George and my brother Fred and my brother James and my sister Shanny and my sister Marion, and all my other siblings too. Ashley and Albertine and Isabelle and Olivia and Kate and Eleanor and David are there too. And Shana and her husband and children. My cats are sprinkled throughout the trees, some asleep, paws stretched far and wide, others blinking up at me. Tabby looks as sprightly as a kitten and is perched on a tree stump next to my in-laws and Andrew.

I lower my hands into the water, cupping my palms together, and lift them to my lips. I take a sip before I close my eyes. I inhale. I exhale. I open my eyes. Everyone is gone. Everyone has left. The water's still flowing, and the trees are still standing, but there's no one to lean against them.

I'm alone.

But I'm not alone.

"I'm home," I whisper.

ACKNOWLEDGEMENTS

I know it can be difficult reading books on adoption, complex familial relationships and intergenerational trauma. I've often wondered if my story is worth telling—but then, that's the thing, isn't it? For generations, few people wanted to hear these stories. There were systemic policies in place to erase them. I suppose it was only natural, then, for me to believe that mine is a story not worth sharing. And yet here I stand, having shared it, and here you are, having read it. I want to thank you for reading it.

To my editor, Melanie Tutino, thank you for believing in this book, for believing in me. Thank you for still being here. The care with which you've approached these pages has been more than I could've expected. Your endless patience and kindness have overwhelmed me sometimes—in the best way. You've picked up what I've placed in your hands, held it, inspected it and given it back to me, asking if I could share a bit more, if I could know it a bit deeper.

Wendy Sherman, my agent, where would any of this be without you? You researched as much as you could on the Sixties Scoop and the history of residential schools, and went so far beyond professional duty or courtesy. I felt your care immediately. You're a formidable force and, more importantly, the way you care for your authors makes me feel so lucky our paths crossed. Of note—thank you to Richelle Fredson for helping me write the proposal for this book and introducing me to Wendy.

My thanks to the team at Doubleday Canada, including Talia Abramson, Amy Black, Kristin Cochrane, Aruna Dahanayake, Marion Garner, Valerie Gow, Madison Hendricks, Carla Kean, Ruta Liormonas, Melanie Little, Kaitlin Smith, Rachel Taylor, Daniella Zanchetta and Noelle Zitzer.

Dad, I know there's a high likelihood you're not reading this. But if, per chance, you are, I want you to know this: I'm thankful you're my father and I'm proud of your family, of your parents, of you. We don't say things like "I love you," but also know that I do. I know you don't understand how I feel or have felt or my need to write about it, but thank you for maintaining the belief that "a crooked toe is a crooked toe."

Mom, I understand this book might've been difficult for you to read. I think you'll forever be the one person who makes me laugh so hard no sound comes out and I have to pinch my legs together to stop from peeing myself. If you read this book, please also read this: you don't need to question your motherhood, you don't need to ask if you're still my mom. You are.

Baba, there's so much to say. You somehow found me endlessly fascinating—or at least you made me feel like I was—and what more could a child ask for? You've always been a firecracker, everyone knows this, but I also know something I don't think anyone else does: how tender your core is, how deeply you care, and how this sometimes gets lost in translation on the way out.

It has never been lost on me.

To my extended adoptive family, I know parts of this book might have been hard to read. I've shared everything from a place that is honest and true to my experience, but I also recognize it might look different from yours. I hope you can feel the love I have for our grandparents and our family in these pages.

To my extended birth family, I know there are still so many things about this family I have yet to learn, that I may never realize, but I'm forever grateful for the opportunity to even ask the questions, to be considered your family at all. Crystal, your generosity in embracing me will never go unnoticed. Thank you for the love you have for me and your willingness to listen to what I have to share. I can't imagine it's always been easy. I'm forever thankful to know you.

I included photographs of my three grandmothers in the part openers of this book—Grandma first, then Baba, and finally my biological grandmother—to honour the influence these women have had in my life.

Mom and Dad P, your family holds more energy in one room than fills some stadiums, I swear. It was difficult for me to figure out how to keep up with you until I realized maybe I don't have to, and maybe you'll love me anyway. And you do. You always have.

To my sisters and our family, *miigwech* for inviting me to be a part of your lives, a part of your family. Albertine, I hope you're at peace, spending your days and nights with friends and family on your side of things. Please know how much you're missed, how deeply you're still loved. Ash, I order carrot cake sometimes just so I can feel closer to you. I wish we'd had more time. I love you.

Shana, I'm not sure I could have survived without you these last few years. I wonder if I'll ever be able to repay you for your love, your kindness, your compassion. Tim and Cru, you literally fed me. Charlee, I can't count the number of times you called me to look through all forty-four pages of your fashion book. Those nights saved me and you didn't even know it.

Eddie, you've been more of a brother to me than you realize. *Miigwech.* Your sons are growing up proud and connected to their culture because you are their father. Isimeli, the way you carry your culture with you has helped me feel more connected to my own. *O kemuni o ni iliuliu vinaka.*

Matthew, I started writing because of your encouragement. Gav, my world has changed since meeting you and this book would not exist without you.

George, thanks for being the only one to have read this back when it wasn't even this. You've survived so much and no one even really knows. I hope you feel like the little George who existed so long ago is still here, on these pages and within you, even after all of it. I hope your kids understand the significance of that stuffed dog one day.

Dr. Raven Sinclair, my heartfelt thanks for taking that unexpected call with an adopted kid from Manitoba you'd never met before.

I wrote the bulk of this manuscript while a writer-in-residence through the Aspen Words partnership with the Catto Shaw Foundation, and I'm continually grateful for the dedicated time I was offered to write. Isa Catto and Daniel Shaw, your kindness and hospitality has stayed with me. I hope all the love and generosity you've offered to those around you returns to you tenfold.

Dani Shapiro, Michael Maren and Hannah Tinti, I never could have predicted the community I'd find through Sirenland. Michael, before I left that first year, you told me, "You're a Sirenlander for life now," and for this, among so much else, I'm grateful.

Animals have been some of the greatest loves of my life and, yes, I know they can't read but, yes, I imagine I'll read this out to my cats anyway. Tabby, Shadow (cat), Nala, Cocoa, Ed, Babe (pig), Candy (horse), Shadow (dog), Bronx, Shelby, Toby, Dakota, Jimmy, Kitty, Abby, Nebeeti, Caesar and Rua, thank you for loving me, for letting me love you. And for waking me up in the middle of the night by standing on my chest because you're hungry and reminding me what life's really all about anyway.

Andrew, I'm looking through the window as the rain falls onto the grass your parents once tended, in the house your grandparents built, which is now our home. So many years later and you're still offering me ways to fall deeper in love with you. You help me feel safe to share the parts of myself I still feel unsure about sometimes. So far, I've found no greater joy, I feel no luckier, than when I am simply walking alongside you.

Love,
Brittany

FURTHER READING

If you've made it to this section of the book and are interested in learning more, I want to offer my deep and heartfelt thanks. I know that my story can't begin to touch the surface of what Indigenous Peoples have faced as a result of colonization. Below is a list of resources that might be helpful.

FICTION

Five Little Indians by Michelle Good
Stolen by Ann-Helén Laestadius
House Made of Dawn by N. Scott Momaday
Night of the Living Rez by Morgan Talty
The Break by katherena vermette
real ones by katherena vermette
The Strangers by katherena vermette

NON-FICTION

Bury My Heart at Wounded Knee by Dee Brown
The Story of a National Crime by Dr. Peter Henderson Bryce
Lessons in Legitimacy by Sean Carleton
Truth Telling by Michelle Good
21 Things You May Not Know About the Indian Act by Bob Joseph

Braiding Sweetgrass by Robin Wall Kimmerer
Distorted Descent by Darryl Leroux
Highway of Tears by Jessica McDiarmid
Wînipêk by Niigaan Sinclair
Intimate Integration by Allyson D. Stevenson
All Our Relations by Tanya Talaga
The Knowing by Tanya Talaga
Seven Fallen Feathers by Tanya Talaga
The North-West Is Our Mother by Jean Teillet

MEMOIR

Halfbreed by Maria Campbell
Crazy Brave by Joy Harjo
Bitterroot by Susan Devan Harness
The Reason You Walk by Wab Kinew
Becoming a Matriarch by Helen Knott
In My Own Moccasins by Helen Knott
Heart Berries by Terese Marie Mailhot
Who We Are by Murray Sinclair
Unbroken by Angela Sterritt
From the Ashes by Jesse Thistle
The Heartbeat of Wounded Knee by David Treuer
Unreconciled by Jesse Wente

BOOKS FOR CHILDREN

Braiding Sweetgrass for Young Adults by Robin Wall Kimmerer, with Monique Gray Smith and Nicole Neidhardt

This Is How I Know by Brittany Luby and Joshua Mangeshig Pawis-Steckley
Walking Together by Elder Dr. Albert D. Marshall and Louise Zimanyi
Be a Good Ancestor by Gabrielle Prince and Leona Prince
On the Trapline by David A. Robertson and Julie Flett
When We Were Alone by David A. Robertson and Julie Flett
Every Child Matters by Phyllis Webstad and Karlene Harvey